# Empire and Independence

> All the world's a stage,
> And all the men and women merely players.
>
> *As You Like It.*
> *Act II, Scene 7.*

# 🏵 AMERICA IN CRISIS

A series of eight books on American Diplomatic History

EDITOR: *Robert A. Divine*

---

# Empire and Independence

The International History
of the American Revolution

## RICHARD W. VAN ALSTYNE
*University of Southern California*

*John Wiley & Sons, Inc., New York · London · Sydney*

# Preface

ALL THE WORLD'S A STAGE, and history is a moving stage. Not only does the contemporary scene change from day to day but, with the passage of time, history also changes. Fresh ideas come into play, perspectives change, and old episodes, like the American Revolution, assume new meanings. As interpreters of the past, historians are like play directors; they choose the stage, build the scenery, select the players, put them in their proper positions on the stage, and then, invoking their knowledge of "the facts," make them play their parts. History itself is no better than the historian who writes it or lectures on it. Creative history is imaginative history; and the more intellectually honest the historian, the more reflection he brings to bear on the subject he is studying, the more stimulating and rewarding will his work turn out to be for his readers.[1]

Some fifteen years ago, while a visiting professor at the University of Michigan, I utilized my spare time in a perusal of the several manuscript collections acquired from Great Britain by the William L. Clements Library. On my return to California I set about reading everything that had been said in both houses of Parliament concerning America. In my effort to penetrate and understand the complexity of British thinking on the problem, I read and reread the debates extending through the whole period of crisis, war, and peace, 1763–1783. From these debates, as recorded in the *Parliamentary History of England* and in the

---

[1] See my essays, "American Nationalism and Its Mythology," *Queen's Quarterly*, LXV (1958) pp. 423–436, and "History and the Imagination," *Pacific Historical Review*, XXXIII (1964) pp. 1–24.

*Parliamentary Register*, I eventually moved into the extensive collection of rare books held by the Henry E. Huntington Library. The influence of these books and of much other printed material available in this great library permeates my book.

My preliminary studies at the Huntington Library led me at various times to other great depositories: in America to the Library of Congress and the National Archives, where I systematically examined the unpublished *Papers of the Continental Congress* and other manuscript collections; to the Alderman Library of the University of Virginia and to the American Philosophical Society and the Pennsylvania Historical Society in Philadelphia; in England, to the Public Record Office and the British Museum in London, to the National Maritime Museum at Greenwich, to the Bodleian Library at Oxford, and to a number of manuscript collections privately owned in various parts of the kingdom. The Institute of Historical Research in London has been most helpful, on several occasions, in opening its facilities to me. Having rounded out my research in Britain and America, I found myself asking certain questions relating to French attitudes and activities which could be answered only by resorting to the Archives of the Ministries of War, Marine, and Foreign Affairs in Paris. Through the kindness of Professors W. N. Medlicott and Francis Wormald, I was fortunate in retaining the services of Dr. Clive E. Church of Trinity College, Dublin. Already familiar with the Archives in Paris and with the Bibliothèque Nationale, Dr. Church ably devoted himself in my behalf during the summer of 1964, and the results of his work show up in various places throughout this book.

It dawned on me, even as I began reading the debates in Parliament, that many of the views and "facts" concerning the War for Independence set forth by historians and regarded for many years as "definitive" were refuted by the knowledge and understanding of the situation shown by a number of speakers in both houses of Parliament. An "argus-eyed" British secret service resting on a network of "spies" is, for instance, given a major role in the diplomacy of the Revolution. But if the historians who propagated the "secret history of the American Revolution" had taken the pains to read even a few of the speeches in Parliament and of the books in circulation in London during the war years, they could hardly have been so confident. What they describe as "secret" was really common knowledge. This preoccupation with a nonexistent secrecy is not only misleading, but it also diverts attention from the major problems bearing on the international history of this conflict.

International history, let me say at this point, is not diplomatic history. I have not in this book confined myself to diplomacy, much less to foreign policy. I have searched for deeper currents in my effort to understand basic attitudes and motivations that come to light only after long study and detached thought. Hence I have not hesitated, whenever occasion demanded, to stray from the well-worn path of diplomatic history and venture into fields commonly labeled domestic or internal history. The British attitude in the crisis year 1775, for instance, makes little sense unless it is studied in terms of the complex of forces bearing down on the government at home as well as abroad. Accordingly, in writing Chapters 2 and 3, I deemed it essential to look closely at the internal scene in both Britain and America and to take into account the play of personalities in both countries that became clear to me as I probed deeper in my study. Similarly, the British persistence in prosecuting the war so far away from home and in the teeth of mounting difficulties in Europe makes no sense without an appreciation of the intelligence reports from America. It was an axiom of British policy that the rebellion was organized and carried on by a minority in America against the wishes of the vast majority of the people who wanted peace and reconciliation under the Crown. Throughout the book I have endeavored to keep this point of view to the fore, but in writing Chapter 8 I felt it appropriate to give it special attention. Finally, I have made a studied attempt at an international approach to this War for American Independence. The center of the stage was the sea, not the American Continent. Sea power was the determinant, and France was a participant even before the rebellion broke into open war. The American leaders appealed to France as their champion and savior.

In my previous book, *The Rising American Empire* (Oxford and New York, 1960), I included two chapters on the international characteristics of this War for Independence, setting it in the context of American expansion which was a continuous process from the seventeenth to the twentieth century. But these chapters were only a distillation of a very large and complex subject, which, I was fully aware, demanded deeper study and more extended treatment. Professor Robert A. Divine, the editor of this series, noted my intention in this respect, and he kindly invited me to write the book for it. Professor Divine's steady encouragement and constructive criticisms, given as he read the book chapter by chapter, have been invaluable. The University of Southern California and the American Philosophical Society both came to my support with grants adequate for financing Dr. Church's work in Paris. To the United States Educational Commission in the United Kingdom I am grateful for my Fulbright year in that country, where I was attached to the staff of University College, London. The *Huntington Library Quarterly* has published three articles of mine on which, with its permission, I have drawn heavily in the writing of this book; and my warm thanks go to my many friends on the staff of that library for their cordial hospitality and assistance. Finally, as on many other occasions, my wife has demonstrated exemplary patience and unflagging interest.

RICHARD W. VAN ALSTYNE

*Los Angeles, California*
*September 1965*

# Contents

# CHAPTER I

## The Pre-Revolution Conflict of Interests

Interest rules all the World—*Dr. John Mitchell, 1757*

IN OCTOBER 1755 JOHN ADAMS, age twenty, wrote a friend a letter which is a masterpiece of realistic thinking. Without any wastage of words, the letter places the nation soon to be born in perspective and shows a knowledge of how the forces of history operate:

All that part of Creation that lies within our observation is liable to change. Even mighty States and Kingdoms are not exempted. . . . Soon after the Reformation, a few people came over into this new world, for conscience sake. Perhaps this apparently trivial incident may transfer the great seat of empire into America. It looks likely to me. For if we remove the turbulent Gallicks, our people according to the exactest computations, will in another century become more numerous than England itself. Should this be the case, since we have I may say all the naval stores of the nation in our hands, it will be easy to obtain the mastery of the seas, and then the united force of all Europe will not be able to subdue us. . . .[1]

When this precocious youth was thus expressing himself, the Great War for the Empire was just beginning. The Acadian French, whose presence in Nova Scotia had irked certain ambitious interests in New England for almost half a century, were at last forcibly being removed from their homes and deported to various parts of the Empire; and hopefully, as young Adams plainly indicated, the bulk of the "turbulent Gallicks" who lived in Canada would soon suffer a similar fate.

---

[1] To Nathan Webb, Oct. 12, 1755. Alexander Biddle, ed., *Old Family Letters* (Series A, Philadelphia, 1892), pp. 5–6.

This indeed was the purpose of the new war, the fourth in a series begun nearly seventy years previously over the issue of domination of the North American continent and its adjacent seas, the Atlantic and Caribbean. In each of these wars the Americans—British Colonials, if we must be literal about their allegiance—were in the vanguard. New York interests, notably the Livingston family with the support of the governors, had been prodding the British government ever since the 1670s into coming to their assistance in pushing the French back from the Great Lakes and confining them to the narrow strip of settlement in the St. Lawrence valley.

Robert Livingston's son-in-law, Samuel Vetch, a Scot who settled in Boston, in 1708 formulated the plans for squeezing out the French altogether. With the enthusiastic support of the governor of Massachusetts, of the merchants, and of the Puritan clergy, Vetch submitted to the Board of Trade in London a lengthy paper on Canada called "Canada Surveyed." This was based on his own personal observations and travels in that country. Vetch described his thesis as "The French Dominions upon the Continent of America, briefly considered in their situation, strength, trade and numbers, more particularly how vastly prejudicial they are to the British interest, and a method proposed of easily removing them." Vetch showed how the conquest could benefit the trading and colonizing interests of the Empire, especially those of his native Scotland which had just consummated the Union with England. With the French out, Canada could be repopulated with Scottish Protestants, the British West Indies could be used as leverage to pry Spain from the Caribbean, and England herself would feel the effects of a greatly expanded transatlantic empire.

The Boston clergy reacted with pleasure to the thought of ridding themselves of the hated "Papists" to the north: Cotton Mather, still the leading preacher in Boston, declared that here was "another matter which I had to spread before the Lord." But best of all was a favorable response by the Board of Trade, which the Whigs—the war party in Britain representative of the banking and trading interests—controlled.[2]

In consequence two volunteer armies recruited from the

[2] G. M. Waller, *Samuel Vetch, Colonial Enterpriser*, Chapel Hill, 1960, pp. 94–141.

Colonies north of Pennsylvania assembled in June 1709, one at Albany for a march overland against Montreal, the other at Boston for an amphibious expedition up the St. Lawrence. Fleet support from Great Britain was, of course, essential, but the expected aid did not arrive. Instead the ministry in London diverted the vessels to the Caribbean for operations against the Spanish. Not daunted, Vetch and his friend, Lieutenant Governor Nicholson of Massachusetts, assembled another force of Colonials in the summer of 1710 and, with the addition of four hundred British marines, captured Port Royal. In this manner, Acadia was effectually subjugated and incorporated within the Empire.

Quebec was another matter. Vetch and his Boston friends talked of it as a new Carthage, and the analogy which they implied as existing between Boston and ancient Rome found a permanent place in the New England mentality. French Canada must be wiped out, as Rome had wipe out Carthage, if New England was to be secure. In June 1711 the much-needed British expedition did arrive in Boston harbor in force—six thousand soldiers and sixty or more vessels—and, with Colonial reinforcements, sailed for the St. Lawrence in August. But the expedition was badly led; without even encountering the enemy it did not get past the mouth of the river.

A contemporary French observer of this failure perceived the divergence of interest between Massachusetts and the mother country. The former was zealous for conquest—business and religion both stood to benefit—but could not achieve its desired end without substantial British help. The British on their part were half-hearted and indecisive. Presbyterian Scots shared the outlook of the Boston Puritans, and between them these groups wrung pledges of support from the British government. But to the *English* mind the advantages of conquering Canada were by no means so apparent. Motivation lacking, or at least being much weaker, doubt and hesitation were natural. But no English commentator at the time remarked, as this anonymous French writer did, that if Canada fell the Colonies would "then unite, shake off the yoke of the English monarchy, and erect themselves into a democracy." [3]

---

[3] *Ibid.*, p. 218.

Antagonism between Massachusetts—"God's American Is-rael," as her assertive Puritan ministers liked to depict her—and the mother country was no novelty. There was a basic conflict of interest between the two which cropped up from time to time in the course of the seventeenth century. Massachusetts was separatist by nature—its uncompromising Calvinism, among other things, ensured that it would be. But Massachusetts was not strong enough to go it alone, and to realize its sweeping ambitions it had to have British support. Britain's half-hearted-ness, however, seems to have done more damage than a down-right refusal to give any help would have inflicted.

Disappointments and ill feelings piled up in the several Colonies during these three years of frustration. The funds they laid out on their own military preparations—Massachusetts and New York, for example, together expended £52,000 on the forces assembled in 1709; the inevitable irritation which spread through the populace against the British government for falling down on its promises; and then the disagreeable surprise at learning, when the troops and sailors did arrive in 1711, that Massachusetts was expected to foot the bill for feeding them—these and other lesser causes of friction compounded an ill will which subsided with the war's end, only to flare up again some thirty-five years later at the end of the next war when Britain once more declined to do all that New England interests demanded of it.

In between the wars was a long peace, lasting twenty-six years. Britain, France, and the other European parties concerned came to terms in a general peace at Utrecht in 1713. Britain kept Acadia and renamed it Nova Scotia, thus pleasing the Scots, who had been claiming this country as theirs for nearly a century. Samuel Vetch was Nova Scotia's first governor, but he did not get the chance to invite in either Scots or Yankees: against his advice, the local French population was allowed to remain. When, a few years later, France built the great stone fortress of Louisbourg on Cape Breton Isle to the north, the French monarchy demonstrated its determination to hold Quebec and the vast interior of the Great Lakes which was naturally tributary to the St. Lawrence. Louisbourg's security rested partly on its ties with the French farmers of Nova Scotia—they furnished the garrison with its food. And thus it was to be expected that, considering the strong religious feeling, a militant priest from Quebec should appear among the Acadians and work on their ancient loyalties to France. This, of course, was subversion in the eyes of the British officials and the New England businessmen who now had more reason than ever for wanting to break French power in North America.

Louisbourg, charged Governor Shirley of Massachusetts, was a dagger pointed at the heart of New England, and in 1745 an army from New England succeeded, with the help of a British fleet, in capturing the fortress. Canada must be destroyed! This was again the cry of New England, shriller and more popular now than even in 1711. But it was not to be. The British government disagreed and at the end of the war in 1748 again balked Yankee ambition by handing Louisbourg back to France. The Acadians were not molested but, to offset Louisbourg, Britain built the naval station of Halifax. This highly significant step failed to appease New England in spite of the benefits which its wealthy business interests reaped from government contracts. One may wonder whether young John Adams, in his youthful confidence in 1755 that empire would soon pass from the Old World to the New, had not absorbed the ambitions, not to say the resentments, of his money-minded elders.

Meanwhile the steady advance of the French in the interior, resting on their control of the magnificent lake and river system, alarmed the trading and landed interests of the Colonies to the south. Men from New York, Pennsylvania, and Virginia added their voices to Samuel Vetch's in appeals to the British government to stand behind their claims to the country west of the Alleghenies. In 1721 the Board of Trade, influenced especially by James Logan, a Quaker merchant of Philadelphia, ranged itself on their side. Then began a long period of fort building on the frontier, extending arc-shaped from Nova Scotia to the Carolinas and looking more and more like an armed peace. Each side aimed to keep ahead of the other in the race, and to win the loyalties of the Indian nations which felt more and more bewildered as time wore on.

The natural friend of the aborigine was the Frenchman who came to trade and not to settle; the natural foe was the British-

American, who came both to trade and to bargain the Indians out of their lands. But the choice, even to the warier of the Indian chiefs, was not so easy as it might seem. The British-American pressed his rum, his weapons, and his utensils on the Indian—he had an abundance of all kinds to offer at prices which his French competitor found difficult to meet. Against these temptations the tribes could not unite. By the middle of the century the Indian desire for things had been so whetted that they lost their independence. One tribe, the Delawares, in a fit of religious fervor tried unsuccessfully to turn back the clock and resume their earlier more primitive way of life. And in 1761 at a gathering of four hundred Indians in Pennsylvania, a chief said to the sympathetic Colonel Henry Bouquet, a Swiss in the service of the British army: "We . . . are penned up like hogs; there are forts all around us, and therefore we are apprehensive that Death is coming upon us." [4] Colonel Bouquet made an honest effort to stop the cheating and keep the whites from intruding on the Indians' lands—he refused a bribe of 25,000 acres offered him by an agent of the Virginia speculators. But the latter then made it so difficult for him that he finally asked to be transferred.

Meanwhile Logan, like many other Americans including Franklin, whom Logan influenced, pressed forward with the argument that the Colonies were being encircled. The French, he told the British government in 1732, "now surround all the British Dominions on the Main." But Logan viewed New England skeptically. He would leave France on the latter's northern flank as a safeguard against too much independence exercised by Boston. The people of New England, he warned, "are naturally and peculiarly stiff." [5] This suspicion of New England was by no means original with Logan. Pennsylvania's acquisitive interests had already had their eyes on the land to the west and on the riches that they could wring from the Spanish Caribbean to the south, but they rejected Boston's special animus against Quebec.

---

[4] Gipson, IX, p. 89.
[5] As quoted in Van Alstyne, *The Rising American Empire*, New York, 1960, p. 16.

In spite of their apparent confidence, the French on their part really had more cause for alarm than the Americans. The security of their inland empire rested, in the last analysis, on their success in preventing Americans from breaching the Alleghenies, a natural barrier as seen from the vantage point of Quebec. To accomplish this they needed Britain's consent to a permanent boundary line running along the mountain watershed. Such consent would mean that Britain would withhold its support of Colonial interests; but it was too late—the Board of Trade had already taken the side of the Americans. Failing to win this entente with the British government, the best the French could do was to erect and garrison barrier forts at points where encroachment from the coast could be intercepted. It was this thin line of barrier forts to which American Colonials pointed whenever they protested that they were being "encircled."

When the handicaps under which they labored are considered, French Army officers did remarkably well in building their defenses. They had an unerring eye for strategy in choosing sites for their forts. Fort Duquesne, erected in 1753 at the head of the Ohio River, was a classic example: from it the local commander drove the Virginia militia under Washington east of the mountains. Britain subsequently mounted two major offensives against this invaluable post: the first one, under General Braddock in 1755, was a tragic failure; the second, led by General Forbes in 1758, yields in importance only to Wolfe's triumph at Quebec in hastening the fall of France in North America. But the volatility of the Indians was, in the long run, fatal to the French cause. The redmen, as we have seen, could not resist the allurements which the traders from the coast dangled before them. Theoretically the Indians held the balance of power. Properly organized under French leadership and promoted by a common interest in surviving, they could constitute a formidable buffer barring the way to expansion in the West. But Indian discipline and political ability could not even reach for such heights, nor were French resources equal to the job of offering leadership.

Americans like Franklin exaggerated the dangers of encirclement by drawing alarming pictures of possible annihilation at the hands of the French and Indians. Such talk was good for

firing the war spirit among the Colonial populace and for spur-
ring enlistments, always lagging, in the Provincial regiments.
Franklin played on this fear in his famous "Join or Die" cartoon
of 1754. But could he really have believed his own propaganda?
He shows his hand much more convincingly in his pamphlet on
*Observations concerning the Increase of Mankind*, which, published the same year, made a profound impression on influential
men in Britain. Prophesying that the Colonial population would
double itself every twenty-five years, Franklin demanded more
living room and admonished his British readers that a prince
"that acquires new Territory, if he finds it vacant, or removes
the Natives to give his own people Room" deserves to be
remembered as the father of his nation. Franklin aimed his
rhetoric at the British sense of grandeur, painting a graphic
picture of the brilliant future in store for the Empire if Britain
would be behind its Colonies; but, for immediate purposes, he
hoped to induce the government to set up two new colonies west
of the Alleghenies and south of the Great Lakes. This would
serve the dual purpose of pushing the British government into
an all-out war in North America and of appeasing the land
hunger of an increasing number of men in the Colonies.

Selling goods to the Indians and speculating in lands on the
expectation that the tribes would be displaced were part and
parcel of the same tangled operation. Individual traders and
speculators spun the web but, by the time Franklin wrote his
pamphlet, Colonial governments and the British government
itself were hopelessly caught. George Croghan, an emigrant
from Ireland, made himself the foremost of the traders in the
1740s, buying up lands in the upper Ohio, proposing new
colonies, and getting a job as agent for the Crown with authority
to conclude treaties with the tribes. Croghan operated out of
Philadelphia, and it was through him that Franklin entered the
game about 1748. Franklin had a personal encounter with the
Indian chiefs at Carlisle five years later, and learned first hand
of their anxiety to keep the whites out of their country, but this,
of course, had no effect on him. Of the two, Croghan identified
himself directly with the West: he consorted with Indian squaws,
begot offspring both red and white and, after the expulsion of
the French, rose to be the leading man in the upper Ohio. During

the 1760s he was in the enviable position of adviser to General Gage, in command of the British garrisons after the war, of finding choice lands for his friends and business acquaintances like Franklin and the influential Wharton brothers of Philadelphia, and of adding substantially to his own holdings. Franklin in London circulated among prestigious friends, such as Peter Collinson, the distinguished naturalist and antiquarian; Dr. John Mitchell, the cartographer, whose map of North America, first published in 1755, had made him famous; Richard Jackson, a barrister, and Thomas Walpole, an eminent merchant, who responded readily to opportunities to participate in the spoliation of the Indian country.

While these interests were working for new colonies, chartered by the Crown but developed by land companies who would control them, Virginia planters found it to their advantage to bring the Ohio valley directly under the jurisdiction of Virginia. To this end they collaborated in 1748 with their British correspondents, notably the great London merchant, John Hanbury, to found the Ohio Company with a grant of 200,000 acres in the upper part of the valley. Then in 1754 Governor Robert Dinwiddie, eager to dislodge the French from their stronghold of Fort Duquesne, promised 200,000 acres to volunteers in an expeditionary force. These promises, made to and accepted by veterans in the Virginia service, such as George Washington, led to trouble after the war with the competing Pennsylvania interests and with the British government, which was making futile efforts to honor its obligations to the Indians to restrain the whites from taking their lands. By creating a separate Indian Department in 1751 the government tried playing the role of mediator but, with fiercely antagonistic interests clamoring for satisfaction, this new agency was not destined for a happy career. When the Great War started in 1755, it was made subordinate to the army.

What led Great Britain to the point where in January 1755 Parliament voted to go the limit in supporting this war in the North American wilderness? Governor Dinwiddie, aware that the Virginia Provincials were unequal to their task, had been pressing hard for two British regiments; but opinion even inside the British government was divided, the King himself being opposed to using the Army. The head of the ministry, the Duke of Newcastle, favored such action, and in September 1754 the powerful head of the army, the thirty-three-year-old Duke of Cumberland, declared himself for a comprehensive campaign aimed at expulsion of the French from all of the interior.

Cumberland's voice seems to have been decisive in overcoming the hesitancy inside the government. But in back of these personal decisions was the network of interests, tied in with the Board of Trade, which were working for the enlargement of the Empire and which viewed the French as no better than trespassers who should be ejected. The French, asserted Mitchell, had no right to be in North America at all. What they had obtained "they have got by usurpation and encroachment." Mitchell wrote these words in 1757, in the midst of the war, but twenty years of prior residence in the Colonies, where he had associated with Franklin, Cadwallader Colden of New York, and other expansion-minded men, certainly must have given him this idea. When he returned to England, the Earl of Halifax, who headed the war party at the Board of Trade, opened the Board's archives on which Mitchell drew in the making of his famous map.

Mitchell was a thorough believer in, and a convincing advocate of, the cause of the Colonies. But unlike Franklin he had, so far as is known, no personal stake in trans-Allegheny lands. On his map he showed all of the country south of the St. Lawrence as being rightfully British, and then in a book published in London in 1757 developed his viewpoint at considerable length. The date of publication suggests that he hoped to spark the lagging war effort, for Britain at that time was still losing the war. "Interest rules all the world," wrote Mitchell. "Why should it not rule our Colonies?" The Colonies were Britain's support, not merely for the commercial wealth they yielded and the "incredible number of seamen and mariners" they furnished, but they were also the bulwark of Britain's own safety:

The result of this contest in America between the two nations must surely be to gain a power and dominion, that must sooner or later command all that Continent, with the whole trade of it, if not many other branches of trade; which must all fall into the hands of France, sooner or later if we suffer her to secure her present encroachments on the British dominions.

France controlled the "prodigious water-carriage" of the St. Lawrence and the Mississippi. If allowed to secure itself in those places it had "usurped on our frontiers"—viz., Crown Point on Lake Champlain, Niagara between Lakes Ontario and Erie, and Duquesne at the head of the Ohio—"we seem to have no way ever to be free from constant danger, and perpetual sources of wars, charges and expences from them." In his zeal to root out the French, Mitchell thought Britain was really to blame for the war: the British had been so dilatory in coming to the aid of the Colonies.

Many people had doubts about all this, and Mitchell made a strong effort to reassure them. "There is a false and groundless notion," he wrote, "that seems to influence many people's opinions and conduct with regard to the Colonies—the fear of their rebelling, and throwing off their dependence on Britain." Yet he wondered how they could do so. Since they could not defend themselves against a handful of French, how could they withstand the whole force and naval power of Britain? Hence he proposed to *let the French stay in Canada.*

Unconsciously Mitchell reiterated the position of James Logan: Canada would serve to deter New England. But most of all, as a good mercantilist, he relied on a sound British economic policy for discouraging rebellion. The thing that bred jealousy between Britain and the Colonies was not power but manufactures. However, Mitchell believed there need be no occasion for jealousy; one should encourage the Americans to make and produce the things that Britain needed—hemp, potash, iron, naval stores, and other primary products. Possession of the hinterland would promote this type of supply and thus make for a stronger empire.[6]

But although under the new leadership of William Pitt the tide of war now changed decisively in favor of the British, doubts apparently persisted. It was still feared that the Americans would take advantage of the victory over France to throw off their allegiance. Arthur Young, who was later to make a name for himself with his books on agricultural reform, realized this

---

[6] *The Contest in America between Great Britain and France,* London: printed for A. Millar, 1757. The quotations from Mitchell in the text are all from this rare book.

possibility but, sharing the views of Mitchell, he did not believe it. Young was at this time only eighteen years of age, John Adams's junior by six years. A more incisive writer than Mitchell, he published in 1759 a small volume dedicated to Pitt, repeating all of Mitchell's arguments and adding a few of his own.

It was a false notion, Young maintained, to imagine that the Americans would make themselves independent. An intelligent economic policy would take care of that. To Mitchell's list of products Young, probably at Collinson's suggestion, made some interesting additions to be introduced once the back country was secured: flax, silk, wine, oil, raisins, currants, almonds, indigo, etc. These would be for the advantage of both the Colonies and the mother country.

Next in importance in Young's mind was a union of all the Colonies: a parliament of eighty-six members should be chosen proportionately and a viceroy appointed by the Crown. Thus he revived Franklin's abortive Albany Plan of Union. With Louisbourg, Frontenac, and Duquesne all in British hands by this time, Young would stop at nothing short of total victory. He would go on and take the French islands in the West Indies, a cause of jealousy in the past; and he spared no words in showing his dislike for "our pretended friends the dutch," who were exploiting their neutrality to earn rich profits as carriers in the French trade.[7]

Doubts expressed during the war regarding the future loyalty of the Colonials were swallowed up in the feeling of triumph that came naturally with the sweeping victories of 1759–1760. Pitt, declared his admirer and follower, the editor and printer John Almon, had "raised the power and grandeur of England to the highest summit of glory and respect." In a word Pitt "was the spirit of the war, the genius of England, and the comet of his age." But Almon wrote in bitterness. The new King, George III, had forced Pitt to resign in favor of a more moderate government headed by the young and inexperienced Scottish peer, Lord Bute. Almon considered it a crime to hand back Havana to

---

[7] *Reflections on the Present State of Affairs at Home and Abroad.* By Arthur Young, Esq., author of the *Theatre of the Present War in North America*, London: printed for J. Coote, 1759.

Spain, Martinique and Guadeloupe and the nearby island of St. Lucia, with its magnificent harbor, to France, and St. Pierre and Miquelon with all the fishing rights in the Gulf of St. Lawrence as well. With these valuable islands again in their possession, the Bourbon powers could prepare themselves for the next war. *"O may the conditions of such a peace be engraved on the tombstones of its advisers!"* Almon exclaimed.[8] Plagued with gout, Pitt had spoken for three hours in Commons in much the same vein.

On questions relating to the mainland of North America, however, there was consensus. The duc de Choiseul, the King of France's chief minister, had tried to save Canada north of the St. Lawrence and the Great Lakes, and also a corridor through the interior down the Wabash River and the lower Ohio to connect with Louisiana and the lower Mississippi. Under this scheme, all the waters emptying into the Gulf of Mexico would remain French. In Britain there was an initial period of indecision over this, even Pitt at first entertaining some doubt. But, as Lord Shelburne put it in a speech in Parliament in December 1762, the war had been fought for the security of the British Colonies in North America; and by this was meant the exclusion of France from the continent. The Americans had been making this their goal over a period of forty years.

Books published in London in 1763, supplementing the brief debate in Parliament over the peace terms, show a disposition to accept as gospel the traditional American argument of "encirclement." The Reverend John Entick, in his five-volume *History of the War*, for instance, charged the French and the Spanish with motives of ambition, envy, and hatred:

The French perfidiously encroached upon our American territories and, in time of profound peace, formed a plan, and began, with its execution, to drive the English out of America, and thereby to annihilate, or to reduce our trade and navigation to a dependence on their naval power and commerce.[9]

---

[8] *A Review of Mr. Pitt's Administration*, 2nd. ed., London: printed for G. Kearsly in Ludgate St., 1763.

[9] The Rev. John Entick, M.A., and other Gentlemen, *The General History of the Late War* . . . , 5 vols., London, 1763, V, p. 466.

Should the French unite Canada with Louisiana, wrote the author of *A Compleat History of the Late War*, the "Colonies must lose all share in the Indian trade in time of peace; and in time of war be exposed to continual dangers, or to the ruinously chargeable defence of a frontier more than 1,500 miles in length." [10] The most graphic presentation of the "encirclement" argument came from an army officer addressing the House of Commons:

They [the French] hold our Colonies between the two Ends of a Net, which if they tighten by Degrees, they may get all of them into the Body of it, and then drown them in the Sea. . . ." [11]

Even Franklin had not put the matter so neatly.

Some people expressed misgivings that the Empire was already too large and that it could not absorb more territory, but these views were overborne by a general feeling of optimism. Just ahead lay a rosy future. Speakers in Parliament echoed the mercantile arguments of Mitchell and Young and showed they had read Franklin. Freed from fear of their enemies and in un-challenged control of their territory, the Colonials would multiply in number and furnish such a demand for manufactures as to ensure full employment in Britain. "Such . . . is that America we now securely possess," reflected one writer, "rich in Towns and Cities, rising Colonies, and every other flourishing Circum-stance of Population, Trade and Industry, the certain Means of Power and of Opulence. . . ." Or, as it was put in Parliament, not trade alone, but also the extent of territory and the number of people were matters of interest "to a state attentive to the sources of real grandeur." The next step was to plant a new colony in the heartland, where the Ohio fell into the Mississippi "which, like another ocean, is the general receptacle of all the rivers that water the interior parts of that vast Continent." And with Britain keeping up her Navy on the Atlantic, how easy it would be in a subsequent war to carry on any attack against the French islands from North America and in addition, to strangle

---

[10] *A Compleat History of the Late War; or Annual Register of its Rise, Progress, and Events* . . . , Dublin, 1763, p. 3.
[11] Quoted in *Chronological Annals of the War* . . . by Mr. Dobson, Oxford, 1763, p. xiv.

the homeward bound trade of Spain. In short, the peace would endure as long as Britain wished.[12]

Optimism, then, appears to have been the prevailing note in Britain in 1763. Writers and speakers, echoing ideas expounded previously by Franklin, Mitchell, Young, and others predicted a golden age of Imperial harmony. The picture they drew was rational and intellectually convincing, but tragically unreal. In the American West, the focus of so much hope, divergent forces, never in harmony with one another during the war, broke once more into the open. The Indians could not be reconciled with their lot; the more intelligent of them were frightened, sensing the steady attrition of their tribal society at the hands of the whites. Even an "honest" purchase, as an Indian Council told George Croghan, had no real value: what the Indians got, in the form of goods or money, was temporary; what they lost—their lands—was permanent and irreparable. Like Sir William Johnson, the Indian Department's agent to the Mohawks, Croghan lived among the Indians and knew their point of view. But his speculative instincts were insatiable; he helped his friends as well as himself to secure choice tracts; and he was active in all three of the large land companies that incorporated after the Great War. "One half of England is now land mad," he told Johnson in 1763, "and everybody there has there Eys fixt on this cuntry. . . ."[13]

Contemporaneously Pennsylvania and Virginia interests spurred their plans for new colonies as far distant as Detroit and

---

[12] The quoted excerpts in this paragraph are taken from *The Parliamentary History of England*, XV, cols. 1271–1272, and from several rare books of the period, viz.: *Reflections on the Terms of Peace*, 2nd ed., London: printed for G. Kearsly, 1763, pp. 40–45; *Thoughts on Trade in General, Our West Indian in particular, our Continental Colonies, Canada, Guadeloupe, and the Preliminary Articles of Peace, addressed to the Community*, London: printed for John Wilkie, 1763, pp. 80–81; *The History of Louisiana, or of the Western Parts of Virginia and Carolina*, translated from the French, by M. LePage Du Pratz; with some Notes and Observations relating to our Colonies, London: printed for T. Becket & P. A. De Hondt, 1763, p. xviii; and *An Appeal to Knowledge; or Candid Discussions of the Preliminaries of Peace, signed at Fontainebleau, Nov. 3, 1762, and laid before Both Houses of Parliament*, London: printed for J. Wilkie, 1763, p. 48.

[13] As quoted in Albert T. Volwiler's, *George Croghan and the Westward Movement, 1741–1782*, Cleveland, O., 1926, p. 234.

the Mississippi. Governor Dinwiddle's wartime promise of 200,000 acres of Ohio lands brought in the veterans as a new pressure group; and this was the medium that whetted George Washington's appetite for Western lands. In 1763 Washington owned 9,581 acres of plantation lands east of the mountains but, not to fall behind in the new wave of speculation, he joined with forty-nine other men in forming the Mississippi Company which aimed at a grant large enough to give 50,000 acres to each shareholder. By 1773, through his interest in the older Ohio Company, Washington achieved a total holding of 32,885 acres.

The British government had been trying, even before the war, to put a brake on this type of activity, and so long as the French were masters of the interior, the Colonial governments cooperated. It was necessary to outbid the French for the friendship of the tribes if the war was to be won, and the authorities took care to reassure the Indians that, in return for their aid, they would be protected on their lands. Indeed, the Albany Congress of 1754 invited the Board of Trade to assume this responsibility and prohibit settlement west of the Alleghenies. The government, acting through the army and the Colonial governors, accepted the obligation and issued orders to stop white men from trespassing on Indian lands.

With a second offensive against Fort Duquesne pending in 1758, both the army and the Governor of Pennsylvania sent emissaries to lure the Ohio Indians away from the French; and to these emissaries, a Moravian missionary from Philadelphia and Colonel Bouquet from the army, goes the credit for opening up the road for General Forbes. At Easton, Bouquet concluded a treaty guaranteeing the Indians possession of their lands and promising them more trade in the future. Bouquet did his best to make good on these promises; he went so far as to post a price list on goods to discourage the cheating. But no sooner were the French expelled from the region than Virginia speculators led by the Ohio Company's representative renewed their old game of land grabbing and, failing to corrupt the Colonel, instituted a lobby in London for direct action on the British government. New York speculators, with eyes on the rich Mohawk Valley, instigated similar pressures.

With the French still on the Mississippi encouraging the

Indians to fight, the latter fought two wars for survival: the Cherokee war in the South (1759–61) and the bloodier uprising of May–October 1763 in the North, led by the Ottawa chieftain, Pontiac. In retrospect we see the natives fighting a hopeless cause. Among other things, they were now habituated to the white man's goods: from the private traders both the Colonial governments and the Army had taken up the practice of making frequent "presents" to the Indians—a form of aid bearing a similarity to today's practice of subsidizing "underdeveloped" nations. But in both wars the backbone of Indian rebellion was broken by the British Army, manning the forts in the interior while the Colonial Assemblies looked on impassively and rendered practically no assistance. It was Colonel Bouquet who brought the northern tribes to terms in the fall of 1763.

Profiting from these lessons and drawing on the advice of Johnson, Croghan, General Jeffrey Amherst, and others with experience in America, the Board of Trade devised plans for pacifying and administering the interior. These plans were foreshadowed by the famous Proclamation of October 7, 1763, drafted by John Pownall who, as secretary to the Board, had almost twenty years of contact with men who knew the problem intimately. As a starting principle, it was agreed that the promises made to the Indians must be kept, and that therefore the whole wilderness west of the Alleghenies must be left for the time being in the hands of the tribes. To persons in the Colonies expecting to migrate westward the Board offered the alternative of moving into one of the new colonies constituted in 1763—East or West Florida in the South, or the Province of Quebec in the North. All three of these had land in abundance to settle—the British Governor of Quebec reserved the country south of the St. Lawrence (subsequently known as the Eastern Townships) expressly for the purpose. But, with the exception of West Florida, settlers failed to come, and even there the number of arrivals was sparse.

The British government, in the meantime, assumed the sole responsibility for the trans-Allegheny West, excluding both Quebec and the seaboard Colonies whose jealousies had for so many years obscured the issue, and keeping the forts under

Army control. Lieutenant General Gage was made commander, with headquarters at Detroit. It was his plan to strengthen the garrison system by introducing colonies of military families at certain posts, notably at Forts Niagara and Pitt. Finally, trade with the Indians was to be encouraged, but the white traders were to be licensed and to post bond for their good behavior. After circularizing the governors in the Colonies and the two superintendents over Indian affairs, the Board was ready at the end of July 1764 to put these plans into effect.

Vested interests lost no time in thwarting these plans, however. Over the next ten years various rival groups of speculators compounded the confusion both in London and the Colonial capitals by their petitions and undercover activities in quest of government support. One of these was the Illinois Company of George Croghan, represented in London by the barrister Richard Jackson, who was also serving as agent for Connecticut. Another group, with eyes on the Ohio Valley, formed in Philadelphia under the name of the "Suffering Traders" of Pennsylvania. Benjamin Franklin and his wealthy Quaker friend, Samuel Wharton, were both among the "sufferers," but they met with opposition from Lord Hillsborough, the President of the Board of Trade who was against these inroads into the Indian country. As Secretary of State for the American Department, set up in 1768 to cope with the increasing gravity of relations with the Colonies, Hillsborough maintained his opposition to these interests; but the latter, Wharton taking the lead, so managed to weaken Hillsborough's position with the other ministers that in 1772 they forced his resignation in favor of Lord Dartmouth, who was disposed to favor colonization of the American West.

Actually, the government's intentions of shielding the Indians from encroachment had collapsed long before this: American resistance to the new taxes, earmarked for financing the defense system in the interior, had made the cost insurmountable, and Hillsborough himself considered it more important to settle the score with the Colonies than to maintain an army in the West. In 1768 he cut the number of garrisons, transferring the troops to the centers of disaffection on the seaboard, and obtained a new treaty with the Indians whereby the Crown agreed to pay £10,-640 for moving the boundary farther west from the mountains.

Meanwhile the Illinois Company and the "Suffering Traders" joined hands in London to form a new group which they called the Walpole Associates. Thomas Walpole, Franklin's merchant friend and Member of Parliament, was a participant. The Walpole Associates then organized, in 1769, the Vandalia Company with the object of getting control of a block of 2,400,000 acres around Fort Pitt on the upper Ohio which the Six Nations had ceded to the Crown under the treaty of the preceding year. The Walpole Associates were composed of a close-knit group of business friends in Philadelphia and London and of high officials, including John Robinson of the Treasury and Lord Camden (Charles Pratt), who was the Lord Chancellor. Wharton was the prime mover of the venture. Franklin held two shares in the Vandalia enterprise but had to keep in the background, as he was out of favor with the ministry, particularly with Hillsborough and the Crown Law Officers, Thurlow and Wedderburn.

Wharton in 1772 devised a ruse to persuade the Crown to concede the desired grant: he had George Croghan send over a number of petitions bearing forged names in the hope of convincing the Privy Council that people were already on this land and needed a government. But despite this concerted pressure brought by the Associates—the parade of dubious evidence put on before the Privy Council, the gift of shares in the company to several members of the government, the displacement of Hillsborough as head of the American Department—the Vandalia Company met with defeat. It had strong opposition from inside the government, notably from the Law Officers who adopted delaying tactics.

Basically the British government was averse to handing over the American West to speculators. Since the Proclamation of 1763 it had entertained hopes of a gradual transition from Indian occupation to bona fide colonization by small settlers, but it, too, of course, found itself thwarted. Unable to administer the country itself or to induce the seaboard Colonies to cooperate in the task, the government in 1774 transferred all of the country north of the Ohio to the Province of Quebec, the only one of the Colonies unhampered by private designs on the Indians' lands.

At one stroke the British government by this Act threw its influence to the side of the ancient Catholic fur-trading colony on the St. Lawrence. The populace of Quebec was, of course, still French; but since the Conquest, the leadership and the driving energy had passed largely into Scottish hands. Far from being defeated and on the road to extinction, as its American rivals had wished, Canada experienced a rebirth and was now stronger than ever. To the rebellious minds to the south, especially in New England where religious prejudice was second nature, the Quebec Act seemed an intolerable insult.

# CHAPTER II

# A Crisis Emerges, 1763-1774

A ship might as well attempt to carry her lading hung at the end of her bowsprit, as a government to manage a people widely dispersed, and more numerous towards the extremities than towards the center.—*Arthur Young, 1772*

STRONG TENSIONS AND OUTRAGED FEELINGS PREVAILED just below the surface of American life in the 1760s. To attempt to rationalize or "justify" such emotions seems pointless. They stemmed from frustrated ambitions and resentments which, in certain colonies, notably in Massachusetts, had filtered down to the lowest levels of society. These emotions had boiled up from below during the wars at the beginning of the century. Now aggressive and ambitious, straining to wage war against the French, the Americans at the top realized their dependence on Britain for help, but they felt no gratitude for the help it gave. Young John Adams in his letter of 1755 reflected this attitude perfectly. He remained wholly unaware of any "debt" to Britain; rather, he coolly calculated the prospect of a transfer of wealth and power; he conceived of an impregnable American empire obtaining mastery of the seas, an empire self-sufficient and independent of Europe. And he rejoiced in the prospect.

Among the populace the passions were easily aroused. At this level the feeling was strongest in Boston, the town that had had the first contact with British soldiers and sailors. In Britain the one-time practice of quartering troops on private householders had been outlawed in the previous century; in America, Parliament not having provided the means for separate camps and supply, the commanders often had no alternative other than to require the local community to sustain their troops. Lord

Loudoun, in command of the forces in 1757, pleaded with the government to make the army self-sufficient. The war, he insisted, would have to be fought by and directed from England. The Provincials could not be trusted. Loudoun's officers complained of the Provincials' lack of discipline, their tendency to desert, their opposition to enlistments, their drunkenness. Colonel Bouquet reported from Philadelphia that the magistrates had refused quarters for his men. The jealousies and obstructionist tactics of local politicians, exercising power through the provincial assemblies, were notorious: they insisted on having their own separate command; they refused to cooperate with the regular army except on their own terms; they frequently required that Provincial troops be used only for local defense and not for offensive campaigning against the enemy. As the French and the Indians operated in the remote interior, no sense of danger could have been felt in the settled parts of the country east of the mountains. The war was far away, and the fear of an incursion or even a raid was nonexistent.

Far from being welcomed as saviors from the enemy, the British forces appear to have been received as sullenly as occupation troops would be. What distant writers like Dr. John Mitchell and Arthur Young in London conceived as a glorious common adventure against a common foe was realistically a sorry scene of mutual distrust and animosity. Even at the outset of the Great War the "redcoat" was a symbol of oppression. Yet opposition, reported Loudoun, came "not from the *lower* People, but from the *leading* People, who raise the dispute, in order to have a merit with the others, by defending their Liberties, as they call them." [1]

The "leading People" were, of course, the merchants of the seaboard towns as well as the planters and speculators of the country. As in Europe, ownership of land in America meant social position and prestige; hence the moneyed merchants joined in the scramble for Western lands and married into the landed gentry.

---

[1] Loudoun to Cumberland, Nov. 22, 1756, in Stanley M. Pargellis, *Military Affairs in North America, 1748–1765. Selected Documents from the Cumberland Papers in Windsor Castle*, New York, 1936, p. 273.

During the war the merchants pressed their opportunities to the limit, turning large profits in the sale of provisions to the enemy and expanding their smuggling operations long made safe and easy by a lax and inefficient British customs service. Thus Thomas Hancock and his son John of Boston, Stephen Hopkins, John Brown, and Andrew Whipple of Rhode Island, Charles Thomson and John Dickinson of Philadelphia, to name but a few who were directly or indirectly mixed up in this business, did not hesitate to turn their wrath on the British government when it started to interfere with their "liberties."

The smugglers brought in dry goods, gunpowder, tea, and so forth from France, Holland, Germany, and even Sweden; wine from Madeira and the Azores; and molasses from the West Indies, which they turned into rum. An estimate in 1765 valued the illicit trade with the European countries at £500,000 per year. Smuggled tea was believed to account for ninety per cent of the total import of that product; Philadelphia, New York, and Newport were the principal centers for the business. Providence, the home of John Brown, ran Newport a close second in rum distilling which was rendered profitable by the smuggled molasses from the West Indies. Richard Oswald, a native American merchant who transferred his business to England before the outbreak of the Revolution, advised Lord Dartmouth in February 1775 that in his opinion a confederacy of smugglers "contrived, prompted and promoted" the union among the Colonies.

It was William Pitt, the "friend of American Liberty," who first instigated measures against these people. Indignant at reports of their trading with the French, he sent a circular dispatch in August 1760 to the Colonial governors, ordering them to tighten up the customs service. But there were difficulties: the vice admiralty courts, where such cases were tried, were locally controlled and, as the governor of Pennsylvania reported, the smugglers were able to buy the services of the best lawyers. Perhaps more subversive than these corrupting influences was the success of leading smugglers in recruiting mobs for attacks on the customs officers. The most notorious incident occurred in 1772 when John Brown and his fellow distillers of Providence personally led a mob against the revenue cutter *Gaspee* after it had run aground and burned it to the waterline. The *Gaspee* had been too efficient in capturing hogsheads of smuggled molasses landed by night in the coves of Rhode Island.

Meanwhile lawyers like James Otis of Boston, with a flair for courtroom oratory, had succeeded in making popular idols out of their wealthy clients, picturing them as defenders of "the rights of man" against a tyrannical government which was trying to "enslave" them. Otis had a personal score to settle: he had been disappointed in not getting the appointment to the chief justiceship of Massachusetts; on the bench, where he thought he ought to be himself, sat his hated rival, Thomas Hutchinson, who later became lieutenant-governor and eventually governor of the Colony. Hutchinson was an able man of high intelligence, a well-to-do merchant himself, but reticent in manner and independent in judgment. At least twice previously he had breasted the opposition of powerful groups with a popular following; and in 1764–1765, he again showed his independence by taking a position against the British government on the Sugar Act and the Stamp Act. He did this *privately*, working directly through his friend Richard Jackson in London and scorning the favor of the populace at home. Eventually Hutchinson, while lieutenant-governor, paid the price of his courage: his home, one of the show places of Boston, was invaded by a mob and systematically wrecked. Inside the house were papers incriminating a group of speculators who eyed lands in Maine.

In Britain the overriding issue was fiscal. At £122,600,000 in 1763 the national debt was not far short of double its size at the beginning of the war. The carrying charge of approximately £4,500,000 absorbed more than half of the annual budget. In its search for new revenue at home the government ran the risk of open defiance, notably from the cider counties of the southwest. During the war Parliament had revived an earlier practice of making grants to the Colonies, sometimes as gifts, other times as compensation for expenditures on the war. Because Massachusetts had made the best showing during the war, it received the largest single reimbursement from Britain: a total of £328,000. The practice was a forerunner of American lend-lease to Britain in the Second World War.

The problem that most directly obtruded itself on the British government in 1763 was the one of keeping the army in the

American West at proper strength. Indian troubles alone made any other course unthinkable. This was the consideration that required the Grenville ministry to formulate plans for a Parliamentary tax on the Colonies. Grenville's first measure, the Sugar Act (1764), was a disappointment; smuggling merchants had already shown they could beat the game. The Stamp Act, which followed, received a full year of careful planning and consideration before being submitted to Parliament, yet it turned into a complete disaster. This measure in particular is often treated as *the cause* of the American Revolution and the inference drawn is that except for it and other fiscal measures enacted by Parliament, no revolution would have occurred. Such an interpretation is, however, extremely superficial; we must keep in mind the tensions accumulating through the years before, especially the war years—the unappeased ambitions of the landowners and merchants, the passions vented at the tavern level among the masses.

Unfortunately only a corner of the veil has been lifted to expose these deeper causes. Antagonism in the Colonies was so violent and so bitter as to make one incredulous that a single Act, or series of Acts, could have caused the Revolution. With the forced departure of the French in 1763, the psychology of the whole situation changed. Previously the Americans had been obliged to accept British help, indeed, they had pleaded for it; now they no longer needed it and were unwilling to assist in supporting it. They were in a position to pursue their own interests.

From the British standpoint there was no alternative to the Stamp Act. Funds were required to maintain the troops in the American West, and no reason could be given as to why the Americans should be excused from their share of this burden. The Act was drawn in the Treasury Department with due care; the four Colonial agents, including Franklin, then in London were consulted and, moreover, a reasonable time was allowed for counter-proposals to come from the Colonies. None came. The best that Franklin and his colleagues could suggest was that the British government fall back on Colonial good will and await the voluntary offerings of the thirteen different assemblies. To any practical-minded statesman such a proposal could hardly have carried conviction. To make compliance doubly sure, after the Act was passed and the tax collectors had been appointed, Grenville gave explicit orders to turn over the proceeds directly to the paymaster of the forces in America. No money was to leave the Colonies. From a pragmatic standpoint, recourse to the statutory power of Parliament was the only possible method, short of letting the whole matter go by default. In the Commons the bill passed 245–49, and in the Lords it elicited so little interest that there was no division.

"I am assured by the Officers," General Lord Loudoun had reported from New York in 1756, "that it is not uncommon for the People of this Country to say, they would be glad to see any Man that dare exert a British Act of Parliament here." The governors, advised Loudoun, were ciphers; unless the provincial governments were remodeled so as to acquire authority, "you will not have a force to exert any British Acts of Parliament here." [2] The universal execration and sudden wave of violence that greeted the news of the Stamp Act in the Colonies substantiated this forgotten warning. The Act was nullified even before the date set (November 1) for it to take effect. Boston mobs, attacking and demolishing the homes of Andrew and Peter Oliver and then of Thomas Hutchinson, set off a chain reaction which spread south as far as Charleston. Local citizens who had consented to serve as stamp distributors were the immediate objects: it was standard procedure for the mob to hang or burn its intended victim in effigy, and then, if that failed to intimidate him, to threaten him with bodily harm. Many of the stamp distributors were men of accomplishment—Colonel George Mercer, who had served in the Virginia forces as aide to Washington in the Great War, was a good case in point.

Encouraging these mobs and indubitably responsible for them was a network of seditious bodies who dubbed themselves "Sons of Liberty." The "Sons" were recruited from the classes who would have to buy the stamps—the merchants, the lawyers, the printers, and in the South, some of the planters. Some of them kept their names hidden or, like the Adamses of Boston, chose the role of silent supporters; others, like the Philadelphia merchants Robert Morris and Charles Thomson, apparently did not

[2] *Ibid.*

mind if their names were linked with violence; a few, like Samuel Langdon, the Congregational minister of Portsmouth, boasted of it.

This sudden outburst of revolutionary temper in 1765, which took experienced and reasonable men completely by surprise and brought effective government to a standstill, was in puzzling contrast to the lack of a war spirit displayed toward the French during the prolonged conflict so recently terminated. No comparable propaganda or expression of hatred had manifested itself against the ancient enemy at any time during the Great War. Now what appeared on the surface as a rational and orderly society suddenly dissolved into a confused and irrational regime of violence and agitation. The Stamp Act was a dead letter, and there was no means to enforce it. Nonimportation agreements among the merchants, coupled with a refusal to honor existing debts to their British counterparts, put the latter in a hard position. The Sons of Liberty exploited the Stamp Act as a symbol of tyranny and drew lurid pictures of the Americans as "slaves" if they submitted to taxation. If Parliament could tax them at all, it could tax them into poverty, so the Sons alleged; and the practical issue of raising a revenue vanished in a heated talk about "rights."

Dismay swept over Britain at news of these many troubles. The merchants were the immediate losers and naturally were the first to react. Working closely with Lord Rockingham, whose ministry had come to power just as the first reports from America were filtering in, a committee of twenty-eight London merchants circularized the commercial and shipping centers of the entire kingdom pleading for cooperation in persuading Parliament to repeal the Stamp Act. When Parliament sat again in January 1766 a flood of petitions greeted it, all of them recounting losses already suffered and voicing fears of bankruptcy and ruin. A business that in 1764 had produced a two-million pound profit shrank to almost nothing by the end of 1765. Whether much of the shrinkage would have occurred anyway, in view of the depression, there was no means of knowing and the protesting merchants hardly took this into account. The cause and cure of their misfortunes, they believed, centered on the Stamp Act.

Certain observant writers went beyond these natural fears

and realized that the advantages all lay with the Americans. "We should tremble at the least apprehension of Revolution," warned Dr. John Fothergill, a prominent London physician who had numerous friends and even family ties in America. Like Dr. John Mitchell, Dr. Fothergill postulated the inestimable importance of the Colonies to Great Britain. If they found it to "their interest to attempt in earnest a dissolution, and either concert the means of shaking off their dependence upon us by their own force, or court the protection of some other power till they were able to unfetter themselves from the temporary aid they had chosen to rely on . . . ," Britain could not prevent them from doing so. The Colonies brought the kingdom great wealth; they consumed vast quantities of its manufactures; they were so situated and their population was increasing so fast that they greatly enhanced Britain's position in the world. "The maritime Powers well know this," Dr. Fothergill continued. "They see, they feel our growing influence; and that if we encourage and protect our Colonies, as we have done, the enemies of Great Britain have everything to dread, its friends everything to hope from the wise management of the power we possess." To him wise management meant going farther than mere repeal of the Act:

If we promote scholarships for Americans in our universities; give posts and benefits in America, to such Americans as have studied here, preferably to others. If the Government permit such youth as come to Europe on account of their studies, to come over in the King's ships *gratis*, we shall still unite them more firmly. The Americans, by mixing with our own youth at the University, will diffuse a spirit of Enquiry after America and its affairs; they will cement friendships on both sides, which will be of more lasting benefit to both countries, than all the armies that Britain can send thither.[3]

Josiah Tucker, the well-known Dean of Gloucester who wielded a vigorous pen on political and economic subjects, thought the Americans wanted to be independent. "You wish," he charged, "to be an Empire by itself. . . ." He favored repealing the Stamp Act, and leaving the Americans to themselves. They would be the losers, he maintained; they would face the prospect

---

[3] John Fothergill, *Considerations relative to the North American Colonies,* London: printed by Henry Kent, 1765, p. 48.

of being a variety of little colonies under a variety of petty governments, jealous of one another. Britain, Tucker believed, could win not by invoking force but by withdrawing its protecting hand; the Colonies would trade with the kingdom as their interest required. But the British could offer better terms than the Americans could get elsewhere. Without a common head, moreover, anarchy and confusion would prevail. As soon as this became clear to them, they would lose the "fit of false patriotism." [4]

Nicholas Ray, a native of New York living in London, would do essentially the same thing: repeal the Stamp Act and remove the troops. There would then be no further need for taxation. But Ray, even more than Dr. Fothergill, grasped the strategic advantage held by the Americans and the necessity of keeping them friendly. With pardonable exaggeration, he asserted they surpassed most of the kingdoms of Europe in power and size of population:

The ruling policy of every State is unquestionably self-interest; the policy therefore of every State of Europe, and particularly our inveterate enemies, must induce them to wish a revolt of our Colonies on the Continent of North America; and they would not fail of supporting them, either openly or secretly, in doing it, whereby that whole Continent would be thrown open to them in point of trade, which this kingdom now alone enjoys. The part which both England and France took when Holland revolted from Spain, proves that my apprehensions are not ill grounded; if therefore severity is used to enforce an unpopular act . . . it would not only be a matter of great joy to our inveterate enemies, but they would second such disobedience with all their power to confirm it, and thereby hope to reduce the dignity and power of Great Britain. . . . We ought therefore to be very careful in our conduct toward the Americans, whom, in all probability, every power in Europe would encourage to rebellion . . . [5]

---

[4] *A Letter from a Merchant in London to his Nephew in North America, relative to the present posture of affairs in the Colonies,* London: printed for J. Walter, 1766.

[5] *The Importance of the Colonies of North America, and the Interest of Great Britain with regard to them considered.* By Nicholas Ray, now of London, a native and formerly a citizen of New York, London; N. Y. reprinted, 1766, p. 8.

On face value Ray's proposal to withdraw the troops would seem the perfect solution. Benjamin Franklin, arguing likewise for the repeal of the Stamp Act, turned history upside down to achieve this end. The Colonies, he blandly told the House of Commons, had had no part in bringing on the last war. They were only attacked after Braddock had come. Until then, they were "in perfect peace with both French and Indians."

The troops were not therefore sent for their defence. The trade with the Indians, though carried on in America, is not an American interest. The people of America are chiefly farmers and planters; scarce anything they raise or produce is an article of commerce with the Indians. The Indian trade is a British interest; it is carried on with British manufactures for the profit of British merchants and manufacturers; therefore the war, as it commenced for defence of territories of the crown, the property of no American, and for the defence of a trade purely British, was really a British war.[6]

This distortion of the facts, done for a specific purpose, apparently went unchallenged at the moment. The Members of Parliament who heard Franklin were probably too concerned with the immediate issue to bother themselves over an historical matter. But this myth—Denys de Berdt, the agent from Massachusetts, had actually voiced it before Franklin—was to become very potent, and therefore we should notice it. It involves a statement which is directly contrary to fact; namely, that the Americans were innocent bystanders, in a sense even victims, of a war which the British had waged solely for their own selfish ends. This being so, the Americans, of course, had not even a moral responsibility for sharing the burdens left by the war. Franklin performed a convenient mental somersault for the benefit of his fellow countrymen. Other writers, notably his fellow Pennsylvanian John Dickinson, embroidered upon his misstatements and Tom Paine in his revolutionary manifesto of 1776, *Common Sense,* put the finishing touches to the myth. Here lay the ideological heart of the Revolution: the passionate affirmation that America was separate from Europe, that it had fallen prey in the past to European selfishness, and that it would not again permit itself to be exploited.

---

[6] *Writings of Benjamin Franklin,* Albert H. Smyth, ed., 10 vols., New York, 1905–1907, IV, p. 439. (Hereafter cited as Smyth.)

After a month of debate Parliament repealed the Stamp Act. The complaints of the British merchants could not be ignored, and there was no way of enforcing the Act. Unwittingly the Grenville ministry had commited a political blunder of the first magnitude. A Pandora's box of disagreement and propaganda was now open. Emotional arguments about "freedom," "rights," "slavery," "tyranny," and so on became common. The more elevated argument, whether Parliament had violated the British constitution by imposing a tax on people who were not represented, did not lend itself to an easy answer. The Rockingham ministry straddled this question by passing the Declaratory Act, a simple affirmation of the established principle of Parliamentary supremacy. It was a jealously guarded principle—the great constitutional legacy of the English Revolution of 1688—and its restatement was a political necessity for the government if it was to secure a majority for repeal. Repeal was an event, said the official record, "that caused more universal joy, throughout the British dominions, than perhaps any other that can be remembered." Franklin credited the British merchants with accomplishing the feat, and reproached his fellow countrymen for not showing their gratitude. "I think," he wrote to his friend Joseph Galloway in Philadelphia, "we should stand in truth greatly obliged to the merchants, who are a very respectable body, and whose friendship is worth preserving, as it may greatly help us on future occasions." [7]

Repeal left the revenue problem just where it had been. But, as in America, argument in Britain over high points relating to the constitution tended to take precedence over practical matters. The Americans, George Grenville flatly declared, wanted to be independent. This was the real cause of all the tumult. The Stamp Act merely furnished the pretext. To repeal it now in the face of threats was a fatal confession of weakness and a virtual surrender. This uneasy thought that Parliament had betrayed itself in its hasty retreat of 1766 weighed on the minds of Grenville and his associates, the Bedford Whigs. A serious crisis had arisen, Grenville insisted, and it had to be met with vigor and firmness. The Declaratory Act was *only a delusive and nugatory affirmance of the right of the legislature of this*

---

[7] June 13, 1767. Smyth, V, no. 430.

*kingdom*, if not followed by some bill which shall exert it." [8]
Repeal of the Stamp Act was realistically an admission that the
Colonies were independent; the resolve to retrieve this lost
position furnished the mainspring for much of the action that
was to follow.

The original question of finding the money to support the
troops in the American West now dropped out of sight, and
the problem of how to make government in the Colonies effective came to the fore. The crux of this matter was to make the
Colonial governors independent of their legislatures, and to
bring this about a separate source of revenue resting on the
authority of Parliament was essential. By putting a tariff on certain *British* goods, notably paper, paints, glass, and tea, which
were imported into the Colonies and were in wide demand there,
and by empowering the Board of Customs in the Colonies to
collect the duties, Charles Townshend, the Chancellor of the
Exchequer, believed that this desired result was in view. The
slogan of the American resistance to the Stamp Act was "No
taxation without representation," and men like Franklin in working for repeal of the Act had distinguished between direct and
indirect taxation, making no claims that indirect taxation, which
involved the customs laws, was outside the power of Parliament.
They protested only that direct taxation was unconstitutional.

Townshend, Hillsborough, and Barrington, the key members
of the new British ministry in 1767, proposed to evacuate the
American West, leaving it to the individual Colonies to defend
their own frontier, and to deal with the Indians by treaty. In
the expectation that this meant reopening the West to colonization, the speculators who constituted the Walpole Associates
favored this policy of military retrenchment. With the army
gone, they could effectively resume their old policy of playing

---

[8] Charles Lloyd, *The Conduct of the late Ministry Examined; from July
1765 to March 1766*, London: printed for J. Almon, 1767, p. 158. This
pamphlet went through two editions and was considered one of the most
formidable attacks on the Rockingham ministry for repealing the Stamp
Act and substituting the high-sounding, but empty Declaratory Act. Charles
Lloyd was George Grenville's secretary, and it was thought by some, at
the time, that Grenville was the real author. In any event, the pamphlet
reflects Grenville's ideas.

off the tribes against one another. But these expectations did not materialize; the Crown withheld its consent to the Vandalia grant; and the situation in the West deteriorated by 1774 to the point where Parliament took the whole country away from the Americans and put it back under control of the Canadians.

Meanwhile, however, the Townshend duties met with the same disaster in the seaboard towns as had the stamp taxes two years previously—the duties on sixty-seven different grades of paper furnished the quick-tempered newspaper press an opportunity for a field day of propaganda and vituperation—and the arrival of British soldiers in Boston, September 28, 1768, had just the opposite of the intended effect. The newspapers spared no effort in fabricating stories of misbehavior on the part of the troops; and a publication cleverly written up in diary form and gotten out every two weeks supplied editors all the way down the coast with free copy of accounts of the alleged brutality and sexual misconduct of the British soldiery in Boston. With the Patriots maliciously watching their every chance to make trouble, the inevitable street incident occurred on March 5, 1770 when a detachment of regulars tormented by a crowd, opened fire and killed five persons. The Patriots, Samuel Adams assuming the lead, quickly exploited this as the "Boston Massacre," which they dramatized as a symbol of "British tyranny." Thus they "made folk heroes out of street loafers and hoodlums," to borrow the words of Professor Schlesinger.[9]

The Townshend duties having failed, they were (the tea duty alone excepted) rescinded the very same month as the unfortunate episode in Boston. British merchants and manufacturers were opposed to them too, since they were levied against British goods; and as smuggled tea continued to enter America freely, the tension there relaxed in spite of the efforts of the seditious elements. In London, meanwhile, Franklin had been watching the political situation and doing apparently all he could to keep it from becoming explosive. "The popular inclination here is to wish us well," he observed in June 1770, "and that we may preserve our liberties." But Parliament had been challenged, and

---

[9] A. M. Schlesinger, Prelude to Independence. The Newspaper War on Britain, 1764–1776, New York, 1958, p. 21.

Franklin feared lest a wave of anti-American feeling whipped up by the Bedford Whigs sweep over it. Men were divided on the subject: some were for severe measures and others for lenient measures; still others for leaving things alone. "Which of these opinions will prevail and be acted on, it is impossible to say," Franklin wrote. " I only know that generally the dispute is thought a dangerous one, and that many wish to see it well compromised in time, lest by a continuance of mutual provocations the breach should become past healing."

By this time Franklin had acquired a distrust of Parliament and he deplored the reiteration of phrases that stressed its supposed supremacy over the Colonial legislatures. Such phrases meant nothing, he insisted, but they might lead to some action that would break up the Empire. "Let us hold fast our loyalty to our King . . . as that steady loyalty is the most probable means of securing us from the arbitrary power of a corrupt Parliament that does not like us. . . ." If his chief critic, William Knox, is to be believed, Franklin by now had a reputation in Britain that gave him "a degree of credit little short of *proofs of holy writ.*" [10] His friends were men who believed in the principle of Parliamentary supremacy as laid down in the Declaratory Act; and Franklin, it appears, was too practical to risk a frontal attack on so universally accepted a doctrine. But he hoped that eventually the doctrine would fall asleep, Parliament recognizing that it had no alternative but to leave it up to the individual Colonies to make their contributions to the common defense. Britain, he wrote to his friend Dr. Dubourg of Paris, had lost millions from the dispute, while the Americans were proportionally the gainers.

Fresh economic difficulties in Britain, resulting from the troubles of the East India Company, precipitated a new crisis in the winter of 1772–73. Dutch traders had captured the Company's American market—the tea duty had made this easy for them, and all the efforts to check the smuggling had been

---

[10] Franklin to Jonathan Williams, June 6, and to Samuel Cooper, June 8, 1770. Smyth, V, nos. 524 and 525. Wm. Knox, *The Controversy between Great Britain and her Colonies Reviewed.* London, printed for J. Almon, 1769.

in vain. The Company now had £2,000,000 worth of tea on its hands, and it could not meet its current expenses. Other firms connected with it were going into bankruptcy, and there was now such a shock to credit, according to Franklin, as had not been felt since the great South Sea Bubble of 1720. The government itself was losing revenue to the tune of £400,000 per year. Parliament passed an emergency measure in May 1773, authorizing the company to sell its tea directly to the retailer in America. Actually, despite the retention of the three-penny duty, the law meant cheaper tea to the consumer because it bypassed the wholesaler. The only persons really hurt would be the smugglers, whose business would now become unprofitable. Yet somehow or other the Sons of Liberty and their allies, the smuggling merchants, managed to capitalize the situation in a massive campaign of propaganda and personal vilification against the tea agents, who were subjected to the same sort of abuse as had been meted out to the stamp distributors in 1765. The crowning act in all the agitation that ensued was the Boston Tea Party of December 16, 1773, maliciously planned and executed by Samuel Adams, John Hancock, and their fellow conspirators among the "Sons." These were now organized throughout the Colonies as revolutionary committees of correspondence. Fifteen thousand pounds worth of private property went into the sea in this audacious raid.

Meanwhile Franklin in London, seeing no reason to protest against the tea duty and uninformed of the machinations against it in America, felt encouraged by the prospects for a lasting reconciliation. Moderation on Britain's part and decent behavior in the Colonies, including patience with the infirmities of the British government, he felt, would bring their reward. "We have here many friends and well-wishers," he reported in July 1773. Even among the landed gentry there was a sense of the Colonies' growing importance and a wish for reconciliation. But the politicians dared not make an open move, for fear of a challenge from their adversaries. Time was needed to heal the wounds. "The general sense of the nation is for us," he told his same correspondent in November, "a conviction that we have been ill-used and that a breach with us would be ruinous to this country." But news of the Tea Party destroyed all these chances.

Franklin recognized that a crisis was now at hand—public indignation in Britain would force the government to retaliate, but he did what he could to avert this. If the Massachusetts Assembly would volunteer to repair the damage and compensate the East India Company, the breach could still be healed. But that body made no such offer.[11]

"We have very few friends in Parliament now," Franklin wrote his Boston friend, Thomas Cushing, in April. The unreasoning violence and the personal abuse heaped on Governor Hutchinson and other royal officials in America had brought demands in Britain for strong action. Some of the British merchants, fearful of more losses, actually volunteered to put up the money to indemnify the East India Company. But otherwise the general feeling seems to have been that a stand must be made if British sovereignty were not to be given up for good. The king, reflecting the prevailing mood, recalled the impression left by the repeal of the Stamp Act: that Britain had then backed down in the face of threats. The government had shown weakness. This must not happen again. At Boston, Lord North told Parliament, "we were considered as two independent states." The question was not one of legislation or taxation, it was "whether or not we have any authority there; that it is very clear we have none, if we suffer the property of our subjects to be destroyed." The choice was plain: punish, control, or yield. "If this threat is yielded to, we may as well take no remedy at all." [12]

There were objections to force. The usual one was that trade would suffer. Apprehension was expressed that Parliament, in authorizing the Crown to use force, was undermining the principles of 1688. Most significant of all perhaps was an expression of foreboding from Edmund Burke. An attempt to punish Boston

---

[11] Franklin to Thomas Cushing, July 7 and Nov. 1, 1773, Feb. 2 and 15, Mar. 22, 1774. Smyth, VI, nos. 679, 709, 720, 722, and 736.

[12] *The Parliamentary History of England*, XVII, cols. 1163–1189, 1215–1223, 1303–1304. (Hereafter cited as *PH*.) See also Anon., *A Letter to a Member of Parliament on the present unhappy disputes between Great Britain and her Colonies*, London: printed for J. Walter, 1774; and Jack M. Sosin, "The Massachusetts Acts of 1774: Coercive or Preventive?" *Hunt. Lib. Quart.*, XXVI (May 1963), pp. 235–252.

would be the first step to full-scale war. "You will draw a foreign force upon you, perhaps, at a time when you little expect it; I will not say where that will end; I will be silent upon that head, and go no further. . . ." [13] "Think before you leap" was the gist of Burke's counsel. But Lord North, as the responsible minister of the Crown, felt that he could not make such a choice. Citing cases involving British cities, he proposed a fine to be levied against Boston for the damage done, to be enforced by four or five frigates blocking up the port. This was the Boston Port Bill. North expressed confidence in the measure's bringing speedy results, but in any event he was willing to back it to the hilt. He appealed for unanimity and got it. The bill passed the Commons without a division on March 25, 1774. Three other measures designed to check the seditious elements in Massachusetts rounded out the ministry's program.

Meanwhile the government had been resisting the pressures of the Walpole Associates and other interests to give the American West to them for speculative purposes. Ever since 1763, moreover, it had wavered on its position toward the alien French-Canadian population on the St. Lawrence. This colony had not merely survived the conquest, disappointing wartime hopes that it would be extinguished; by 1774 it was stronger than ever, a model dependency when compared with the quarrelsome seaboard colonies to the south. During the decade a new class of merchants had risen to the front in Canada, mixing readily with the *habitants* and making Montreal again the fur-trading capital of North America, its historic ties with the Indian tribes of the interior fully restored. Furthermore, with the sympathetic backing of the British military governors, Quebec kept its language, its French customs of law and government, and its Catholic faith, contrary to the intentions of its original conquerors to Anglicize and Protestantize it. Parliament sanctioned this situation by the Quebec Act, passed after a year of careful study inside the North ministry.

The Quebec Act was a great piece of statesmanship, the cornerstone of the future Dominion of Canada. But, in common with the Boston Port Act, it furnished welcome fuel for the propa-

---

[13] *PH,* XVII, cols. 1182–1185.

ganda mills to the south. Religious bigots who never tired of
venting their hatred of the "Romish religion," and disappointed
speculators who found themselves shut out of the West could
meet on common ground against this new proof of "British
tyranny." In Boston effigies of Lord North, Governor Hutchinson, the Pope, and the Devil were solemnly paraded through the
streets and burned on the Common. Samuel Langdon, D.D.,
soon to be president of Harvard, preached a sermon "explaining" how the Act "punctually verified" the Vision of the Two
Beasts in the Book of Revelation, and Edes & Gill, leaders in
the Boston Committee of Correspondence, promptly published
the sermon.[14] Men as unlike as John Hancock and the youthful Alexander Hamilton dipped their pens in gall against Parliament and the ministry for "enslaving" the American people.
And since the Quebec Act did verify the ancient claims of
Canada to the trans-Allegheny hinterland north of the Ohio,
the extremists could appeal with some semblance of fact to the
fear, rooted in earlier days, that the Americans were being
"encircled." Quaker speculators of Philadelphia were therefore
readier to accept the charges of the New England committees
of correspondence that the Acts of Parliament were "intolerable." The committees of correspondence sedulously employed
this word as an epithet; and the so-called Intolerable Acts, conceived in Britain as measures necessary for the prevention of
violence and the restoration of orderly government, had just the
opposite effect. The British government seems to have been unaware of these committees—it knew nothing of the network of
organization they had built up since the Stamp Act, of their
untiring zeal, their skill in playing on the fears and prejudices
of the ignorant masses, their success in silencing opposition
through methods of intimidation, and their readiness to exagger-
ate or falsify the facts or to resort to violence whenever their
interests could be served.

"I conjure you by all that is dear," orated John Hancock in
Boston on March 5, 1774, "that, if necessary, ye fight and even

---

[14] *A Rational Explication of St. John's Vision of the two Beasts* [Rev. xiii]
*shewing that the beginning, power and duration of Popery are plainly
predicted in that vision . . .*

die for the prosperity of our Jerusalem. . . ." At this time the so-called "Intolerable Acts" had not even been passed in London, yet Hancock was determined to provoke a revolution. As one of the ringleaders in the Tea Party, he still had reason to fear arrest and deportation, and he was invoking the anger of the mob to protect him. "I am a friend to righteous government," he began, and then he proceeded to accuse Lord Hillsborough personally of planning "the unprovok'd murders" committed four years previously by "a knot of treacherous knaves" (British regulars) under "the cruel hand" of Captain Preston "and his sanguinary coadjutors." [15] After this demagogic beginning, larded with the usual phrases about tyranny and slavery, Hancock made known his wish for the committees of correspondence to promote a union of all the Colonies through a meeting of a general congress. Parliament's "Intolerable Acts" subsequently gave the committees the push they needed for this purpose, and in September they succeeded in assembling the First Continental Congress in Philadelphia.

Better men than Hancock were at first in control of this Congress. Joseph Galloway led the moderates in a new plan of union with Britain: a separate American legislature was to be created, theoretically as a branch of Parliament but actually with full law-making powers of its own. Galloway's plan was recorded in the minutes as receiving the votes of six delegations out of the eleven present. Against this conciliatory attitude Hancock and the two Adamses from Boston pushed a set of die-hard resolves demanding a resumption of the nonimportation agreements aimed at forcing the British Parliament to back down, as it had in 1766. These resolves were then adopted, and the Galloway Plan was expunged from the record. Galloway distrusted the committees of correspondence—they were in his eyes a "licentious tyranny"—and he was confident that, if the king and Parliament were properly addressed through the regular provincial assemblies, they would reconsider. Subsequent developments in Britain proved him right; but the shelving of his Plan, which he regarded as a piece of trickery on the part of the radicals,

---

[15] J. Hancock, *An Oration . . . to Commemorate the Bloody Tragedy*, Boston: printed by Edes & Gill, 1774.

indicates that the revolutionary temper in America had passed the point of no return.[16]

Galloway's Plan was really a new edition of Franklin's old Plan of Union presented to the Albany Congress back in 1754, but now Franklin would have none of it. He charged his friend with appeasement, even implying that he was furnishing Lord North with secret intelligence. From London, Franklin, in touch with Thomas Cushing, a member of the Boston Committee of Correspondence, threw his support to the extremists. He and his friends had been thwarted in their plans for the American West, and he made no secret of his desire to see the North ministry forced out. He was also trying to oust Hutchinson from the lieutenant-governorship. If the Americans stood fast in boycotting British goods, he told the men in Boston, "this ministry must be ruined and our friends succeed to them, from whom we may hope a great Constitutional Charter to be confirmed by King, Lords & Commons, whereby our liberties shall be recognized and established, as the only sure foundation of that Union so necessary for our common welfare."[17]

Franklin on his part had every reason for wanting the quarrel patched up, and he counted on the Earl of Chatham (the former William Pitt) returning to power and making a practical adjustment of the difficulties. He was right with reference to Chatham's intentions, but wrong in gambling on American defiance of Parliament bringing down the North ministry. By now he had developed a new concept of the British Empire as a *union* under the king. This would get around the moot question of Parliament being supreme; and to try to drive his point home to his English acquaintances, he employed all of his dry humor in a skit which he called *An Edict of the King of Prussia,* which he published anonymously in 1773. The *Edict,* in which he has the Prussian king issuing a set of absurd orders regulating the internal affairs of England, a country colonized "in ages past" by primitive Germans, at first brought astonishment and then laughter from

---

[16] J. Galloway, *A Candid Examination of the Mutual Claims . . . with a Plan of Accommodation.* New York: Rivington, 1775; *ibid., A Reply to an Address.*

[17] Franklin to Cushing, Sept. 3, 1774; to Galloway, Feb. 25, 1775. Smyth, VI, nos. 747 and 768.

its British readers. Franklin contrived to be present at a meeting where the piece was read aloud. As the reading went on, the joke dawned on the audience and the general verdict was that it was a fair hit. It even made an impression on Lord Mansfield, the chief justice, who like Lord North was a firm and consistent believer in the principle of Parliamentary supremacy.

Two books, one published in London in 1769, the other in Williamsburg, Virginia in 1774, discoursed at some length on this idea of a union of equals under the king. Dr. Edward Bancroft, a roving American physician from Massachusetts, was the author of the first and Thomas Jefferson was the author of the second. Bancroft argued that the Colonies were really independent states; they were outside the realm of England, chartered by the Stuart kings who were free to do things that the sovereigns since the Revolution of 1688 had not been entitled to do. As Bancroft saw the situation, the Colonies qualified for the best of all possible worlds; they were independent, yet they could lean on Britain for protection if they chose. Submission to Parliament would be "slavery." Independence was something to which Britain should accede for England's own good. Bancroft's arguments—even his claim that the Great War had been solely a "British war"—were so like Franklin's as to arouse the suspicion that either the great man had put him up to writing the tract or, which seems more probable, he was trying to curry favor. At any rate, Franklin did develop a strong attachment for this man, and he became one of the Walpole Associates.

Jefferson's little piece, *A Summary View*, was much more concise and imaginative. He would have the deputies in Congress address the king directly:

We do earnestly entreat his majesty, as yet the only mediatory power between the several *states* of the British empire, to recommend to his parliament the total revocation of these acts . . .

Developing an argument that circumstances had changed, Jefferson then proceeded to ask his majesty to revive the royal veto. He said:

The addition of new *states* to the British empire has produced an addition of new, and sometimes opposite interests. It is now, therefore, the great office of his majesty, to resume the exercise of his negative power, and to prevent the passage of laws by any one legislature of the empire, which might bear injuriously on the rights and interests of another. . . .[18]

On its surface the argument was attractive. But to ask a Hanoverian king to step back into the shoes of the Stuarts was to expect the impossible. As Samuel Seabury of New York put it, the king was king by Act of Parliament.

Meanwhile the developing crisis evoked considerable reflective thinking and writing in Britain. Dr. John Mitchell published a new book in 1767 reinforcing his earlier mercantilist arguments in favor of hastening settlement on the Ohio and the Mississippi, asserting that the Colonists were already sharing the costs of empire through the goods and services they bought from Great Britain, and dismissing the taxes as a total loss even if collected: "The right [to tax] can never be worth a groat; and it would be the greatest loss and detriment to the nation, ever to exercise it." John H. Wynne in a three-volume *History of the British Empire in America*, published in 1769, echoed these thoughts, deplored the empty dispute over "rights," and insisted that the defense of the Empire lay, not with a few troops dispersed through the American interior, but in a healthy seagoing trade protected by a strong fleet. Sir William Draper, a prominent army officer with a background of extensive travel in the Colonies, reacted to the tense atmosphere of 1774. Regretting that the tax issue had not been buried with the Stamp Act, he agreed that the Americans had the advantage. Militarily they could be formidable. They had the resources to form a great naval power and to seek dominion over the sea. "In short, the country is impregnated with all the seeds of a mighty Empire, waiting only for the maturing hand of time and good management to bring it forth. . . ." Draper feared the American politicians, "fierce, intractable men who would gladly fell monarchy to the ground: These are the men we should now watch and guard against; or they will renew the days of Cromwellian fanaticism. . . ." He

---

[18] Edward Bancroft, *Remarks on the Review of the Controversy* . . . , London: printed for T. Becket & P. A. De Hondt, 1769; Thomas Jefferson, *A Summary View of the Rights of British America*, Williamsburg, Va., 1774.

contended that experience from Britain's own blunders came too dear. Draper urged his countrymen to extinguish the flame: meet all of the grievances of the Americans, withdraw all the regiments except the garrison at Castle William in Boston harbor, and then arm powerfully by sea. This was the only way to make Britain respected.[19]

Other writers, following the example of Nicholas Ray the former New Yorker, coupled these warnings of the dangers of revolution with forecasts of a war of revenge by France. Two works published in New York in 1768 pictured France and Spain as the only gainers from a disruption of the British Empire. Recognizing that the intrinsic advantages in the dispute lay with the Americans, and that "the ambitions of turbulent men would spur them to designs of the most dangerous nature," both of these writers urged a cautious policy on Britain. An attack on the Empire from the Bourbon powers would inflict a deadly wound. The price of disunion was ruin; but America, "after many revolutions, and perhaps great distresses, will become a mighty empire." [20]

Franklin was fully cognizant of these possibilities, particularly after paying a visit to France. "All Europe is attentive to the dispute . . . ," he wrote to a Boston friend in April 1770, "and I own I have a satisfaction in seeing that our part is taken everywhere. . . . At the same time the malignant pleasure, which other powers take in British divisions, may convince us on both sides of the necessity of our uniting." Yet he was quite ready to stimulate the feeling on the Continent and to get several pro-American pamphlets translated and printed in Paris. French

---

[19] John Mitchell, *The Present State of Great Britain and North America*, London: printed for T. Becket & P. A. De Hondt, 1767; John H. Wynne, *The History of the British Empire in America: in three volumes*, London: printed for W. Richardson & L. Urquehart, 1769; Sir William Draper, *The Thoughts of a Traveler upon our American Disputes*, London: printed for J. Ridley, 1774.

[20] *The Power and Grandeur of Great Britain, founded on the Liberty of the Colonies and the Mischiefs attending the taxing them by Act of Parliament demonstrated*, New York: printed and sold by James Parker, 1768; Stephen Sayre, *The Englishman Deceived: a political piece; wherein some very important secrets of State are briefly recited, and offered to the consideration of the public*, London: printed N. Y., 1768.

being the polite language of Europe, no better means could be found for propagating the American side of the quarrel.

These Continental ties helped to make life in London very agreeable for Franklin, as he pridefully told his son William:

Learned and ingenious foreigners, that come to England, almost all make a point of visiting me; for my reputation is still higher abroad than here. Several of the foreign ambassadors have assiduously cultivated my acquaintance, treating me as one of their *corps*, partly I believe from the desire they have . . . of hearing something of American affairs, an object become of importance in foreign courts, who begin to hope Britain's alarming power will be diminished by the defection of her colonies. . . .

And, hearing rumors of an approaching war between Britain and the Bourbon powers, Franklin hoped that the British would get embroiled; they would then have to give in to the Americans and, moreover, would want their help for, "as the House of Bourbon is most vulnerable in its American possessions, our hearty assistance in a war there must be of the greatest importance." [21] Clearly Franklin looked forward to the next war as the opportunity for completing the conquests which the British government had foregone in 1763.

The talented writer, Arthur Young, belonged to the same school of thought, advocating an all-out war of conquest and regarding Lord Chatham as its natural leader. Young was influenced by Franklin too, paying the doctor a handsome tribute and quoting him directly in his own writings. But, being English, Young differed from Franklin in that he aspired to see Britain remain in the lead for as long in the future as possible. Even at thirty Young was mature beyond his years, as he demonstrated in a comprehensive work on the Empire published in 1772. Recalling the experience with the Stamp Act and bearing in mind, as Franklin did, that the margin of power between Britain and America was steadily narrowing in favor of America, Young set himself the problem of discovering how Britain might keep

---

[21] Franklin to Samuel Cooper, Sept. 30, 1769 and Apr. 14, 1770; to William Franklin, Aug. 19, 1772; to Galloway, Apr. 6, 1773. Smyth, VI, nos. 512, 522, 597, 659.

ahead. "A certain concatenation of events," he warned, "might give the Colonies an opportunity of not only striking the blow, but preventing all future hopes in the mother-country of reversing it. The effect of *external* circumstances therefore must be great." Then Young proceeded:

It is impossible to state exactly the balance of power between Great Britain and North America; but the latter enjoys some peculiar advantages, which are of very great consequence. In case of a rupture between them, it is the interest of all those powers in Europe, whom Britain rivals either in general power, naval dominion, trade, commerce, or manufactures, that the colonies should become independent; —that is, it is the interest of all our neighbours:—consequently we should not only have the precise power of the rebels to deal with, but the probable assistance they would receive from others, in respect of supplies of military stores, artillery, or whatever else might be most wanting to them; and this in an especial degree, if we were engaged in a war. The most sanguine admirers of the power of this country will allow, that we *might* have our hands so full at home, as to be able to give but a weak attention to the rebellion of several millions of subjects above a thousand leagues off.

Young anticipated that the American Empire would in time become "absolutely invulnerable and universal," that it would be able to engross the whole commerce of South America, to reign not only lords of America, but to possess the dominion of the sea throughout the world. And it would differ from other empires because it was geographically isolated. What could Britain, an island kingdom, do to meet such a situation as this? First, Britain must remain powerful at sea. "I lay it down as a maxim," wrote Young, "that the dependence of the British colonies on the mother-country can only be made a question, while Britain is superior at sea: the moment she loses that superiority, her colonies can be dependent on her only through the courtesy of others. . . ." Secondly, Britain could slow down the process through careful political management, designed especially to encourage the Colonies to continue as staples. Any other conduct on its part "will be vain and useless." And finally, displaying a masterful knowledge of world geography and pointing to the British genius for colonization, Young urged that new colonies be founded among the islands of the Pacific, including the great southern continent of Australia. Emigrants should be directed toward these new colonies rather than to the old ones.[22]

Arthur Young's work was by far the most candid and searching on the subject; and as he belonged to the Rockingham Whigs and associated personally with Lord Rockingham and the Duke of Portland, the leaders of this group, we may infer that his book authentically reflected their ideas. But other pens also were employed in 1774 to warn of the dangers of Britain finding itself in the middle of a great war. Chief among these was Matthew Robinson-Morris, an independent Whig who had retired from Parliament some years before. Interestingly enough, Edes & Gill, the fiery Patriot printers of Boston, Massachusetts, reprinted Robinson-Morris's book the same year. Using his historical knowledge with telling effect, the author developed a temperately worded and meaty argument for ending the dispute. He put before his readers a picture of the disaster which overtook Spain in trying to suppress the Dutch revolt, and predicted that Britain would expose itself to a similar fate. "The wish, the hand of every man will be against us," Robinson-Morris wrote. All the trading nations of Europe would traffic with the Americans, giving them aid, assistance, encouragement, and protection. Britain could not possibly watch such immense coasts. And, he asked, "what if one or more of the greatest powers in Europe should in a most critical and difficult moment declare war against us?" [23]

Arthur Lee of the Virginia Lees wrote in the same vein. Lee mixed with the more radical elements in English politics, notably with John Wilkes. He had the ambition to become a barrister and even a Member of Parliament, but although he was neither of these, in 1774 he published a book which he pretended had been written by "an old Member of Parliament." Lee was alert to the posture of France, to which he paid a visit in 1774 although whether before or after he wrote the book is not clear. He warned:

There is not a part of the world upon which France looks with a more attentive eye than upon America. There is not the smallest

---

[22] Arthur Young, *Political Essays concerning the Present State of the British Empire*, London: printed for W. Strahan, 1772.

[23] M. Robinson-Morris, 2nd, Baron Rokeby, *Considerations on the Measures carrying on with respect to the British Colonies in North America*, London, Boston: reprinted by Edes & Gill, 1774.

event, relative to our proceedings towards the colonies, of which they are not minutely informed. If they should be idle spectators of such a contest, it would be one of the most extraordinary events that ever happened. . . ."[24]

Meanwhile the French were well aware of the impending crisis within the British Empire, which had inflicted such a humiliating defeat on them. They were asking questions about the attitude they should assume and, more specifically, about the policy that the ministers of His Christian Majesty should pursue. The questions raised were exceedingly complex and, although the thirst for revenge was a potent factor, it was not necessarily the controlling one, as so many American writers seem to take for granted. Nor is it to be supposed that, with a population in excess of twenty million (greater by at least four-fold than that of Britain), France was submissive to the will of a few ministers acting in the name of an absolute, although weak, monarch. Conscious of a great, long-established, cultural tradition, the French were too articulate and too sophisticated a people to be so easily dismissed. Indeed, the leaders of the French Enlightenment, of whom Voltaire and Montesquieu were the shining examples, regarded Britain (or, more accurately in this case, "England") with respect and admiration: England had mastered the art of self-government or, to express it as it was said in the eighteenth century, it possessed a balanced constitu-tion—one wherein the three great branches of government were so nicely poised one against the other as to make tyranny im-possible. That portion of the French aristocracy that identified itself with the ancient *parlements*, or legislative assemblies, shared these sentiments.[25]

Skeptical and quite unfriendly, but still not belligerent nor revenge-minded, were the Physiocrats, an influential school of thinkers permeating French society and believing firmly in the superior virtue of an agrarian civilization. To their minds

---

[24] Arthur Lee, *An Appeal to the Justice and Interests of the People of Great Britain, in the present disputes with America, by an old Member of Parliament*, London: J. Almon, 1774.

[25] These pages on French thought, including the direct quotations, are based on the excellent monograph by Frances Acomb, *Anglophobia in France, 1763–1789. An Essay in the History of Constitutionalism and Nationalism*, Durham, N. C., 1950.

England was a *republic* under the heel of its merchants, who had perverted its social institutions and corrupted its politics. England, remarked the Marquis de Mirabeau, is "a nation where the cries of the people frequently prevail over good reasons." To Turgot, Louis XVI's finance minister, William Pitt was the "famous demagogue." And, Turgot added, "there is no greater enemy of liberty than the people." With their belief in America as a purely agricultural society, sympathy for the American cause came easily to the Physiocrats.

Near them in thought, but different, were the Liberals. Among them were the Encyclopedist, Denis Diderot, and, better known to modern students, Jean-Jacques Rousseau, whose book *Du Contrat Social* (1758) was already famous and familiar reading to American thinkers such as Franklin and Jefferson. Egalitarians at least in theory, the Liberals were not as discriminating as the Physiocrats. They got their impressions of England in no small measure through personal contacts with the erratic and notorious journalist-politician, John Wilkes, the idol of the London mobs who had insulted the king. Jean Paul Marat, a physician who had lived in England, commented unfavorably on English courts and laws. Years later Marat would be one of the leaders of the Terror in the French Revolution, himself to die by the hand of an assassin in 1793. These men drew a fanciful picture of a "republic of virtue," which England could never be because it had fallen victim to contending interests. The Liberals were partisan to the English Whigs, through whose eyes they viewed America. Like Charles James Fox, they came to believe that the Americans were fighting the battle for English liberty, which meant preserving the gains of the English Revolution of 1688. But, like the Physiocrats, the French Liberals were lacking in first-hand knowledge of America.

The Conservatives in France, who held the reins of power, took quite a different view, although there was an area of agreement between them and the other groups. In particular they shared the faith in the superiority of an agrarian society, of which France itself was their symbol, over a crass commercial state, as represented most by England. As Dr. Quesnay, the founder of the Physiocratic movement, put it, "moneyed fortunes are clandestine riches which know neither king nor country."

To the French Conservatives their king was the head of the family, which was the French nation. Courtesy, sociability, generosity were the distinguishing characteristics of *la patrie* in contrast to the vulgarity of "those haughty islanders."

Defeated in war, France remained the stronger of the two; Britain was the modern Carthage, showing the strain of wars it could not afford and already traveling the road toward ultimate destruction. The disaffection of its Colonies spoke for itself in this respect. Courtiers like Caron de Beaumarchais, who was ready to indulge his taste for intrigue, could consort with English radicals like John Wilkes, yet feel scorn for "republican Britain" whose government he described as "mixed and turbulent," a "royal-aristo-democracy." The British Navy was an instrument of oppression, a threat to freedom which had to be humbled. The French Conservatives, it need hardly be said, were no more in contact with America than were the Physiocrats. Most of them came from the landed aristocracy, the *frondeur* nobility who harbored notions of honor and glory. The king being head of the family whose honor Britain had so insultingly impugned, he must be avenged. These were the people who assumed a posture of belligerence toward the British, and the American revolt gave them their opportunity to exercise it.

Foremost among this governing class were the duc de Choiseul and his cousin, the duc de Praslin. Choiseul was Louis XV's minister of marine for a portion of the decade 1761–1772, but he also held at times the portfolios of foreign affairs and of war. He and Praslin worked tirelessly for the improvement of the Navy, the one instrument capable of retaliating on the British rival; and by appealing to national pride they raised thirteen million livres through popular subscription for the construction of fifteen ships of the line. Choiseul's goal was a fleet of eighty ships of the line and fifty-five frigates, to be ready before 1773, his target date for opening a war on Britain. Although he fell short of this goal, the French fleet was nevertheless a formidable force whose strength was well known and appreciated in Britain.

Choiseul's agents surveyed the southern coast of England, the plan calling for a sudden landing near the mouth of the Thames and a quick attack on London in expectation of demoralizing the populace. Meanwhile new commanders were appointed, some of whom like de Grasse were to make their reputations in the future War for American Independence; a fleet was constituted for cruising in the Bay of Biscay; Corsica was occupied to the advantage of the French position in the Mediterranean; exploring expeditions were sent to the Indian Ocean and to the Pacific; and important technical improvements, including chronometers, were introduced. Equally substantial were the improvements to the existing naval arsenals—Brest and Rochefort on the Atlantic side, Toulon in the Mediterranean—and the addition of two new ones, Marseilles and L'Orient. Louis XV in his old age dismissed Choiseul in 1770, apparently because of Choiseul's impatience for war. The Navy was again temporarily allowed to stagnate, but in 1774 Louis XVI appointed as minister of marine the able and popular Gabriel de Sartine, who had been serving as lieutenant-general of police. Sartine was a zealous follower of Choiseul, and he lost no time in resuming Choiseul's policies.[26]

With such definite intentions toward Great Britain in mind, Choiseul, of course, kept himself informed on the internal dissensions of the British Empire. He had tried at the end of the Great War, to save Canada and its Mississippi hinterland for France. Failing at this, he held the opinion that, unless checked, the British Empire would take over the western half of North America and advance into the Caribbean and South America at the expense of the Spaniards. Firm ties between France and Spain were accordingly very important in his view. In the French Embassy in London, particularly in M. Durand, who was minister resident from 1766 to 1768, Choiseul had a capable staff who kept the British government and the politicians who ran the factions in Parliament under close observation.

With the exception of Lord Chatham, the French had a poor opinion of British politicians, including the king. They regarded them as weak, but this very weakness, they sometimes feared, might lead them into rash action. Chatham's chronic gout was notorious, but the French wondered whether this was not a cover-up for insanity. As they feared his possible return to

---

[26] G. Lacour-Gayet, *La Marine Militaire de la France sous le Regne de Louis XV*, Paris, 1902; Margaret Cotter Morison, "The Duc de Choiseul and the Invasion of England, 1768–1770," *Royal Historical Society Transactions* (1909), 3rd series, IV, pp. 83–107.

power, they were solicitous about his health, and by June 1768 Choiseul was convinced that Chatham was done for. This was the comment Choiseul made to his ambassador in London:

The Earl of Chatham will not be henceforth a redoubtable bugbear who makes Ministers tremble. The poor state of health in which he finds himself suggests that he will die very shortly, the object of pity of those who once were jealous of him. Besides, even if his health does recover, the party which appears at the moment likely to be dominant, the one led by the D. of Bedford, will never consent to admit to their administration a man whose character, vain, proud and imperious does not allow him to have any partners in public esteem. . . . One only sees in him now the artificial facade of national zeal and the oft demonstrated reality of insatiable greed and ambition.[27]

Urged by Durand, who apparently developed a strong curiosity about the Colonies, Choiseul sent an experienced naval officer named Pontleroy to America. Pontleroy performed his mission in 1764, the year before the troubles really started, yet he felt confident of the inevitable separation. The Americans, he reported, were "too rich to be obedient, eager to be the sole masters of their fur trade, and restive to shake off the fetters and restraints on their commerce."[28] Remembering the wartime prosperity of the American merchants and their undisguised resistance to authority, we can see that Pontleroy had no trouble in sizing up the situation. His mission took in the New England coast and the Middle Colonies, and after inspecting the principal harbors, he recommended plans for their capture. Another agent covered much the same territory the very next year, while the resistance to the Stamp Act was at its height, and arrived at the same conclusions. No country was better situated for independence, the people were so inclined, and the subject was a matter of common conversation.

But the French were cautious about committing themselves to any policy concerning America. Choiseul thought it astonishing that "England which is a very small part of Europe, domi-

---

[27] Choiseul to du Chatelet, June 10, 1768, AAE cp Ang. 477, ff. 30–41.
[28] As quoted by Claude H. Van Tyne, "French Aid before the Alliance of 1778," *Amer. Hist. Rev.*, XXXI (1925–1926), p. 25.

nates more than a third of America and that this American domination is only used for commercial purposes." Even Durand, to whom the American economy and particularly the rapidly growing population were very impressive, reacted against France coming to the aid of the Americans in the event of the Americans revolting against Britain. In December 1767 he reported on warlike preparations in America pointing toward a revolution. At the height of the Stamp Act controversy a certain secret committee had sent an emissary to London who was permitted to continue on to France. This person, so Durand said, sounded him out on the prospects for French official intervention, but the minister laughingly discouraged him with the remark "that we would never help to form a power which would be a threat to our own colonies, that we received certainly vital foodstuffs from America, but that we could find no advantage in exchanging them for sugar in which America dreamed of establishing a monopoly. . . ."[29]

Du Chatelet, Durand's successor at the London Embassy in 1768, recommended a more positive policy of capitalizing a revolt which was sure to be successful. He advised sending agents to America, men "sufficiently prudent and intelligent to breathe on a fire which [is] covered by cinders at a time when it only asks to break out." Like his predecessor, Du Chatelet was fascinated by the size of the American population, against which the British Army would have no chance, and thought France should be on the winning side in a revolt "which the world foresees but dares not give a date to."[30]

Nothing so definite as this emerged from Versailles. A modernized and strengthened navy and an intimate alliance with Spain—these were the assets on which France could really rely

[29] Durand to Choiseul, Aug. 11, 30, Sept. 4, Dec. 1, 8, 17, 1767; Choiseul to Durand, Dec. 13, 1767. AAE cp Ang. 474, ff. 241–245, 265–280, 336–337; 475, ff. 3, 195–198, 235–241, 263, 276. These citations from the French Archives are from notes and transcripts sent to me in translation by Dr. Clive H. Church of Trinity College Dublin, who carried on the investigations under my direction.

[30] Du Chatelet to Choiseul, Mar. 12, 1768. AAE cp Ang. 47, ff. 348–353. All direct references hereafter to the French Archives are from Dr. Church's notes and transcripts which are in my possession.

in the next round with Britain. There was no call for France to foment a revolution in America or to decide on a policy before such a revolution materialized. Then with Choiseul fallen from favor, French policy grew still more cautious. Louis XV rejected the minister's timetable for war, and other voices expressed disagreement. The aged comte de Maurepas was recalled to power and made head of the king's council. Turgot, temporarily marine minister and then at the finance post, believed that the British Empire would break up in due course anyway and that therefore France should hold back; Charles Gravier, the comte de Vergennes, who took the portfolio for foreign affairs in 1774 and was far from eager to indulge in provocative acts on behalf of the Americans, felt apprehensive lest Britain find a way out of its domestic troubles by instigating another attack on France. This was most likely should Lord Chatham regain power. Chatham never ceased to regard France as the main enemy, an attitude with which the French were entirely familiar. Chatham's program of reconciliation with America called for a solid front against France, and warnings from the ambassador in London convinced Vergennes that this was at least a possibility. Responding to these warnings in January 1775, the French foreign minister admitted:

We fear above all the return of Lord Chatham who although without a party will once again follow only the movements of his effervescence and his hate for us. Happily his Britannic Majesty has the most weighty reasons for not giving his confidence to this former minister, even though the situation of his enemies leaves that Prince with a free hand, and even though he remains the master, able to amalgamate different parties without letting any one of them dominate.[31]

With or without Chatham's leadership, however, the prospects for a reunited British Empire were poor, and the French had little to fear from a recurrence of aggressive war at the hands of their old enemy.

---

[31] Vergennes to Garnier, Jan. 1775. AAE cp Ang. 508, ff. 59–62.

# CHAPTER III

## The Revolution Bursts—1775

America will soon be the seat of empire—yet my fear is, they will not accept our king to rule them, but chuse one of their own; by which means we, who bought in, at a severe price too, shall lose our bread . . .—*Private Letters from an American in England to his Friends in America*, London: printed for J. Almon, 1769, p. 78

IN FEBRUARY 1775 ALEXANDER HAMILTON, age eighteen, published a pamphlet which, for sheer candor and brilliant exposition of the forces of history, was reminiscent of the view expounded by John Adams twenty years previously. Hamilton had been reading Robinson-Morris's diagnosis of Britain's vulnerable situation. Like Robinson-Morris, he spoke out against the "unnatural quarrel," and expressed his ardent wish "for a speedy reconciliation, a perpetual and mutually beneficial union." Hamilton considered this easy to achieve: a compact had been made whereby the kings of Great Britain were also kings of America. "We hold our lands . . . by virtue of Charters from the British Monarchs; and are under no obligations to the lords or commons for them. . . ." There was a difference between being subjects of his majesty and being subjects of Parliament.

Young Hamilton seemed to have no lack of confidence that Parliament would yield the point: Britain's position was so weak, America's so strong. France and Spain could not possibly pass up the opportunity, and the Dutch merchants would resort to their old practice of making profits out of war. These powers would undoubtedly take every clandestine method to introduce among us supplies of those things, which we stood in need of to carry on the dispute. They would not neglect any thing, in their power, to make the opposition on our part, as vigorous as our affairs would admit of. . . . And, in whatever light we view the matter, the consequence to Great Britain would be too destructive to permit her to proceed to extremities, unless she has lost all just sense of her own interest.[1]

Concluding his discourse, Hamilton declared himself a thorough supporter of limited monarchy and a well wisher of the royal family. The idea was by no means original with him. Franklin had said as much a few years before and in fact had based his whole conduct in London on the belief that the leaders of Parliament would be practical enough to see the necessity for altering the relationship. Parliamentary supremacy over the Colonies was a tiresome and unrealistic concept. The idea of a personal union between America and Britain under the king was much sounder historically. Edward Bancroft and Thomas Jefferson both had argued to the same end, contributing the thought that the Colonies were really independent states; and Jefferson had gone so far as to call on his majesty to veto acts of Parliament that were repugnant to the interests of the Colonies. Jefferson relied less on history to make his point than on the change of circumstances which had come about in the eighteenth century. The Colonies, he said, in effect, had come of age: they were states which had been added to the British Empire.

But the king had not invoked the veto for the better part of a century; for him to do so now was totally out of the question. It would mean a repudiation of the Revolution of 1688, an outright challenge to the authority of Parliament, whose position the Revolution had firmly secured after a century of dissension and war with the Stuart kings. No one in 1775, on either side of the water, stated this issue more accurately or more lucidly than the New York conservative, Samuel Seabury, whose writings Alexander Hamilton singled out for refutation. Seabury was exactly twice Hamilton's age; he was well established in the public life of his province; and he represented the agrarian interests of New York, who were incensed against the nonimportation and exportation agreements and distrustful of the

[1] "The Farmer Refuted" in *The Papers of Alexander Hamilton*, Harold C. Syrett and Jacob E. Cooke, eds., New York, 1960–, I, pp. 159–160.

revolutionary committees which controlled the city mobs. "To talk of subjection to the king, while we disclaim submission to Parliament is ridiculous," Seabury wrote. "It is a distinction made by the American Republicans to serve their own rebellious purposes. . . . *The king is king by act of Parliament*." [2] Some alternative had to be found if the Empire was to be held together.

In Britain a number of proposals emerged, but all of them in some measure or other were anchored to the established principle of Parliamentary supremacy. Baffled by the reception the Americans had given the so-called Intolerable Acts, the government seemed unable to decide on the next step. But, thoroughly alarmed by the gravity of the crisis—a prospective civil war within the Empire, or a foreign war, with Britain exposed to a direct attack from France—Lord Chatham forced the issue. First he demanded that the government recall the troops from Boston— an idea to which others, notably Josiah Tucker, had previously given expression. Then, on the first of February, 1775, he introduced a bill into Parliament designed to heal the wounds and bind the Colonies more closely than ever to Britain. Chatham's bill began with an assertion that Parliament possessed supreme legislative and supervisory power over the Colonies. It then proposed the repeal of the Quebec Act, declared that no tax or other charge would be levied against the Americans, sanctioned the meeting of the Continental Congress scheduled to open in Philadelphia in May, and stipulated that the delegates, on assembling, rec-

---

[2] *The Congress Canvassed: or an Examination into the Conduct of the Delegates at their Grand Convention, held in Philadelphia, September 1, 1774, addressed to the Merchants of New York.* By A. W. Farmer (Samuel Seabury). I have repeated and italicized for the sake of emphasis. Seabury's writings are vital to an understanding of the constitutional issue. Since, under the Act of Settlement of 1701, Parliament controlled the throne, Seabury's position was unassailable. See also his *Free Thoughts . . .* and his *A View of the Controversy . . . in a Letter to the Author of a Full Vindication*, both published in 1774. In the last-named pamphlet Seabury charged that not one-hundredth part of the people of New York had any voice in sending delegates to the Congress. While Seabury may have exaggerated, there is no doubt that the opposition to the Revolutionary movement was very strong in New York. For the most recent study of this matter see Roger J. Champagne's, "New York's Radicals and the Coming of Independence," *The Journ. of Amer. Hist.*, LI (1964), pp. 21–40.

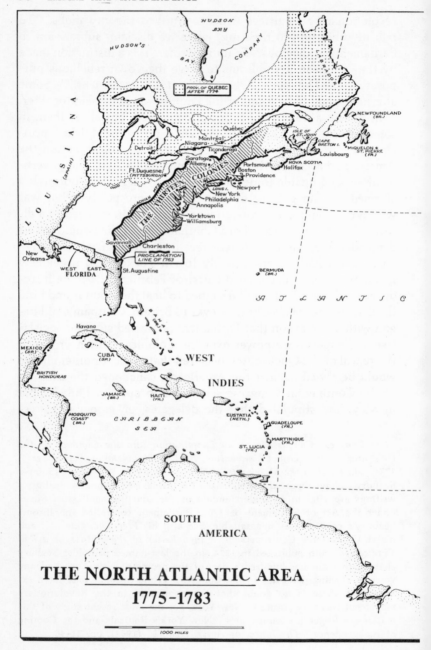

# THE NORTH ATLANTIC AREA
## 1775-1783

ENGLAND
Glasgow
Dublin
IRELAND
Southampton
Cork
Plymouth
London
Portsmouth
CHANNEL IS.
St. Malo
Brest
QUIBERON-BAY
Nantes
BAY OF BISCAY
Bilbao
Corunna
PORTUGAL
Lisbon
Cadiz
Hamburg
NETH.
Amsterdam
Dunkirk
Le Havre
Paris
FRANCE
Angoulême
Bordeaux
Metz
Berlin
PRUSSIA
Toulon
Madrid
SPAIN
GIBRALTAR (BR.)
AZORES (PORT.)

O C E A N

AFRICA

T.R.M.

ognize the supremacy of Parliament and make a free grant of a certain perpetual revenue to the king.

Chatham is revered in history as "the friend of America" in contrast to Lord North and his government who were known as "the wicked ministry"—to copy the epithet used against them by their opponents on both sides of the water. But actually the differences between the two were not very real: Chatham was groping for an avenue of escape; the government was standing firm on the abstract principle of Parliamentary supremacy but prepared to go equally far toward satisfying the Americans. Lord Mansfield, the great chief justice who the very next year was to rule Negro slavery unconstitutional in Britain, stated the government's position clearly. "We were reduced to the alternative," he declared in Parliament, "of adopting coercive measures, or of forever relinquishing our claim of sovereignty or dominion over the colonies. . . . [Either] the supremacy of the British legislature must be complete, entire, and unconditional or on the other hand, the colonies must be free and independent." To Mansfield, a jurist, this was the choice: either the supremacy of Parliament or an "independent American empire." The Scottish peer readily conceded that the taxes had been a mistake, but it was "utterly impossible to say a syllable on the matter of expediency, till the right was first as fully asserted on one side, as acknowledged on the other." [3]

We can better appreciate the predicament of the British government in 1774–1775 by comparing it with the problems of the Lincoln administration in 1861. In both cases the authority of the central government had been denied. In both cases the central government was threatened with civil war. The Americans, as Lord North correctly stated, had entered "an almost universal confederacy" to resist the will of Parliament. This meant secession and dismemberment of the Empire, from which all thinking men in Britain recoiled. As William Eden, a young member of Parliament who joined the government, put it:

. . . There was at that moment no alternative but "War or Separation." All retrospect to the causes of such an alternative were idle;

[3] *PH*, XVIII, cols. 269–271. For a full treatment of this subject see Richard W. Van Alstyne, "Parliamentary Supremacy versus Independence: Notes and Documents," *Hunt. Lib. Quart.*, XXVI (1963), pp. 201–233.

it was necessary to take a choice; and in so doing I was not influenced either by the popular cry or by political connections. As an individual of a family possessing considerable interests both in Great Britain and America I was naturally indisposed to a separation evidently mischievous to both countries, . . . I could not bear to see a dismemberment of the Empire without running every hazard to prevent it. Nor did I give in to these feelings under a misconception that the task we were undertaking would be an easy one. I was aware of the difficulties which existed in the one Continent and would spring up in the other and I should have learnt them indeed indirectly from Dr. Franklin if I had had no other access to them.[4]

Eden's friendships with Americans in London gave him, as he said, "no inconsiderable knowledge of their [the Colonies] natural strength and advantages." Subsequently he was to play a prominent role in British affairs and to demonstrate an untiring effort to bring about peace and reconciliation between the two countries. But, although conscious of the formidable task ahead, he could not acquiesce in secession.

With the support of the king, Lord North on February 20, 1775, offered a resolution which passed the House of Commons by a vote of 274–88. The resolution represented the utmost the government had decided it could concede. Thereafter there was no real variation in policy until 1782 when, the North ministry having lost the war, a different ministry with great reluctance admitted independence. North's resolution stated that whenever any of the Colonies made provision "for contributing their proportion to the common defence" and for the support of the governor and the courts of the Colony, Parliament would "forbear . . . to levy any duty, tax, or assessment, or to impose any farther duty, tax, or assessment, except only such duties as it may be expedient to continue to levy or to impose for the regulation of commerce; the net produce of the duties last mentioned to be carried to the account of such province or colony respectively."[5] In a supporting speech Lord North drew a fine line between Parliament's "right" to tax and the *exercise* of the right by the Colonial assemblies. He also said he favored leaving the Colonies at liberty to contribute voluntarily to the common

---

[4] British Museum Add. MSS. 46,490–491, Pkt. 2.
[5] *PH*, XVIII, col. 320.

defense, with Parliament as a matter of legal form retaining the right to reject or increase the amount of the aids offered. However, it was plain from the context that the government did not intend to exercise its "right."

Between Lord Chatham's bill of February 1 and Lord North's resolution of February 20 there were only shades of difference. Chatham was perhaps closer to the political realities then prevailing in the Colonies; he and his friends were in touch with the Americans in London, including Franklin, who were partisans of his against the government. Chatham went further than the ministry in advocating the repeal of the Quebec Act and in giving Parliamentary approval to the meeting of the Continental Congress, but his bill stipulated recognition of the supremacy of Parliament, and it made an American grant of a perpetual revenue a requirement. North's resolution all but shelved this issue. Chatham was ready to recall the troops, and the followers of Lord Rockingham, including Edmund Burke, were in agreement on this. But the latter, who constituted an influential minority group in both houses of Parliament, stood firm on the Declaratory Act which Rockingham had pushed through Parliament in 1766 when the Stamp Act was repealed.

Chatham's bill failed in the House of Lords on its first reading, while North's resolution subsequently got strong support in the House of Commons. The real difference between the two lay not in these details, North's resolution being really more generous, but in the attitude with which the two men viewed the crisis. Chatham and his followers had no faith in Britain's ability to force the Colonies into submission. To block the American ports against commerce was, as Lord Camden said, to sap the life blood of Britain herself. Compared with the several powers of Europe, Britain without commerce was no more than a "bird's nest floating on a pool." Beyond that the Chathamites were terrified at the prospect of the Bourbon powers joining in a general war, with Britain in the middle and facing hopeless odds. Not only would all the gains of the previous war be lost, but also Britain herself would again become merely an island off the coast of Europe. "What can France desire more than to see her rival sinking every year, from being mistress of the world, land and sea, into the bubble of her enemies, and the scorn of nations?" So Chatham had asked in 1773.[6] In this state of mind he was grasping at any straw to prevent the disaster he was certain would otherwise befall. But for the ministry the constitutional issue was overriding. It could not go beyond the North resolution. It had to have some answering gesture from the Americans. If the Americans would make a gesture of "submission," that would be enough.

Lord Camden, speaking for the Chathamites in the debates of February, ridiculed "the high sounding unintelligible phrases of legislative supremacy and parliamentary omnipotence." But it proved impossible to get past them. In March David Hartley, who belonged to the Rockingham group but who was closer to Chatham in spirit, proposed making a fresh approach through the king. His idea was that the king send to each of the provinces a letter of requisition, which Hartley himself had actually written. Stressing the importance of the Royal Navy and the need for contributing to its support, the letter proceeded to state that his majesty regretted that "needless and imprudent discussions of speculative points, from mutual misapprehensions, have been converted into anger and animosities, which threaten the most fatal consequences." And in conclusion, it said, his majesty wished to see "unanimity restored . . . in one common obedience to the supreme legislature," so that the provinces may join "to support the dignity of his crown, the just authority of parliament, the true and combined interests of Great Britain and America. . . ." [7]

It was an ingenious idea: the king to assume the initiative in sending a letter written for him and approved in advance by Parliament. Parliament's ultimate position was safeguarded, at least in theory, but the hand of friendship was to come from the king. The results would be the same as those sought from the North resolution, but the stress was on voluntary action rather than on "rights." Hartley and Franklin had been friends before Franklin had taken his departure from England, and Hartley hoped to mollify the Americans through an informal

---

[6] Chatham to Baron Bridport (Adm. Hood), June 6, 1773. Bridport Papers, II, British Museum Add. MSS. 35, 192.

[7] PH, XVIII, cols. 565–566.

approach. But unfortunately his motion received scant attention. Lord North saw it setting a dangerous precedent for a revival of the royal prerogative. He said that it suggested King Charles I's methods of imposing taxes without Parliamentary consent, and the motion was negatived without a division. A strictly constitutional monarch who implicitly accepted the principles laid down in 1688, George III at no time showed any disposition to act independently of Parliament.

Clearly the British government pinned its hopes to a belief that its efforts at conciliation would meet with a response from America. Far from any sense of playing the role of "tyrant," the government had paid meticulous attention to the requirements of the British constitution; in all its measures it consistently deferred to the will of Parliament. It could do no less, and it assumed that tempers would cool and reason prevail in the Colonies. A "little time," Lord Dartmouth had written to an American correspondent shortly after the passage of the "Intolerable Acts," would convince all who "can think with coolness and temper, that the liberties of America are not so much in danger from any thing that Parliament has done, or is likely to do here, as from the violence and misconduct of America itself." [8]

Nevertheless, the behavior of the First Continental Congress and its rude dismissal of the Galloway Plan did not point in this direction. Apparently the Americans felt confident that through continued resistance they could bring on the downfall of the North ministry and the restoration of Chatham to power—as Franklin had advised his Boston friends. In that case, they believed, they could get all they wanted from Britain. Thus, when the Second Continental Congress opened in May 1775, it did not act on Lord North's resolution.

Before this the first battles had been fought at Lexington and Concord, and the British forces in Boston were under siege. Denouncing the "sanguinary zeal of the Ministerial Army," John Hancock, speaking for a provincial congress of Massachusetts,

---

[8] As quoted from the Dartmouth Papers by Jack M. Sosin, whose article, "The Massachusetts Acts of 1774: Coercive or Preventive?" *Hunt. Lib. Quart.*, XXVI (1963), pp. 235–252, shows admirably the care which the North ministry took in preparing these measures.

demanded that the Congress in Philadelphia authorize a powerful army on the side of America. With such a force, he declared,
"we can hope that the authors of our miseries can be punished
by the just indignation of our brethren" in Britain.[9]

Hancock no doubt had the zealous followers of Lord Chatham
in mind; and the pages of the *London Evening Post*, if Hancock
had read them, would have fully justified his optimism. John
Almon who published this paper, spared no efforts to denounce
the "wicked ministers" and to slant the news heavily in favor
of the Americans. Almon demanded to know how the ministers
were to keep Britain from becoming a province of France. Others
had voiced this fear not once, but many times. Thus David
Hartley, addressing Commons on May 2 when the Battle of
Lexington was still not known in Britain, said:

It is next to infatuation and madness, for one moment, to suppose
that we can have an American without a French and Spanish war.
I am clear that they will keep off while there is any possibility of
the American dispute being made up, but when once the war is
begun, and neither party can withdraw, then, Sir, in spite of all
those assurances . . . gained at Paris from the French ministers,
you will find them take a determined part—a part plainly pointed out
by both interest and ambition. . . . Nothing but the most infantine
credulity can believe the contrary; you will then find yourselves
engaged in a French war, in a Spanish war, I think, in a Prussian
war; and wars are so catching, Sir, when they spread, in I know not
how many other wars likewise. . . .[10]

Nevertheless, despite these scattered protests, it was unrealistic
to hope for the overthrow of the North ministry. Many Whigs,

---

[9] Peter Force, *American Archives: Consisting of a Collection of Authentick
Records, State Papers, Debates, and Letters and other Notices of Publick
Affairs*, 4th series from March 4, 1774 to July 4, 1776, 5 vols., Washington,
D. C., 1839, II, cols. 1826–1828. (Hereafter cited as Force.)

The Battles of Lexington and Concord, April 19, were not reported in
England until May 28. This was about the average lapse of time for
news to cross the Atlantic. Lord North's resolution of February 20 is
printed in Force, II, cols. 1899–1900, but without North's accompanying
speech. It was considered by the Continental Congress on July 31 and
rejected. *Ibid.*, cols. 1900–1902.

[10] From the *London Morning Post and Daily Advertiser*, May 5, 1775,
British Museum, Burney Collection.

including their leader, Lord Rockingham, shared the fears of the Chathamites, but for reasons of internal politics, these two groups would not cooperate. Even so the government possessed a safe margin of support in both houses of Parliament.

Meanwhile the Second Continental Congress was moving steadily ahead toward war. Massachusetts had demanded the creation of a regular army, and New England militia captured the fort at Ticonderoga on Lake Champlain and moved its cannon south for use against the British forces in Boston. The capture of this fort cut off the British invasion route from Canada, yet the Congress voted a resolution that "indubitable evidence" existed that the British government was preparing a "cruel invasion" from that direction. Just the opposite was the case. Governor Carleton's forces in Quebec were so small as to make an offensive campaign unthinkable; and, still ignorant of the Battles of Lexington and Concord, the government in London had not even begun to formulate plans for suppressing the rebellion. Overlooking the ancient dislike that Americans harbored for the Catholic French of Quebec, and failing to appreciate that, with the Quebec Act now in force, the French Canadians would of course look to Britain as their protector, the Congress now addressed them as "oppressed inhabitants" and "fellow sufferers." The Canadians were warned of the perils of "slavery" and of the danger of enjoying their religion at the hands of a legislature in which they had no voice. A thousand copies of this message were ordered translated and printed, to be dispatched to Canada for distribution among the populace.

Next, Massachusetts got its wish for a regular army when, on June 16, George Washington was named general and commander-in-chief. If John Adams is to be taken at his word—even more than his more radical cousin Samuel, John Adams was in the forefront in pushing for vigorous measures—Washington's appointment served to silence the mutterings against New England and advance the cause of union.[11] Preparations, originating in New England, were undertaken shortly thereafter for

[11] John Adams to his wife Abigail, June 17, 1775. *Letters of Members of the Continental Congress*, Edmund C. Burnett, ed., 8 vols., Washington, D. C., 1921–1936, I, pp. 130–132. (Hereafter cited as Burnett.)

an invasion and permanent subjugation of the colony on the St. Lawrence.

Early in July the Congress approved successively a declaration on the causes and necessity of taking up arms, a petition to the king, an address to "the inhabitants of Great Britain," and finally a speech to the Iroquois Indians who, as "Brothers and Friends," were exhorted to lend a hand in the defense of "liberty." Now as previously, it was important to bid for the friendship of these tribes. "Our cause is just. Our union is perfect. Our internal resources are great, and, if necessary, *foreign assistance* is *undoubtedly attainable*," concluded the first document, which Jefferson and John Dickinson composed together.[12] All of these documents studiously ignored Parliament, and gave the impression of being designed as propaganda. The strong language and the tone of defiance they adopted express a spirit of revolution rather than of conciliation. Beyond that, the Americans realized they were playing from strength and could afford to take risks: at home they were strong, abroad Britain's enemies would come to their support.

Dickinson, voicing the hesitancy and the last-ditch hope for peace displayed in the Middle and Southern Colonies, drafted the petition to the king. In it the ministers were made the butt of attack; they were guilty of "delusive pretences, fruitless terrors, and unavailing severities," and his majesty was entreated personally to assume the initiative in re-establishing harmony within the Empire. But the king under the constitution could take no such step, nor did the petitioners themselves propose reform beyond the repeal of the measures precipitated by the Boston Tea Party. Franklin discounted the value of this document, whereas John Adams, exasperated by the divisions of opinion in Congress, rejected it but recognized its practical necessity. An absolute refusal to petition and negotiate would spell discord and total disunion. But, he wrote Joseph Warren, "my hopes are that Ministry will be afraid of negotiation as well as we and therefore refuse it."[13] The procedure followed ensured that this would be the case.

The address to the British public repeated the charge that the

---

[12] Force, II, cols. 1866–1869. Italics inserted.
[13] July 6, 1775, Burnett, I, pp. 151–152.

ministry aimed at "the reduction of these Colonies to slavery and ruin," and blamed the same source for fabricating the notion that the Americans desired independence. "Have we called in the aid of those foreign powers, who are the rivals of your grandeur?" This was the proof offered that the Colonies were innocent of any such intention. And then the address noted:

It is alleged that we contribute nothing to the common defence. To this we answer, that the advantages which Great Britain receives from the monopoly of our trade far exceed our proportion of the expense necessary for that purpose. But should these advantages be inadequate thereto, let the restrictions on our trade be removed, and we will cheerfully contribute such proportion when constitutionally required.[14]

Although the Americans repudiated the notion that they intended to be "independent," their attitude revealed a different purpose. Unmistakably they were prepared to insist on their de facto independence. The original controversy over taxation had become submerged in larger and more indefinite issues, and nothing short of a complete abnegation of its powers on the part of Parliament would be satisfactory. The Americans were no longer pleading their case for the redress of specific grievances, they were talking of their "rights " and framing their demands in terms of power and prestige. A personal union under the king would do, and some of the American leaders, including Jefferson, seemed to have convinced themselves that if Chatham were again at the helm in Britain, an organic change of this kind would result. But Chatham, no less than Mansfield and North, accepted the principle of Parliamentary supremacy; and, although ostensibly more anxious than the ministry to accommodate the Americans, he would have faced the same cruel dilemma had he been in power. Possibly, with Chatham supplanting Lord North, the atmosphere would have cleared and a compromise would have been worked out along the lines of Hartley's proposal. Chatham was a hero in America, whereas the distrust of Lord North was such as to make a peaceful settlement impossible. But the point is only speculative, for the

---

[14] Force, II, cols. 1872–1875.

Americans were ill-informed if they really hoped for an over-throw of the ministry.

Indeed there was no disposition in America to view Lord North's resolution on its merits. Jefferson assembled a number of arguments against it, which were incorporated in the Virginia Resolutions of June 10, 1775, but these arguments seem quite unfair, especially in the context of Lord North's speech in support of his resolution. Although the resolution was really a formula for escaping from an impossible situation, Jefferson chose to attack it on legalistic grounds and ignore the spirit with which it was offered. It only changed "the form of oppression without lightening its burden," he declared. "We must saddle ourselves with a perpetual tax adequate to the expectations and subject to the disposal of Parliament alone."

Jefferson found other arguments against the resolution, including a complaint against the Quebec Act, an assertion that the British were "planning to invade us by sea and land," and a final charge that "on our agreeing to contribute our share to the common defence, they do not propose to lay open to us a free trade with all the world." Then follows an allusion to Lord Chatham, blaming the ministers for all the trouble. Under them "the component parts of the empire have . . . been falling asunder, and a total annihilation of its weight in the political scale of the World seems justly to be apprehended." [15] In this spirit the Continental Congress on July 31 rejected the resolution.

At home in Monticello, Jefferson seemed more composed and anxious for a reconciliation. Still it depended, he believed, on "the returning wisdom" of Britain, and not on any concession the Americans should make. The British public, even "those in parliament who are called friends of America, seem to know nothing of our real determinations." And he was of two minds on the subject of foreign intervention:

If indeed Great Britain, disjoined from her colonies, be a match for the most potent nations of Europe with the colonies thrown into their scale, they may go on securely. But if they are not assured of this, it would be certainly unwise, by trying the event of another

---

[15] *The Papers of Thomas Jefferson*, Julian P. Boyd, ed., 15 vols., Princeton, N. J., 1950–1958, I, pp. 170–174. (Hereafter cited as *Jefferson Papers*.)

campaign, to risque our accepting a foreign aid which perhaps may not be obtainable but on a condition of everlasting avulsion from Great Britain. This would be thought a hard condition to those who still wish for reunion with their parent country. . . ."[16]

Thus Jefferson hesitated before venturing out on uncharted seas. Not possessing Adams's cocksureness, he was aware that foreign aid would become a necessity, and he was apprehensive of its consequences. But the price for reunion, on which he held out, was that Parliament relinquish its right to legislate. Paradoxically this was what Lord North's resolution proposed to do by indirection.

Meanwhile the Congress entrusted its several communications to Richard Penn, a former lieutenant-governor of Pennsylvania, who arrived at Bristol, England, on August 13, one day behind a vessel bearing the news of the tragedy at Bunker Hill. Accompanied by Arthur Lee, who had been having secret meetings with the Frenchman, Caron de Beaumarchais, Penn formally presented the petition not to the king personally, but to Lord Dartmouth, the minister in charge of American affairs. Lee's part in this transaction can probably never be understood; only the bare facts are known, but from the scanty record his conduct seems highly equivocal. On the one hand, he was plotting with Beaumarchais to enlist the aid of the French Court; on the other hand, he was still an aspirant to membership in the House of Commons. In a speech which he published in London, but never delivered orally in Commons, he made a moving appeal for the restoration of Imperial unity, reminding his British readers of the previous war when the Americans had made common cause against the "ancient inveterate enmity" of France.[17]

The petition being directed against the ministry, it is hard to see how it could have borne results. However that may be, the government had already determined its course. Lord North advised the king on July 26 that the war had become such that it would have to be treated as a foreign war. And the king

---

[16] To John Randolph, Aug. 25, 1775. *Ibid.*, pp. 240–243.
[17] Arthur Lee, *A Speech intended to have been delivered in the House of Commons, in support of the Petition from the General Congress at Philadelphia*, London: J. Almon, 1775.

expressed himself simply and straightforwardly in a letter written to the minister on the same day:

I am clear as to one point that we must persist and not be dismayed by any difficulties that may arise on either side of the Atlantick; I know I am doing my duty and therefore can never wish to retract; the Resolution proposed by the House of Commons is the utmost that can be come into; and if people will have patience this must in the end be obtained.[18]

These decisions led to a royal proclamation, August 23, announcing a state of rebellion in the Colonies. In retrospect this drastic step may be regarded as too hasty: also it is not clear why it was taken so soon. Sizable French shipments of arms and gunpowder to the rebels were already being reported, but no attempt was made to stop them. The government continued to make the mistake of supposing it was dealing with an insurrection, whereas actually it was confronted with a revolution. Lord Dartmouth wrote General Gage in Boston to say that it was hoped the rebellion could be confined to New England—that the Middle Colonies would prove more reasonable and accept the conciliatory North resolution of February 20. Loyalist sentiment among the back-country settlers of the Carolinas was also taken into account; these men to be rewarded with land grants and organized into a provincial corps on equal terms with the regulars. General Gage, in the thick of things in Boston, was pessimistic, but Major General Haldimand, who had seen service in Canada, advised that with reinforcements sent to that country the insurrection could be suppressed by the following spring. On that basis it was decided to recruit a fair-sized army to be dispatched and ready for action in America when the campaigning season opened, while at the same time holding out the olive branch of Lord North's resolution.

Meanwhile awareness of the crisis produced a small flood of books and pamphlets in Britain. Both Dr. Samuel Johnson and the Methodist leader, John Wesley, took stands against the Americans. Johnson saw anarchy as the consequence of

---

[18] *The Correspondence of King George the Third*, John Fortescue, ed., 6 vols., London, 1927–1928, No. 1683. (Hereafter cited as Fortescue.)

rebellion, and Wesley echoed his sentiments by deriding the American contention that the people of the Colonies were being "enslaved." "The Negroes in America are slaves, the whites enjoy liberty," declared Wesley. "Is not then all this outcry about Liberty and Slavery mere rant, and playing upon words?" And, he wanted to know: "Are women free agents?" [19] John Lind, a brother-in-law of Governor Hutchinson and a political writer who echoed the views of Lord Mansfield, was on a business trip to America in the summer of 1775, and published a book in New York which the next year was republished in London and went through at least five editions. The whole British people believed the Americans should be free, he declared, and that they were entitled to a hearing. Recalling the American appeals for help in past wars, he argued the case for the protection of the Colonies by British fleets and armies. But an empire with such responsibilities required a central legislature, he held; and for Americans to assume that they were not to be bound by this legislature was to invalidate their claims to the benefits of, and to destroy their title to, protection. [20]

Lind's book was paralleled by a tract written by the Massachusetts loyalist, Daniel Leonard, who denounced the tyranny of the revolutionary committees in America. Leonard's book is an excellent expression of conservative opinion: it warned against the exhaustion and load of debt that a war would engender, and predicted that France and Spain would move in as soon as the British forces were withdrawn. In *A Friendly Address to all Reasonable Americans*, Thomas B. Chandler came to Leonard's support with a strong argument that, without the mediatory power of Great Britain, the Colonies with their competing interests would make war on one another and so tempt foreign powers to intervene. Chandler accused New England of starting the rebellion, and suggested that a new American constitution had become necessary, and could be

---

[19] Samuel Johnson, *Taxation no Tyranny; an Answer to the Resolutions and Address of the American Congress*, London, T. Cadell, 1775; John Wesley, *A Calm Address to our American Colonies*, London: Robert Hawes, 1775.
[20] John Lind, *An Englishman's Answer to the Address from the Delegates to the People of Great Britain*, New York: Rivington, 1775.

obtained "by decent, candid and respectful application, not by threats." [21]

In London Arthur Young returned to the arguments of his earlier writings, publishing a two-volume work on *American Husbandry* in which he stressed the growing power and wealth of the Colonies, the likelihood that they would turn against Britain, and the opportunity the latter possessed to delay or prevent independence by stimulating settlement of the Ohio country. An agricultural country with staples to export, Young believed, would not want independence. But if commerce and manufacturing were allowed to get the upper hand, there was no doubt the Americans would assert themselves. Emphasizing even more than Arthur Young this factor of power inherent in America, Hugh Williamson, writing also from the viewpoint of an English Whig, pointed out the dangers from France and Spain. These two countries would be the real victors, if the Colonies became independent. Britain, deprived of its American trade, would cease to be formidable at sea. The French would aid the Americans and benefit accordingly. "Have the French no account to settle . . . ? Is Great Britain like a polypus? Can she remain whole after her limbs are cut off? Can she retain her naval strength when the employment ceases for half her shipping? Will she be a match for France, when the colonies are thrown into the other scale?" [22] These were questions which the ministry, accepting French professions of friendship at their face value, neglected to weigh.

Other writers perceived the tragic position into which Britain was slipping. None shared the hopes of the ministry; all realized that the bargaining power lay with the Americans and expressed

---

[21] Daniel Leonard, *The Origin of the American Contest with Great Britain* . . . New York: Rivington, 1775. In addition to the pamphlet cited above, Chandler issued a second one entitled *What think ye of Congress Now?*, in which he repeated his warning that secession would "leave us open and exposed to the avarice and ambition of every maritime power in Europe or America."

[22] Arthur Young, *American Husbandry* . . . *Observations on the Advantages and Disadvantages of settling in them, compared with Great Britain and Ireland.* London: J. Bew, 1775; Hugh Williamson, *The Plea of the Colonies on the Charges brought against them by Lord M--d and Others*, London: J. Almon, 1775.

themselves as baffled when it came to offering an escape from the dilemma. As an anonymous writer who sympathized with the Americans put it, their real object was independence. If Parliament acceded to the claims asserted in the petition to the king, the era would commence when America would be the ruler of Britain. Conciliation was attractive, but not really possible. Painful as it was, there was no alternative to the recourse to arms. The sole hope, and it was a faint one, was that the Boston rebels would not get the support of the other colonies.[23]

Josiah Tucker returned to his earlier theme of letting the Americans fend for themselves. Parliament could not allow the king to dispense with its authority in order to please them. But to resort to arms could not bring benefits, even if Britain won. It would not mean an increase of trade; that was impossible, "for a shopkeeper will never get the more custom by beating his customers: and what is true of a shopkeeper is true of a shop-keeping nation." Tucker was well acquainted with Franklin's ambitions, and he pulled no punches in deriding the propaganda against "the *imaginary* tyranny and the pretended oppression of the mother country." "You want to be independent," he charged. "You wish to be an Empire by itself, and to be no longer the Province of another. This spirit is uppermost; and this principle is visible in all your speeches, and all your writings, even when you take some pains to disguise it. . . ." Hence Tucker would take the Americans at their word, separate totally from them, and offer to enter an alliance of friendship and commerce. The Americans would pay the ultimate price, he believed; they would fall victims to civil war.[24] But this medicine was too strong to be swallowed, and Tucker's naked realism found little support.

There was another side to the problem and an anonymous

---

[23] *The Present Crisis with respect to America Considered*, London: T. Becket, 1775.

[24] Josiah Tucker, *An Humble Address and Earnest Appeal; The Respective Pleas and Arguments set forth; and the Impossibility of a Compromise of Differences or a Mutual Concession of Rights plainly demonstrated*, Glocester: R. Raikes, 1775.

author, addressing himself directly to Dr. Johnson and to the ministers, put it most comprehensively. Britain was dependent on America for its position in Europe: "It is by the American Continent only that the balance of Europe can be any longer in your hands." By the superiority in numbers there, he wrote, "you command both the Americas, command Spain and Portugal, influence France and other powers of Europe and . . . therefore instead of checking their increase by a jealous and hostile policy, you ought to encourage it by every just and generous institution." Britain would hazard all its American commerce and its American empire for the shadow of revenue, he asserted. Without a large army it could levy nothing; with it the expense would overbalance the receipts. If the army did not stay there, there would be confusion as soon as it left; if it stayed, it would be impossible to keep its ranks filled. Further, it would be difficult to prevent it from becoming American. And even if all these difficulties were removed, an American system could not easily be reconciled to the principle of the British Empire, which was free and commercial. Here in a nutshell was Britain's dilemma, one that Rome had once faced without success.[25]

By their deliberate onslaught on the North ministry and especially by their ostentatious snubbing of Parliament, the Americans made a peaceful settlement practically impossible. The radicals who dominated the stage in Philadelphia did not want such a settlement. As Richard Champion, a merchant of Bristol with many contacts in America, told his Philadelphia correspondents, Willing, Morris & Company: "What has strengthened Administration, and weakened the hands of the Whigs in this country more than can be conceived is this, that it is represented here, that America is adverse to every set of men among us, and [this is] urged as a proof of their aiming at independency." Champion, who kept in close contact with Burke and Lord Rockingham, had good cause for complaining that the Americans made no distinction between the Whigs and the Tories, and so tied the hands of the former in their efforts at conciliation:

---

[25] *An Answer to a Pamphlet entitled Taxation no Tyranny, addressed to the Author and to Persons in Power*, London: J. Almon, 1775.

I repeat it again, and I had it from authority, that the Whig Party which is composed of men of the first rank reputation and knowledge in this country is the only reliance of America, supposing she means honestly and sincerely to be dependent on Great Britain. . . . America, instead of discrediting the Whig Party, must give them credit and support by shewing that it is of a bad system that they complain, and not of the whole country. The quarrel between a party here and all America may be decided in favour of America, without prejudice to this country; but a quarrel between the whole body of the two countries must be injurious to both, and it is hard to say to which of them in the greatest [degree].[26]

Replying to the Duke of Grafton, who had queried him privately on the possibility of the Colonies sending over individuals to state to Parliament their wishes and expectations, Lord North was not sanguine. His view was that:

the leaders of the rebellion . . . manifestly aim at a total independence. Against this we propose to exert ourselves, using every species of force to reduce them, but authorizing, at the same time, either the commander-in-chief or some other commissioner, to proclaim immediate peace and pardon, and to restore all the privileges of trade to any Colony upon its submission. Authority will likewise be given to settle the question of taxation for the future . . . and to put every other matter now in dispute between them and this country in a course of accommodation. Till the Provinces have made some submission it will be in vain to hope that they will come into any reasonable terms and, I am afraid, that declaring a cessation of arms at this time would establish that independence which the leaders of the faction in America have always intended, and which they now almost openly avow.[27]

The king's speech, delivered at the opening of Parliament on October 26 only six days after, repeated this view more briefly and added that there was nothing to fear from France at the time. Nevertheless, lengthy and heated debates in both houses ensued. The Rockingham Whigs now came forward, proposing a review of the whole problem in the hope that Parliament would

[26] *The American Correspondence of a Bristol Merchant*, G. H. Guttridge, ed., Berkeley, Calif., 1934, pp. 62–65.
[27] The whole of this letter, from the Grafton Papers at Bury St. Edmunds, England, is printed in Van Alstyne, "Parl. Supremacy . . . ," pp. 221–222.

not commit itself to making war. But this group could not swallow the challenge to the ultimate authority of Parliament— it took its stand on the Declaratory Act—and it could find no solid basis for opposing the ministry. Only the small minority of the Chathamites were willing to go farther, proposing the repeal of all thirteen acts passed since 1763. These men had France on their minds and saw Britain facing disaster if the situation was not brought under control. Hence they were ready to negotiate with the revolutionary Continental Congress on the basis of the petition. To them events had made the dogma of Parliamentary supremacy an unreal issue; but to the king, North and the ministers, Mansfield, Rockingham, and the majority in both houses, it was everything. Lord North expressed the majority viewpoint succinctly when he said at the end of the debate that if all of the acts passed since 1763 were repealed, of course the dispute would be terminated: the Americans would be independent.[28]

The Chathamites now found themselves in the slough of despondency. "America is lost and the war afoot," wrote Lord Camden. "There is an end of advising preventive measures, and peace will be more difficult to make than the war was. . . . Ye claims of the Americans, if they are successful, will grow too big for concession, and no man here will venture to be responsible for such a treaty." [29] But the ministry felt it was equal to the occasion. On November 20 Lord North introduced a bill forbidding all trade and intercourse with the Colonies until the rebellion was over. He discounted the war spirit in America, believing reports that the rebel army was plagued with desertions and that local uprisings against it had already occurred.

---

[28] *PH*, XVIII, cols. 705–798, 910–936, 942–963, 963–992.
[29] Van Alstyne, "Parl. Supremacy . . . ," p. 230, quoting from the Grafton Papers.

# CHAPTER IV

# The Gathering Storm in Europe

If France will but join us in time there is no danger but America will soon be established an Independent Empire, and France drawing from her the principal part of those sources of wealth and power that formerly flowed into Great Britain will immediately become the greatest power in Europe. . . .—*The Secret Committee to Silas Deane, October 1, 1776*

O N THE EIGHTEENTH OF SEPTEMBER 1775 the Continental Congress in Philadelphia constituted a committee of nine men and pledged them to secrecy. The job of this committee of secrecy, as it was well called, was to make contracts for importing arms and ammunition. With an army ready by this time to start on an invasion of Canada, the Congress by this act showed that, regardless of further proposals that might emanate from Britain, it was resolved to go the limit. The king, it is true, had already proclaimed the Colonies in a state of insurrection, but the Congress acted in ignorance of the proclamation. Moreover, General Washington in Cambridge, Massachusetts, had previously expressed his confidence that Quebec would fall an easy prey to conquest.[1]

A glance at the membership of the Secret Committee provides an insight into how worldly interests on the one hand and purely ideological considerations on the other can get mixed up. Thomas Willing, the senior partner of the Philadelphia firm, Willing, Morris & Company, was the Committee's chairman. In December Willing, who belonged to the recognized social set of his city, stepped down in favor of his partner Robert Morris, a *parvenu*

---

[1] Force, III, cols. 632 and 1882. The royal proclamation was dated, we recall, Aug. 23, 1775.

who was proving himself a genius in business. Second only to Morris in importance on this committee was Silas Deane of Wethersfield, Connecticut, another social climber and businessman of unusual ability. Deane, who was in his early forties, had married a rich widow in 1763 but was already making money on his own account. In 1767 he again ventured into matrimony, this time with Elizabeth Saltonstall of the politically and socially influential Massachusetts family of that name, and henceforth proved himself adept in politics as well as in business. As an active participant in the Susquehanna Company, he qualified naturally for leadership among the local Connecticut Sons of Liberty, and of course wholeheartedly endorsed the jargon and the uncompromising program of these radicals. Like other men of ardent temperament, Deane persuaded himself that Parliament was really trying to "enslave" America. "Liberty or death is before us," he declared to Elizabeth in September 1775, "and I can conceive of no alternative. . . ." [2] Throughout the preceding summer he boasted of the numbers of troops the Colonies were raising, putting the figure at one point as high as 100,000.

Mixing with the New York radicals, Deane had been on the spot when the New Yorkers attacked and destroyed the property of the loyalist printer, James Rivington, and, much to his own personal satisfaction, witnessed the arrest and imprisonment of Samuel Seabury, the conservative judge and writer of Westchester County whose books Alexander Hamilton deemed worthy of challenge. There is no doubt that Deane had a closed mind on the subject of reconciliation. He paid no heed to Lord North's resolution; he appears to have been indifferent to the prospect of Chatham's returning to power, and, in expressing his impatience in September for additional intelligence from Britain, he made clear that his motive was to exploit it not for the purpose of healing, but of widening, the breach.

As late as 1774 Deane kept up his interest in the Susquehanna scheme, talking about an addition of 4,000 immigrants into that valley during the ensuing year; but, discovering that Morris

---

[2] *The Deane Papers*, 4 vols. Charles Isham, ed., in Collections of the New York Historical Society for the year 1886, I, p. 80. (Hereafter cited as *Deane Papers*.)

and other affluent Philadelphians had staked out rival claims to the Susquehanna, he found it convenient forthwith to subordinate his own interest to theirs in anticipation of far more lucrative opportunities that friendship with them would bring.[3] In this he showed excellent judgment. Meanwhile he and his brother-in-law, Gurdon Saltonstall, had acquired an interest in Ohio lands, so that naturally Parliament's passage of "that most execrable Quebec Act" was to them another nail in the coffin of good will for Britain. In this respect at least Deane felt himself on common ground with Patrick Henry, to whom he wrote a long letter in January expressing his sense of frustration aroused by this measure. "Public, as well as private interest," he told Henry, who was also speculating in Ohio lands, "urge to extend settlements of true and well-principled protestants westward." Here seems to be the most powerful motive behind the eagerness for an inter-Colonial union shown by Deane and the many other speculators awaiting their chance for landgrabbing in the West. Deane himself was candid on the subject. A union, he told Henry, would enable us to "break the boundaries of the Quebec empire." Incidentally it would compel Britain to retreat on other fronts as well. The alternative—Deane habitually spoke of alternatives in terms of extremes—was ruin.[4]

Of the other original members of the Secret Committee, Franklin can hardly be ignored. In terms of prestige alone Franklin outranked Morris or Deane, but the network of moneyed interests which gathered around the latter two men put them in the foreground. Franklin's motives were subtler and more complex than theirs; but he too could hardly have been indifferent to his personal interests, made worthless by the Quebec Act. Franklin's established friendships in Britain and in Europe rendered him invaluable to the committee, and two months later he and four others were constituted a Committee of Secret Correspondence, whose purpose was to enlist support

---

[3] Deane to Samuel H. Parsons, Apr. 13, 1774, *Correspondence between Silas Deane, his Brothers and their Business and Political Associates, 1771–1795* in Collections of the Connecticut Historical Society, vols. II and XXIII, II, pp. 131–135. (Hereafter cited as *Deane Corresp.*)

[4] Saltonstall to Deane, Aug. 29, 1775, and Deane to P. Henry, Jan. 2, 1775, *Deane Papers*, I, pp. 4–5, 33–42.

in Europe. Three of the remaining six members of the Secret Committee were prominent merchants whose business activities were so intertwined with those of the committee as to be indistinguishable. These men were John Langdon of Portsmouth, New Hampshire, brother of the theologian and a zealous member of the Sons of Liberty, Paul Livingston of the powerful New York family, and John Alsop of Virginia. John Dickinson, although remembered chiefly as a lawyer, might well be put in the same category because of his speculations in Philadelphia real estate. All six men—Franklin as a seventh member being apparently an exception—used their positions on the Secret Committee for the enrichment of themselves, their relatives, and their friends. Of the remaining two members—Thomas McKean, a fiery lawyer from Pennsylvania, and a Samuel Ward —little is known. Since the committee's account books were subsequently burned, a complete record is beyond our grasp.

During the months preceding—just how many it is impossible to say—Willing, Morris & Company had been handling the deliveries of gunpowder arriving in quantity from Europe. This business, it was reported at the time, paid the firm a net profit of £12,000. Although the charge is difficult to document, the straitlaced John Adams referred to it in his diary and later statements gave it substance.[5] William Bingham, a younger member of Morris's circle, served five years on the strategic French island of Martinique in the West Indies, as agent for the firm as well as for the Continental Congress. Bingham returned home a rich man in 1780, having made a fortune out of the multitudinous commissions and other transactions that passed continuously through his hands. Not unnaturally, he was a flaming patriot. To Silas Deane he wrote enthusiastically, after the former had gone to Paris, of the great progress the Americans were making on land and sea. Bingham expressed his conviction that France would soon enter the war as defender and guarantor of American independence.[6] Presently, Bingham's activities will merit attention again—he was a key man in the

---

[5] *The Adams Papers*, L. H. Butterfield, ed., series I, vol. II, p. 183. (Hereafter cited as *Adams Papers*.)
[6] Bingham to Deane, Aug. 4, 1776, *Deane Corresp.*, II, pp. 27–31.

vast web of interests spun around the Island of Martinique during the war, connecting American merchants and politicians with their French counterparts on the opposite side of the Atlantic.

Closest to Robert Morris and indefatigable in tying business and political intrigue together was Silas Deane, whom the committee selected to represent it in Paris. Deane's elder brother Barnabas stayed out of politics, but resolved to cut into the lucrative munitions trade. A boatload of grain from the Connecticut Valley for Amsterdam, the export center for Dutch-made gunpowder, would get him started, he hoped, and perhaps a voyage to Havana would be worth trying. "If we are unanimous and have ammunition enough," he told Silas, "I believe we may support our liberties." But Deane's friend, Thomas Mumford of New Haven, was already on the job with two ships en route to St. Eustatia, the Dutch island in the West Indies; the captains of the vessels were given authority to buy powder. Mumford wrote to Deane in October for permission from Congress to dispatch all the vessels and cargoes he could assemble for engaging in the powder business.[7] All told, some forty American merchants were believed to have benefited directly from contracts awarded by the Committee.

Other methods of making money included privateering operations out of French ports, in the West Indies as well as in European waters. Morris, Deane, and four Philadelphia merchants participated in this business. Deane was the linchpin binding the Americans to important financiers and merchants in Europe. His mission to Paris took him through Martinique, where he organized an international commercial and land-speculating group which counted among its members Conrad Alexandre Gérard, the French undersecretary of state for foreign affairs, MM. LeRay Chaumont and Ferdinand Grand, Paris bankers, Sir George Grand of Amsterdam, and Thomas Walpole of the Walpole Associates in London. In addition members of four other prominent firms with whom Deane established close relations need to be mentioned: MM. Delap of Bordeaux,

---

[7] Barnabas to Silas Deane, Oct. 18; Mumford to Deane, Oct. 19, 1775. *Deane Corresp.*, XXIII, pp. 10–12.

which Deane described as a capital house, M. Schweighauser of Nantes, M. Limouzin of Havre, and the Moylan brothers of L'Orient. All of these men, as well as others whom we shall have occasion to mention, had influence and contributed heavily to the equipping and financing of the American revolutionaries.[8] Then there were MM. Penet and Pliarne, two merchants of Nantes who visited Philadelphia early in 1776 and established connections with Morris; they were preceded by Achard de Bonvouloir, a former French naval officer who, apparently at the instance of the comte de Guines, the French ambassador in London, went disguised as a merchant from Antwerp to make cautious inquiries of the Secret Committee. On his return to Paris, Bonvouloir reported to Vergennes; hence his mission was politically motivated and marked the first step toward inducing the French government to take a hand.

In the meantime, however, private enterprise, chiefly Dutch, French, and. Spanish, supplied the Americans with their wants. After Bunker Hill the Americans ran short of gunpowder, and the deficiency had to be made up from Europe if the resistance was to continue. The Netherlands was the principal source of supply, and the chances for profit were so good that by the middle of 1776, if not before, the Dutch mills were working at full capacity. Amsterdam merchants handled the business, and the town, according to the British ambassador, swarmed with Americans. But the powder, supplemented with guns, bayonets, and field pieces, reached America by devious routes. Some of these went direct to the Dutch island of St. Eustatia, where on arrival they doubled in price; then they were re-exported to America at a further advance of twenty to thirty per cent. The island importers pleaded with their correspondents in Amsterdam to send them more powder, shot, muskets with bayonets, swords, cannon, and so on for resale to the Americans. This was "the way to make a little fortune," as one of them eagerly

---

[8] Robert A. East's, *Business Enterprise in the American Revolutionary Era*, New York, 1938, is the best analysis of these economic interests. See especially his chapter on "Robert Morris and his Group." See also: Thomas P. Abernethy, "Commercial Activities of Silas Deane in France," *Amer. Hist. Rev.*, XXXIX (1934), pp. 477–485, and Clarence L. Ver Steeg, *Robert Morris, Revolutionary Financier*, Philadelphia, 1954.

put it. The Americans paid for their purchases with indigo and tobacco and also ships, which were put into the service of the contraband trade between Amsterdam and the island. But British vessels were also joining the Dutch merchant marine. If the rebellion continued, remarked the British ambassador, Sir Joseph Yorke, "we run the risk of seeing half the merchant marine of Great Britain employed to make war on the other half." [9]

St. Eustatia is commonly supposed to have been the entrepôt for this trade, but British intelligence, derived from the embassies in Holland, France, Spain, and Portugal, disclosed that more Dutch powder reached the Americans through French and Spanish ports than through the Dutch West Indies. Yorke reported three times during the year of 1776 that most of the powder shipped from Amsterdam went in French bottoms to Nantes and Bordeaux, whence it moved direct to American ports. From the British consulate at Corunna, Spain, came reports on the trade through that country. Dutch vessels brought barrels of powder to Bilbao and St. Ander for transfer to ships belonging to Willing, Morris & Company. The Philadelphia firm transacted its Spanish business with Gardoqui & Co. of Bilbao, which throve on the exchange of American tobacco for guns and powder.

The British also had many other sources of information. Trains of artillery were moving through the French port of Dunkirk en route to America as early as December 1775. Ostend and Nieuport in Belgium were also ports of export for powder. The Isle of Jersey in the English Channel was a good observation post, and its governor was able to send detailed reports on the arms trade through the French ports. On March 4, 1776, for instance, he reported that a Swedish vessel had just arrived at St. Malo from London, carrying a cargo of large guns and ammunition to the account of French merchants. These merchants reship the stuff to St. Domingue, Martinique, and Guadeloupe, he advised, "there being fresh orders daily arriving with great precipitation from the French-American Colonies for these articles, bearing a great price there, on account they sell them

---

[9] Yorke to Suffolk, Aug. 2 and 30, 1776. State Papers, 84/553. (Hereafter cited as *SP*.) Public Record Office, London. (Hereafter cited as *PRO*.)

to the North Americans, as also all kinds of provisions now in great demand and sent to their Colonies in great quantities for the supplying and supporting of the North Americans." [10]

From naval commanders and other officials stationed in American waters the Admiralty learned of the daily arrival of munitions-laden ships in American ports, and of the difficulties and hardships its own cruisers faced in trying to control the traffic. Thus Vice Admiral Shuldham, who reached Boston with his squadron on the thirtieth of December, 1775, after a stormy passage of sixty-one days, reported on the advantages the rebels had over his cruisers through their control of the harbors, creeks, and rivers along the coast. His own supply ships faced capture: out of thirty-five which had sailed from England only eight arrived safely. The king sensibly proposed a blockade of the waters between the French and Dutch islands in the West Indies and the mainland, but this was easier said than done; the navy lacked the ships for a blockade, and much of the gun-running was done in "neutral" French bottoms which British commanders were not allowed to intercept.[11] Obviously British sea power was in a sad state at this time, and it was fated to remain so throughout the war. Here, as in other respects, the Americans played from strength, trafficking with Europe at will and putting the British Navy in a hopeless posture of defense.

Long before the Revolution broke into open war, forecasts had been made repeatedly that the Americans would have Britain's rivals on their side. Fears of encirclement had been freely expressed in Britain. Chatham and his followers were so positive in their dread of this eventuality that they were virtually ready for peace at any price with the Americans. Chatham's ideas centered on a reunited Empire offering a solid front against

---

[10] To Lord Weymouth, the Secretary of State for the Southern Department, CO 5/139, PRO.

[11] *The Despatches of Molyneux Shuldham. Vice-Admiral of the Blue and Commander-in-Chief of His Britannic Majesty's Ships in North America. January–July 1776*, Robert Wilden Neeser, ed., New York, The Naval History Society, 1913, pp. 37–39, 69–75. And for additional evidence and documentation see my article, "Great Britain, the War for Independence, and the 'Gathering Storm' in Europe, 1775–1778," *Hunt. Lib. Quart.*, XXVII (1964), pp. 311–346.

the Bourbon combination in Europe. And when, on its part, the Continental Congress in July 1775 boasted that "foreign assistance is undoubtedly attainable," it was not speaking in terms of private trading. The chances for at least a French alliance had already been canvassed and considered excellent. Franklin, while still in London, had explored the possibilities. But for the moment there was a disposition to temporize, leaving it to private enterprise to secure the necessary supplies. Fears most vividly expressed by Jefferson that, if they moved too fast into a new alignment, the Americans would merely change masters caused them to hesitate.

John Adams, characteristically weighing the alternatives in his mind, scouted the idea of an alliance. Let the French take the initiative, he said in effect, but let the connection be strictly commercial. If the Americans sent an ambassador, their representative "might possibly, if well skill'd in intrigue, his Pockets well filled with Money and his Person Robust and elegant enough, get introduced to some of the Misses and Courtesans in Keeping of the statesmen in France," but there would be no other benefits. The French themselves would realize the flaw in such an alliance: once the Americans got their independence, they would make a separate peace and make common cause with Britain. Such a combination would be more threatening to France than ever.[12]

Adams continued to talk in this vein. How, he mused in March 1776, were French and Spanish interests affected by the war between Britain and America? Were they not exposed to the danger of a reconciliation? "A British Fleet and Army united with an American Fleet and Army and supplied with Provisions and other Necessaries from America, might conquer all the french islands in the W.I. in six Months, and a little (less) more Time than that would be required, to destroy all their Marine and Commerce."[13] This pattern of thought was precisely in line with the previous thinking of both Franklin and Chatham. But by this time Congress was ready to make the first approach to France, and Adams reacted accordingly: "No

---

[12] Adams to James Warren, Oct. 7, 1775. Burnett, I, pp. 218–220.
[13] Diary entry for Mar. 1, 1776. *Adams Papers*, II, p. 235.

Political Connection," he insisted. "Submit to none of her Authority—receive no Governors, or officers from her. . . . No military Connection. Receive no Troops from her." He urged the Congress not to go past a commercial connection, saying it should let the ports of both countries be opened by treaty to each other, and let the French "furnish Us with Arms, Cannon, Salt Petre, Powder, Duck, Steel." [14] But this desire for a lopsided advantage was not so easy to meet, and Adams himself was to change his tune.

Franklin, writing privately but undoubtedly speaking for the Secret Committee, made the first overture. A letter to his friend, C. F. W. Dumas, in The Hague asked Dumas to find out whether, if the Americans declared themselves independent, there was any state or power in Europe willing to form an alliance. The date of Franklin's letter, December 19, 1775, indicates that the Secret Committee had reached at least a tentative conclusion to go ahead; but the arrival immediately after of Bonvouloir, the secret agent from France, and the encouraging replies he gave to the committee's inquiries must certainly have helped to dispel any doubts.[15] By this time the committee must have become aware that aid received through private business would not suffice; subventions and other forms of participation by the French government would be required.

In this same month of December Alexandre Gérard, the undersecretary who was to play a key role in the diplomacy in Paris, composed a lengthy memorandum which gives us an insight into official French thinking on the subject. Gérard found it difficult to understand how the British had been so foolish as to put themselves at such a disadvantage, but now that the rebellion had gone so far there was no turning back. Thus it behooved France to seize the opportunity, give the Americans enough help to "feed their courage . . . and flatter them with the hope of efficacious assistance when circumstances called for

---

[14] *Ibid.,* p. 236.

[15] Francis Wharton, *Revolutionary Diplomatic Correspondence of the United States,* 6 vols., Washington, D. C., 1889, II, p. 65. (Hereafter cited as Wharton.) John J. Meng, *Despatches and Instructions of Conrad Alexandre Gérard, 1778–1780,* Baltimore, 1939, p. 45. (Hereafter cited as Meng.)

it," and retrieve some of the losses she had suffered in the preceding war. Obviously disposed to intervene, Gérard dismissed the fear expressed in France that the Americans would use the war to embark on a program of conquest at French and Spanish expense. They would be too exhausted for that, he decided, and then he added the thought that they would set up as a republic, or perhaps as a number of small republics. Republics, he felt "rarely have the spirit of conquest, and those which will be formed in America will have it all the less, as they know the pleasures and advantages of commerce, and have need of industry. . . ." [16] These *Réflexions* show Gérard more incautious than his chief, less skeptical of the Americans, and readier to commit France to their side. When, about six months later, Silas Deane arrived in Paris, he found that Gérard was to be his principal contact at Versailles.

Vergennes was more reserved, holding that the war had risks for France regardless of who won. Britain might well recoup itself by an attack on the French and Spanish islands, or the British might persuade the Americans to join them, as Chatham and others openly desired. Or, thought Vergennes, the Americans might undertake such a war on their own account, or wage an economic warfare that would have the same effect as conquest. Nevertheless, Vergennes concluded, France had little choice in the matter. The French had to keep the British pacified, but at the same time sustain the Americans "by some secret favors and by vague hopes that would prevent the steps which it is sought to induce them to take for a reconciliation. . . ." Such encouragement, however, had to be kept within bounds, for "it would not accord with the King's dignity, nor with his interest, to enter into a compact with the insurgents." Above all, France had to put itself in a position of strength. Both War Minister St. Germain and Minister of Marine Sartine expressed agreement with these views.[17]

---

[16] B. F. Stevens, *Facsimiles of Manuscripts in European Archives relating to America, 1773–1783*, no. 1310. (Hereafter cited as Stevens, *Facs.*)

[17] *Ibid.*, nos. 1316, 1319 and 1332. Vergennes' *Considérations* bear the date Mar. 12, 1776; St. Germain's Mémoir, Mar. 15; and Sartine to Vergennes, Apr. 27.

Early in March 1776, the Secret Committee decided to send Deane to France, empowering him to make contracts for the shipment of supplies, including a quantity of goods to give to the Indians whom it was necessary to appease, and to sound out the French ministers with reference to a possible alliance. Franklin furnished Deane with letters of introduction to his friends LeRay Chaumont and Barbeu Dubourg in London. Dubourg would put Deane in touch with Vergennes, and Bancroft would come from London and give him intelligence regarding the situation there. Deane sent his first report in June from Bordeaux, after conversations with the Delap brothers in that city in which he learned that both France and Spain were preparing for war. The card he played then and later was the prospect of a rich trade with America which would soon put France in the place of Britain. The French merchants were easily persuaded and agreed to sell on credit against future receipts of tobacco. Vergennes too was impressed, or at least so Deane thought after a three-hour private conversation. Actually the court at Versailles had decided on May 2, 1776, while Deane was still on the high seas, to grant the Americans a subvention of a million livres.

This decision, influenced principally by considerations of high policy and arrived at independently of applications from the Americans, marked the first tentative step on the part of France toward intervention in the war. But at the time it was something of a leap in the dark. Months of vacillation and divisions of opinion lay behind it. Even for those days it was a comparatively modest sum, conceived of as a temporizing measure of encouragement to the Americans in order to give France, in conjunction with Spain, the time needed to prepare for the next war with Britain. For this eventuality the navy first had to be put in shape. Since Choiseul's dismissal in 1770 it had been neglected, as Sartine reported after a detailed inspection of the ports and naval arsenals. With great energy Sartine in 1775 resumed Choiseul's building program and kept Vergennes closely informed of the progress the navy was making. Thus in November 1776 Sartine advised that he would have forty ships of the line nearing completion by the end of the year; in April of the following year he had forty-two ready for sea duty, with thirty more to be built; and in May 1778, at the time of the rupture with Britain, he reported that France and Spain had a combined strength of ninety ships of the line against seventy-two British vessels.[18]

Among the forces working for a policy of intermeddling on the side of the Americans, the French Embassy in London appears to have been in the forefront. Other than the reports of the few agents occasionally sent to America, the ministers in Paris knew little about the situation there. But the Embassy had ample sources on which to draw. Sharing the viewpoint that Britain would be shorn of her strength if separated from her Colonies, the comte de Guines, like his predecessors, regarded the rebellion as France's opportunity.

More positive still in this opinion was Beaumarchais, whom Vergennes sent to London on a special errand, not related to the American crisis, in the summer of 1775. Beaumarchais's peculiar importance rests on his personal ties with Vergennes and Gérard, but as a maker of policy he gets more credit from historians than he probably deserves. While in London he became a zealot for the American cause, but since the record of his activities there is so scanty, it is necessary that we be cautious. We know that he befriended Arthur Lee, John Wilkes, the English radical, serving as intermediary; and apparently Beaumarchais became quite expansive in outlining for Lee's benefit what France could do for the Americans. Lee on his part was temperamentally disposed to intrigue, even daring to hint to the French playwright that France had better lend a hand if it wanted to keep its own islands in the West Indies. But Beaumarchais was way ahead of Vergennes in his schemes, and whatever his persuasive powers with Vergennes may have been, the complete absence of documentation bearing on his conversations with the foreign minister puts us squarely in the realm of guesswork.[19]

By the time that Beaumarchais started his intrigue in London, it seems to have been an article of faith accepted in Paris that

---

[18] G. Lacour-Gayet, *La Marine Militaire de la France sous Louis XVI,* Paris, 1905, pp. 18–56.

[19] For a discussion of the literature on Beaumarchais see the bibliographical essay at the end of this book.

the breach between Britain and its Colonies was irreparable and that Britain might seek compensation through a new war with France. This was the view taken by Louis XVI in urging on Charles III of Spain the necessity of the two countries keeping closely in step. Charles III cordially agreed. "I am convinced," wrote the Spanish king in reply, "that if the English recognize us to be ready or on guard at all points they will leave us in peace, and we will profit from this peace which we desire to preserve. But the great thing is [to] achieve a state wherein we are capable of imposing our will on our enemies. . . ." [20] Vergennes had perhaps a more elegant way of expressing this last sentiment, but his meaning was the same, namely, that France should be ready to resume its true role of "arbiter of peace and war," an aspiration common to all sovereign states.

About the time that the French made their decision to give the Americans a subvention the situation in Europe itself was clouding up. Turgot, the finance minister, concurred with the wisdom of stepping very carefully: Britain obviously was not seeking a war with France, but a reconciliation with America would put France in a dangerous position. From the French and Spanish standpoint, it would be advantageous for the British eventually to win in America, for the victory would exhaust them and oblige them to hold the Colonies down by force. However, Turgot decided, it was more likely that the Americans would get their independence, and such an outcome would have its consequences for the other colonial powers. Hence for France a temporizing policy was best, giving the Americans hope but taking care not to provoke the British.[21]

---

[20] AAE, K 164, année 1775, nos. 21–22. Evidently fear and suspicion of an unprovoked attack was mutual between Britain on the one hand and the Bourbon powers on the other.

[21] AAE, K 1340, no. 10.

Turgot's *Memoir* shows, in lesser degree, the apprehension that Vergennes had formerly held. On October 31, 1775 Vergennes said to Lord Stormont, the British ambassador, "in the most positive manner" that France would *never* extend aid to the rebels. If the Americans got their desired independence, they "would immediately set about forming a great marine, and as they have every possible advantage for ship-building it would not be long before they had such fleets as would be an over-match

At the moment the greatest threat to the peace of Europe came from south of the Pyrenees. Spain, it was feared, was preparing to revive previous attempts to conquer and annex Portugal, and there was also the possibility of a colonial war between the Spanish and the Portuguese in South America. On these issues Versailles and Whitehall found themselves on common ground; Vergennes undertook to restrain his Spanish colleague, the Marquis de Grimaldi, while the British government cautioned the Portuguese. As viewed from London, the Spanish-Portuguese crisis was "extremely critical"; if it led to war, Britain would be obliged to come to the aid of its Portuguese ally, and the war would then become general.[22] Vergennes had equally good reason for not wanting to be dragged in on the side of Spain.

But to the Portuguese foreign minister, the Marquis de Pombal, the time seemed ripe for a showdown. To the British ambassador Pombal proposed that Britain

. . . require of France and Spain to declare whether the great armaments going on at Toulon and at Brest and at Cadiz are designed against Great Britain or its Allies, or against its National Interests: and that in case France and Spain should hesitate to give an answer to this embarrassing inquiry, as probably they would, that then his Majesty should order Brest and Cadiz blocked up by his fleets, so that no ships should come out without falling into the power of the British fleets: that this success against these two powerful fleets would tend to the pacification of the Americans, whose great dependence at this

---

for the whole naval power of Europe. . . . With this superiority and every advantage of situation they might, when they pleased, conquer both your islands and ours. I am persuaded that they would not stop here, but would in process of time advance to the Southern Continent of America and either subdue the inhabitants or carry them along with them, and in the end not leave a foot of that Hemisphere in the possession of any European power. . . ." Stormont to Rochford, no. 19, SP 78/297, PRO.

Of course, Vergennes may have been exaggerating for the benefit of the ambassador, but Stormont did not think so. "I am myself convinced," he added, "that much of the general fate of Europe is involved in this unhappy contest."

[22] Grantham to Weymouth, no. 33, July 25, 1776; Weymouth to Grantham, no. 13, July 9. SP 94/200–201, PRO.

time is on those two nations, and who would upon their defeats be deprived of the resources they at present rely upon.[23]

Pombal's ideas coincided with those of Chatham and his followers in Parliament: Britain's major enemies were the Bourbon powers; confront them, Pombal believed, and the American rebellion would peter out. But this was always too strong medicine for the North ministry, and in any event it was now too late: British naval strength had dispersed to the farther side of the Atlantic. Through the summer of 1776 British diplomacy concentrated on Portugal. If Pombal were encouraged, Europe would burst into flame.

To the Americans, however, a European war was just the thing. Silas Deane was in high spirits over what he heard and saw. "It is by no means probable that Europe will long remain in a state of peace," he told the Secret Committee in August. "The disputes between Portugal and Spain are on the point of producing an open rupture; the former relies on England, the latter will look to this Kingdom, and has already applied to this Court on the subject." Frederick of Prussia was another good prospect, although at the moment he was preoccupied with dividing up Poland. Frederick bore a grudge against Britain for letting him down in the previous war and he was eager, so Deane speculated, to develop overseas commerce. Who but the Americans, asked Deane, could help him so well in realizing this ambition? They could bring him coffee and sugar from the West Indies.

With his imagination thus working, Deane envisaged a grand European coalition, "after which, Great Britain having her whole force employed in America, there could be nothing on the one hand to prevent Spain and France from reducing Portugal to a submission to the former, nor from Prussia and France subduing . . . Hanover and the other little mercenary Electorates. . . ." Then Deane wrote separately to Robert Morris to recommend that authority be given American vessels to make war on Portuguese ships, for in that way "you may depend on the friendship and alliance of Spain. Let me urge this measure. Much may be got, nothing can be lost by it. Increase, at all events,

---

[23] Walpole to Weymouth, no. 39, Aug. 17, 1776. SP 89/82, PRO.

your navy." [24] Morris, now head of the Marine Committee, thought the advice was very good and put it into effect. It was America's first bid for a Spanish alliance, but since war did not break out in Europe, as expected, it did not bring results. Portugal, however, faithful to its British alliance, closed its gates to American shipping in July 1776 and ordered all rebel vessels to leave, whereas the rich Spanish trade in contraband goods continued to flourish under the auspices of the House of Gardoqui.[25]

Meanwhile Deane in Paris plunged into a round of activity which he described at length in a communication to the Secret Committee dated August 18, 1776.[26] At first he passed himself off as a Bermuda merchant, but the disguise was too thin to last long. He established relations with Dubourg and others as instructed, and met with Bancroft on the eighth of July. Thomas Walpole, a much more important figure than Bancroft in London, also came over to see Deane. As a merchant banker, as a Member of Parliament identified with the Rockingham Whigs, and as one with strong business and personal ties in America, Walpole had every motive for patching up a peace even at that late date; but, as he discovered, his only chance of success lay in persuading the ministry to yield to the Americans in time to come between them and the French.

Deane talked freely with both Walpole and Bancroft and showed them the instructions the Secret Committee had given him. Both men then returned to London to lay the facts before the authorities. In addition to a detailed knowledge of the merchandise, arms, and supplies the Americans were getting from France, they knew that Deane was bidding for an alliance and that it was quite possible he would get it. The French court, Walpole reported, "will do everything short of an open rupture with us, and the French nation have already tasted considerable advantages from the interruption of our American trade, and loudly demands a closer connection between the two countries

---

[24] Deane to the Secret Committee, Aug. 18, 1776; to Robert Morris, Sept. 17. *Deane Papers*, I, pp. 195–218, 247.

[25] Walpole to Weymouth, no. 32, July 6, 1776. SP 89/82, PRO.

[26] *Deane Papers*, I, pp. 195–218.

—a war on that account would be popular." Not long after, on the seventeenth of August, the *London Evening Post* published the text of the American Declaration of Independence, an event Walpole concluded that would force the Congress to decide on a policy of seeking alliances with the other powers of Europe.[27] Lord Weymouth, the Secretary of State for the Southern Department, transmitted a full report of the intelligence thus gained to Lord Stormont in Paris, but other than becoming more watchful, the North ministry showed no disposition to alter its policy.

During the very week of July when Deane was receiving visits from Walpole and Bancroft, he had his first encounter with Beaumarchais. So much has been written about Beaumarchais and the mysterious company, Hortalés & Cie., which he set up for the purpose of funneling supplies direct from French arsenals to the Americans, that we cannot ignore him. To Deane, who had come to France to deal with merchants and bankers, especially with four *hommes des affaires*, MM. Penet and Pliarne of Nantes, and Chaumont and Dubourg of Paris, Beaumarchais' sudden entry on the scene came as a surprise. It was even worse to Dubourg, who had expected to serve as Deane's contact man with the Court. Beaumarchais's intrusion caused a quarrel, but when Deane took the matter to Gérard he was told to deal with Beaumarchais. This, thought Deane, was extraordinary: Beaumarchais was so careless in money matters. Lord Stormont, the British ambassador, was equally skeptical; not worth a shilling until recently, he commented, Beaumarchais suddenly had millions at his command. Beaumarchais, on his part, discovering that Deane was the man with whom to negotiate, dropped his underground connections with Arthur Lee in London. Naturally Lee, with a jealous disposition, felt outraged and became a bitter enemy of Deane, whose downfall he and his brothers ultimately brought about.

Beaumarchais' peculiar hold on the French Court remains a mystery. It is indeed puzzling that men as calculating as Gérard and Vergennes would be so ready to entrust him with apparently enormous responsibilities. It is a fact that Lord Stormont, whose

---

[27] Walpole to the Duke of Grafton, July 11 and Aug. 13, 1776. Grafton Papers.

sources of information were excellent, gave him only casual notice and, in his numerous reports to Whitehall, did not once mention Hortalés & Cie. Silas Deane, to be sure, accepted Gérard's decision and dealt with Beaumarchais accordingly. But Deane, a hardheaded schemer playing for high stakes, seems to have regarded the playwright as a convenient tool whose ardor proved useful on occasion. In his reports Deane made very few allusions to Beaumarchais, whom he characterized as "a man of wit and genius and a considerable writer in comic and political subjects," but as "a person of no interest with the merchants."

Obviously Deane felt more at home with the latter and, having much more on his mind than the procurement of supplies, he used every opportunity he could get to communicate with Gérard at the Foreign Ministry and with the *Bureau de Guerre* direct. But by December he had decided to be more attentive. The Americans were feeling the pinch badly, the merchants were refusing further credits, and the court, aware of the British occupation of New York, vacillated over allowing the flow of supplies to continue. "Our affairs," wrote Robert Morris to Deane, "are amazingly altered for the worse within a few weeks." Meanwhile, however, the Court had ordered cargoes which Beaumarchais had prepared for shipment to be publicly unloaded, to Deane's bitter disappointment. The Court reversed itself again in February 1777, permitting three vessels heavily laden with artillery and military stores to sail, but how much influence Beaumarchais had in this change of policy is unknown. On the whole, it would seem that historians have overestimated his importance. He was a willing tool, as Deane originally regarded him, but expendable if the French court so desired.[28]

---

[28] Stormont mentioned Beaumarchais eight times: May 1, Sept. 25, Nov. 6, 13 and 20, Dec. 23 and 25, 1776, and for the last time on May 27, 1777. SP 78/299, 300, 302. Deane's first allusion to Beaumarchais was in his long communication of Aug. 18, 1776. It is clear that he knew less about him at the time than did the British ambassador. He had already fallen out with Lee, and on the twenty-second he wrote both Gérard and Vergennes to protest against Lee's coming to Paris. *Deane Papers*, I, pp. 220–222. There are only four other references to Beaumarchais in this collection for the remainder of the year 1776; and for Jan.–Feb., 1777, there are two letters—one from Deane to Beaumarchais and one from Beaumarchais to Deane.

In the early stages of the conflict the Americans had gone into the European market chiefly for gunpowder and for saltpeter, the raw material required for the manufacture of powder. But as the war spread and as more men came under arms, the list of matèriel and the quantity of things needed expanded accordingly. Deane wanted heavy guns and mortars—seventy or eighty thousand, he reported, were lying unused in French magazines, along with other military stores, where they had been discarded by the army in favor of newer weapons. These could be picked up cheaply through private merchants. Deane had been ordered to buy clothing for 25,000 troops, including coarse woolens and linens for underwear and blankets, and so forth.

As the war lengthened out, the demand for dry goods of the latter kind grew more imperative. It is impossible to separate statistically the quantity and value of the matèriel purchased on private account from what Deane got from official sources. He continued making contracts with Chaumont, Penet, and other private dealers, and paying—or promising payment—in tobacco, indigo, and other produce brought back from America. Willing, Morris & Company had at least three other agents doing business for them in France and Holland in 1776, and got from the Delap brothers of Bordeaux a credit of £4,000 to £5,000 sterling. French shipping documents were the best protection against British attempts at search on the high seas, the American firm advised its correspondents; and to the extent possible the cargoes should be sent direct to American ports, rather than roundabout through the West Indies.[29] Deane preferred Bordeaux to any other French port: its greater distance from England put British frigates at a corresponding disadvantage in patrolling the waters of the Bay of Biscay; relations with the Delap brothers were excellent; and in the neighboring town of Angôulème was the foundry where most of the French cannon were cast.

But Deane had other schemes which he wanted to try out. He heard that the primitive Caribs on the island of St. Vincent, which the British had taken from the French in the last war, were discontented. Since Bingham was near at hand on Mar-

---

[29] Robert Morris Papers. (Hereafter cited as *Morris Papers*.) Accession 1805. Corresp. 1776–1777.

tinique, Deane wished to send agents to agitate an insurrection and promise the Indians arms and ammunitions. Then, Deane noticed that insurance rates on cargoes between London and Jamaica had risen to twenty per cent. A few American vessels enjoying the shelter of French ports and furnished with intelligence regarding the movements of British shipping could profitably engage in privateering in the English Channel. This idea was soon to be put into practice. Next, French merchants, Deane felt, would speculate heavily in the American trade, if the premium on insurance could be kept at a reasonable figure. If the Congress would assume the risk, the trade would benefit accordingly.[30] Moreover, since it was politic to get France involved in the war, Deane wondered what could be more effectual than to go into its debt for supplies and to employ French persons of family and influence in the American service. American ability to pay, he admitted, was a common topic of conversation; already bills were being protested, and his expenses were rising fast. But, Deane argued, there need be no anxiety on this score; with heavy emigration to America certain to resume after the war, land values would rise accordingly. The Americans could pay for the war through the sale of land. He wanted the Congress to make a grant to an international syndicate of 200 square miles along the Ohio River. Proposing that civil government be established in this territory and confederated with the United States, Deane sought the reservation of one-fifth of this land for paying off the public debt, leaving the syndicate title to the other four-fifths. It seemed like an attractive proposition coming naturally from Deane, since he had already organized just such a syndicate consisting of himself, Gérard, Chaumont, Ferdinand Grand, Sir George Grand of Amsterdam, and Walpole. But, for reasons unknown, this idea did not take hold.

---

[30] Deane set forth most of his ideas in his communication of Aug. 18, 1776. In general Morris responded favorably, but to the suggestion that Congress stimulate the trade by assuming the insurance risks Morris countered with the proposal that Deane try the underwriters in London. Morris to Deane, Feb. 27, 1777. *Deane Papers*, II, p. 14. Lord Stormont, in several of his dispatches to Weymouth, declared that rebel purchases in France were being financed through London, but I am unable to corroborate his statements.

More than anything else, however, the political implications of French involvement in the war interested Deane. When he wrote his first report, he had not had word of the Declaration of Independence, but, he stated, "I go on the supposition of an actual unconditional independency, without which little can be effected publickly; with it, almost everything we can wish for." Later, on November 20, 1776, he formally presented Vergennes with a copy of the Declaration, but it failed to have the effect he intended. Meanwhile, scarcely was he settled in Paris when Dubourg brought him memorials from French officers and engineers who wanted to go to America. In spite of Beaumarchais, Deane continued to regard Dubourg as his most helpful French acquaintance; and he instantly discerned the political value of rewarding these volunteers. Several young gentlemen of fortune whose families had intimate ties at court, he explained, were preparing to go. His most valued recruit was Philippe Tronson du Coudray, "a fine acquisition," an adjutant general in the French Army and a trained engineer who was stationed at Metz. Deane proposed to send him over with the rank of major general in charge of artillery, and secured his release from the French Army. Lord Stormont had intelligence by November that Deane had signed up 400 French officers, and he was certainly not underestimating the number: Deane complained he was being "harrassed to death" with applications, and Morris in Philadelphia protested strongly that they were too numerous for him to handle. It was his job to get them commissions in the American Army, "but really," Morris complained, "they are flocking over in such numbers from every port and by every ship that I don't know what we shall do with them." [31]

On or about December 14, 1776 du Coudray and four other officers sailed from Le Havre on the French frigate *Amphitrite*, but under his orders the ship put back much to Dean's chagrin: it was heavily laden with cannon and military stores badly needed on the other side of the Atlantic. Eventually du Coudray

---

[31] Deane to the Secret Committee, Nov. 28, 1776, *Deane Papers*, I, pp. 371–378. Deane said he had been getting offers from Germany and Switzerland, the men to sail from Dunkirk ostensibly for the French West Indies, but actually for America. Morris to Bingham, Feb. 16, 1777, *Morris Papers*.

did join Washington's Army—"the most learned and promising officer in France," as John Adams described him. But his career in America did not live up to expectations, arousing the jealousy of Nathaniel Greene and other American officers who reacted against Frenchmen who were pushed ahead of them. The following September he rode his horse off a boat in the Schuylkill and was drowned, "peut-être un heureux accident," as Lafayette, who had arrived after him, laconically remarked.[32]

Deane in the meantime remained highly confident that a general war was close at hand, and that he could personally hurry it along. Dr. Bancroft kept him informed of the situation in Britain, coming to Paris a second time in order to render a full report. Bancroft thought also that the war would soon spread. On the twenty-fourth of September Deane boldly tackled the French Foreign Office on the proposition that it was time for France to take the plunge. It was within France's power, he argued, to take advantage of "this critical, this extremely Critical Period." Vigorous action by France would advance French "interest and happiness" and make it impossible for Britain ever again "to disturb her repose on the Continent or insult her on the Ocean." If France hesitated, the chance would never recur Deane maintained. Parliament would convene in October, and the opposition was hoping to regain power and make peace. If the British government came under "the management of a Great Genius, a Man of Liberal and extensive views" (meaning, no doubt, Chatham), ran Deane's argument, France would be in mortal peril. With land and sea forces in America superior to those of all the other European powers combined, and with the Americans as possible allies, France would lose its colonies "nor would the Danger in such case threaten the possessions of France only." However, there was a positive benefit which support of America could win for France, Deane asserted; of all the kingdoms in Europe, France was America's "most natural ally. Nor is it possible, while each pursues its own obvious Interest, to find an instance in which they can

---

[32] *Adams Papers*, series I, Diaries, II, p. 263. See also André Lasseray, *Les Francais sous les Treize Etoiles (1775–1783)*, 2 vols., Paris, 1935, I, pp. 344–354. Lord Stormont was well informed on Coudray and the lading of the *Amphitrite*.

interfere with, or rival each other; on the contrary, they are as naturally situated to increase and promote each other's true Interest and happiness as any Two Countries on the Globe. . . ." [33]

In Philadelphia the Secret Committee, nervous over the superior fleet under the command of Admiral Lord Howe in New York and over the large number of loyalists whose presence in every state the committee admitted, took the same view. If the French were serious, let them send a fleet to engage Lord Howe and let them send good muskets, blankets, clothes, and more ammunition. "But alas, we fear the Court of France will let slip the glorious opportunity and go to war by halves, as we have done; we say go to war because we are of opinion they must take part in the war, sooner or later, and the longer they are about it, the worse terms will they come upon. . . ." And then the committee repeated the veiled threat: if France, Spain, and Portugal did not help, they might at some future time find themselves at a disadvantage in holding their American possessions.

Deane meanwhile was writing to the committee to put more ginger into its program: to make war on Portugal, to send over commissions in blank for privateers, above all, to depute someone to go to Prussia to arouse its interest. "I am fully of opinion," he repeated on the eighth of October, "that a war must break out soon and become general in Europe." Still, he felt the committee was not backing him up strongly enough. With the help of du Coudray, he had obtained from French government arsenals 200 brass cannon, arms, tents and accoutrements for 30,000 men, ammunition in proportion, and 20,000 to 30,000 brass mortars. And he had been visited by the duc de Broglie, who had led the French Army in Europe in the previous war. But all of this could be lost just by a word from Versailles. Deane had not heard

---

[33] *Deane Papers*, I, pp. 252–285. The length as well as the vehemence of this Memoir is worth noting. Bancroft wrote Deane two long letters, one on the thirteenth and again on the twentieth, telling, among many other things, of a visit he had received from David Hartley and of a friend in the ministry connected with Lord Suffolk, the Secretary of State for the Northern Department. The friend was probably William Eden (see *supra*, pp. 60–61), and the significance of this relationship will be discussed below. The letters to Deane are in *The Deane Papers*, pp. 237–243 and 249–252.

from Philadelphia for many months, and he was vexed at the silence.[34]

At last on November 20, Deane was able to tell Vergennes that the Congress was preparing treaty proposals to submit to France. But in the meantime he had been preparing his own draft, and on the twenty-third he sent it to Gérard. The document illustrates how extreme he had grown in his pursuit of a "natural" alliance with France. Deane's draft called for a perpetual union of France, Spain, and America to strip Great Britain of all its possessions in North America and the West Indies and distribute the spoils among the three victorious powers. This would be the road to "Peace, Liberty and Safety." To insure the alliance for all time, the three powers should have free trade between themselves, but deny it forever to the British. Should any British ship be found on the coast of North or South America or near the islands thereto, it should be considered lawful prize in peace as in war. "Nor shall France, Spain or the United States ever hereafter admit British ships into any of their Ports in America, North or South, or the Islands adjacent, nor shall this Article ever be altered or dispensed with but only by and with the consent of each of the Three Contracting States." What was more immediately to the point, France and Spain were to dispatch a fleet to defend the coast and trade of the United States, and the three parties were to pledge themselves not to make peace separately.[35] This last stipulation Deane probably thought would put an end to French fears of a reconciliation between Britain and America. But if he imagined he was putting down good bait, he was wrong. The French Foreign Office was too experienced to be attracted.

All of this feverish activity and endeavor to secure massive aid from France and to draw that country into the war had its background in America and to that we must now turn our

---

[34] The Secret Committee to Deane, Oct. 1; Deane to the Committee, Oct. 1 and 8, Nov. 6, 1776. *Deane Papers*, I, pp. 294–300, 287–294, 309–311, 324–327, 340–343. Since France was not moving fast enough to suit him, Deane imagined that the Committee's failure to communicate with him was to blame. But there were other factors which he overlooked. See pp. 109–111.

[35] Deane to Gérard, Nov. 23, 1776, *ibid.*, pp. 361–364.

attention. In June 1775, when Washington first organized the Continental Army, he had recognized the strategic value of taking possession of Canada, and in the following September an expeditionary force of about 1,200 men set forth up the Kennebec River, Colonel Benedict Arnold in command. A similar force under General Montgomery started north from Albany, the plan being for the two to come together on the St. Lawrence and capture Montreal and Quebec. Permanent occupation, as Washington himself stated, was the objective and not mere temporary conquest, for as an officer in Arnold's force well put it, Quebec was "the key to America." The French had demonstrated that fact for all to behold in the century of warfare that had gone on before; and with the Americans in possession of the St. Lawrence Valley, they need have no fear of a British invasion from the north. This would have the further benefit of keeping the Indian tribes pliable, the latter being deprived of their traditional support from Canada. That the "savages" were constantly on the Americans' mind may be seen from the instruction given to Silas Deane for the purchase of goods in France for delivery to them.

Unfortunately the American leaders underestimated their capacity for subjugating Canada. Washington thought the 1,200 men ample and expected Quebec to fall "an easy prey." Not to magnify the error, it is only necessary to mention that the commanding officer in charge of the troops still laying siege to the city in the following April appealed for 10,000 men if he was to do the job. But there were other grave errors: the Americans did not have the powder, the field pieces, or even the clothes for the troops to sustain a successful expedition. Nor, until they actually had the experience, did they realize they were trying to occupy enemy country where the local population was against them. There was no supply line and, without money with which to pay for their food, the troops resorted to plundering the farmers. "The keeping of the country . . . is totally against us," reported Colonel Hazen in charge of headquarters at Montreal, April 1, 1776.

Meanwhile in March, the same month the Secret Committee decided on making the approach to France, the Congress dispatched three commissioners to Canada: Franklin and Samuel Chase and Charles Carroll of Maryland, men who were the least likely to offend the *Canadiens* because of religious bias. The function of the commissioners was to try persuasion, renewing the original call on the French-speaking population to join in revolt, although the Americans made no offer bearing on the crucial issue of the western and southern boundaries of Quebec Province. Franklin discreetly withdrew on May 11, leaving it to the other two commissioners to echo the complaints of the military. "For God's sake send off pork," they wrote on the sixteenth, "or our troops will be greatly distressed . . . and may mutiny and desert to the enemy." And again on the twenty-seventh, remarking on the breakdown in discipline among the troops, they said: "We cannot find words to describe our miserable situation." They had already given their opinion that Canada would have to be abandoned: five British warships, the vanguard of Burgoyne's force, arrived off Quebec on May 10, and the Americans, with only a thousand men fit for duty, were in full retreat.

By early June, before Silas Deane had even reached Bordeaux, the bad news was filtering through to Washington in New York and to the politicians in Philadelphia. The situation was "truly alarming," Washington admitted and ordered General Schuyler, who was stationed at Albany, to strain every nerve to send help. If Canada was lost, everyone would feel "the fatal consequences." Taking the same view, Hancock in Philadelphia appealed to Massachusetts to collect all the gold and silver possible and send the metal to Canada. One hundred thousand dollars in specie was the figure he mentioned. Both Hancock and Washington now feared the British would launch an offensive against New York City. By June 23, after learning that Burgoyne and his main army had reached Quebec, Washington acknowledged the gravity of the defeat. It was much to be feared, he wrote Hancock, that "our scattered, divided, and broken Army . . . have been obliged to abandon the country and to retreat. . . . It will not be easy to describe all the fatal consequences that may flow from it; at least our utmost exertions will be necessary to prevent the advantages they have gained to be turned to our greater misfortunes. . . ." [36]

---

[36] The excerpts in these paragraphs on the Canada expedition are from the original documents printed in Force, III, p. 632; V, pp. 411–414, 869; VI, pp. 449, 558–559, 578, 587–589, 742, 767–768, 886–887, 1035, 1066, 1194–1195. See also Murray G. Lawson, "Canada and the Articles of Confederation," *Amer. Hist. Rev.*, LVIII (1952–1953), pp. 39–54.

"Alas Canada!" was John Adams's comment as the Declaration of Independence was about ready for signature in Philadelphia. "The Romans made it a fixed rule never to send or receive Ambassadors, to treat of peace with their enemies, while their affairs were in an adverse or disastrous situation. . . ." So the Declaration was duly inscribed in the teeth of a threatening military disaster, and with knowledge that the struggle would now be long and bitter. But, despite the courage thus shown, there were political overtones to the Declaration, an admission that the step must be taken as a means of clearing the road to an alliance with France. Richard Henry Lee, who offered the original resolution of June 7, 1776, favoring a formal declaration, recognized the connection in a private letter to Patrick Henry: it was time for an "alliance with proper and willing powers in Europe. . . . But no State in Europe will either Treat or Trade with us so long as we consider ourselves Subjects of G.B. . . . It is not choice . . . but necessity that calls for Independence, as the only means by which foreign Alliances can be obtained and a proper confederation by which internal peace and union may be secured. . . ."[37]

The Declaration, although published first in London and then in Paris, did not have the desired effect. In Britain it occasioned little surprise, as it was interpreted as simply an open announcement of an objective long since resolved on. All parties realized that it made reconciliation more difficult than ever. The Declaration deepened the pessimism of the opposition groups who, like the ministry, could not bring themselves to concede independence. David Hartley, the most liberal of the Rockingham Whigs, paid a call on Bancroft in London in the vain hope of finding a common meeting ground between the Americans and their friends in Parliament. Somewhat later, Lord Shelburne, one of the most prominent of the Chathamites, went to Paris and exchanged views with Silas Deane, but equally without result.

Meanwhile the Americans suffered serious military reverses: General Howe defeated them at the Battle of Long Island, and shortly thereafter Washington abandoned New York to the

---

[37] R. H. Lee to P. Henry and to Landon Carter, June 2, 1776. *The Letters of Richard Henry Lee,* James Curtis Ballagh, ed., 2 vols., N. Y. 1911, I, pp. 176–178, 198.

British forces. Coupled with the retreat from Canada in the previous June, these events pointed at an ultimate British victory. And although Admiral Lord Howe, his fleet in control of New York Harbor, reported his disappointment over the results of a meeting he had arranged with a committee from the Congress, he nevertheless expressed himself as hopeful that the Americans would be ready for reconciliation by the beginning of the new year. The committee, comprised of Franklin, Adams, and Rutledge, was intransigent on the point of independence; but Howe was convinced that a large party in the Congress would settle for less. He learned, moreover, that Washington's Army was in bad shape, suffering from desertion and disease, depleted in number, and short of shoes, clothing, and field artillery. Sir Henry Clinton reported similar intelligence. A few months more and the war would be over.[38]

Fortified with these optimistic reports, the king opened Parliament on October 31 with an appeal for unanimous support in prosecuting the war and with an expression of confidence that peace would continue in Europe. The ministry built its strategy on a quick end to the war in America, accompanied by a generous peace short of independence and followed by a solid front that would discourage the Continental powers. This had been its objective from the outset. But the risks were formidable, as the intelligence received from Lord Stormont in Paris continued to show and as the Opposition speakers in Parliament insisted were the case. Besides reporting on Deane's activities, the ambassador warned of a new crisis pending between Spain and Portugal and of a decision of both France and Spain to strengthen their naval forces in the West Indies. Either one of these moves might precipitate a general war. "War is now the general topic of conversation here," the ambassador advised; "not only the public at large regard it as certain, but persons of the first rank likewise. . . ."[39] Nevertheless, Stormont, conscious of the divi-

---

[38] Bancroft to Deane, Sept. 13 and 20, Nov. 8, 1776; Shelburne to Deane, Oct. 20, *Deane Papers*, I, pp. 237–243, 249–252, 330–331, 345–350. Clinton to the Duke of Newcastle, Sept. 5 and 20, 1776, Newcastle Mss., University of Nottingham.

[39] Stormont to Weymouth, Aug. 21 and 28, Oct. 9 and Nov. 6, 1776. SP 78/299–300.

sions of opinion inside the French ministry, advised restraint. France should be given no excuse to make war. Britain should never betray the slightest suspicion of French honesty: it should leave the door open to a fair and honorable retreat by letting the French believe that their secret maneuvers passed unnoticed. Once the American war was over, the European danger would resolve itself.

But neither the Whigs nor the Chathamites in Parliament were to be reconciled to this course. The followers of Lord Rockingham, still clinging to the creed of Parliamentary supremacy, rejected the American demand for independence but paradoxically feared a British military victory in America. "What a dismal piece of news!" said Charles James Fox to Edmund Burke on learning of Howe's victory in Long Island, and Burke concurred. Custodians of the principles of 1688, the English Whigs shrank from what in the twentieth century has been called "militarism." "I do not know that I was ever so deeply affected with any public event either in history or in life," Fox continued. "The introduction of great standing armies into Europe has then made all mankind irrevocably slaves. . . ." Parliament alone stood between liberty and military despotism. Rockingham framed the issue in terms of a peace without victory: a decisive victory on either side, he argued, "would create such insolence in the conquering part as would render anything like an amicable reunion of the empire impracticable." [40] But, Fox dissenting, the leaders of the Rockingham Whigs had already decided, as their only means of making known their fears for the principles of 1688, to absent themselves from Parliament whenever the government brought up the question of employing military force against the Americans.

The Chathamites, however, were not so ready to retire from the field, and in their determination to challenge the government they were joined by some of the friends of Lord Rockingham. Not surprised by the American Declaration of Independence,

[40] Fox to Burke, Oct. 13, and Rockingham to Burke, Oct. 13, 1776, *The Correspondence of Edmund Burke*, July 1774–June, 1778, George H. Guttridge, ed., Chicago, 1961, III, pp. 294–297. (Hereafter cited as *Burke Corresp.*)

they recognized its international implications and believed that it changed the character of the war. "How can anyone now propose a medium between the two extremes: unconditional submission and independence?" asked Lord Camden. "I dread the firmness of the Congress equally with the pride of England, and see no issue out of this desperate war if it was only waged between the two countries. But if France and Spain take part, which I verily believe is now in agitation, the very existence of England is put to the hazard, and we are forced to unite upon the principle of self-preservation." [41]

Other peers, who had had personal experience in France, denounced the government for scattering the navy and for complacently accepting French and Spanish professions of friendship. Shelburne cited chapter and verse gathered from firsthand information he had collected: a formidable fleet assembling at Brest, the free use of French and Spanish ports for privateering raids on British shipping, the daily departure from almost every French port of vessels laden with military stores for America, and the ill-concealed negotiations of Silas Deane with the Court of Versailles. Here was "irrefragable proof" of French hostility. And then, with reports received that a Spanish fleet had sailed from Cadiz for an unannounced destination, fears were revived for the security of Portugal. In a word, none of the ministry's critics shared its confidence that the war would soon be over or that it could be kept localized in America. One of them, the young and imaginative Charles Lennox, Duke of Richmond, who often took independent positions, drew a graphic picture of Britain's mounting predicament and declared flatly that peace with the Americans was necessary at any price. "Better have them as friends, even though we recognize them as independent states." [42] At the conclusion of the debates in both houses, however, the ministry prevailed.

In France, meanwhile, the American Declaration of Independence received even less attention than in Britain. Scattered references to it appeared in the Paris press, only one newspaper,

---

[41] Camden to Thomas Walpole, Aug. 23, 1776, the Camden Album, Walpole Papers in the possession of David Holland, Esq.
[42] *PH*, XVIII, cols. 1366–1391, 1431–1455.

the *Journal de Politique et de Literataire,* giving it more than a bare mention. Vergennes received his copy of the document from Garnier, the chargé in London, and decided that it meant that the war would go on for some time to the detriment of Britain and the benefit of France. That was enough for him. In a lengthy memoir read to the Royal Council on August 31, 1776, the foreign minister debated, in a somewhat academic manner, the question of France going to war. Although he recognized certain advantages in doing so, he was against it. France was not yet prepared. It should take precautions against a future British aggression in the West Indies, but nothing more. As for entering an alliance with America he said not a word.[43] Such indifference, if known to the men in Philadelphia who had expected tangible results from the Declaration, would have been sadly disillusioning.

Much more impressive were the military reverses suffered at the hands of the British in Canada and New York and the increasing difficulty in getting credit in Europe. British naval efficiency was keeping pace with the victories on land. The Americans depended on exports to meet their obligations in Europe but, the ports being blockaded, ships could not get out. The New England States had lost control of the fishery, and had little therefore to export. Thousands of hogsheads of tobacco were ready in Maryland and Virginia but, Morris informed Deane, the committee could not get the ships to take them. From the Carolinas there was no trade at all. "It is absolutely necessary," urged Morris, "the French shou'd send us aid in the naval line . . . so that ships may get in and out. . . . These considerations induce me to wish you may have negotiated some loans with the French Court, that they may become so interested as to send their Men of War, in order to cover their own remittances. . . ."[44]

Deane was meeting with disappointments, however, and he attributed them to the military defeats. The bad news had ab-

---

[43] AAE cp Ang. 517, ff. 222, 282–285, 385–390. An examination was made of the French newspapers to determine their reaction to the Declaration of Independence.

[44] Morris to Deane, Jan. 11, 1777, *Deane Papers,* I, pp. 456–462.

solutely ruined America's credit, he reported, and the Court was now extremely cautious. The *Amphitrite*, with its valuable cargo, had returned to port, and the three ships which Beaumarchais had loaded were ordered not to sail. Everyone in Paris, Deane told Morris, thinks the Americans are negotiating peace or giving up. Two days later, on December 6, he had a novel idea: why not appoint a prominent European general, such as Marshal Broglie, commander of the American Army? The move would give a much needed lift in prestige. The British also wanted peace, as the French knew, and Deane sedulously avoided seeing his British friends lest he be suspected of negotiating. He did make an exception of Shelburne, Fox, and Lord Townsend, with whom he had "a free and long conversation." But he remained deaf to their pleas for a reunion, and on the last day of the year penned another futile plea to the French Foreign Office to join in the war.[45]

So the year 1776 ended in a situation full of irony: the British anxious for reconciliation and reunion, but adamant against granting independence for fear they would lose their own independence; the Americans unyielding unless independence was granted them, but distressingly aware of their dependence on France if they were to get it; the French seriously compromised by their past record and by their warlike preparations, but hesitant, unready, and choosing to remain uncommitted.

[45] Deane to the Secret Committee, Nov. 28, Dec. 1, 3, 6, 1776; to Jay, Dec. 3, and to Morris, Dec. 4; to the French Foreign Office, Dec. 31. *Ibid.*, pp. 371–378, 392–399, 404, 434–442.

# CHAPTER V

## *The Storm Begins to Break*

If Great Britain should again be united to America by conquest or conciliation it would be vain to menace her with war. America has been felt like
Hercules in his cradle. Great Britain knit again to such growing strength
would reign the irresistible though hated arbiter of Europe. This, then, is
the moment in which Spain and France may clip her wings and pinion her
forever.—*Arthur Lee to the Spanish Court, March 8, 1777*

IT WAS IN SEPTEMBER 1776, when the British were beginning to
close in, that the leaders in Philadelphia decided to risk their
fortunes with the French. France, they perceived, would determine the outcome: it was disposed to help, although not to enter
the contest. "We must cultivate her good disposition, draw from
her all that we can, and in the end their [the French] private aid
must assist us to establish peace or inevitably draw them in as
parties to the war." Franklin and Morris made the decision, but
kept the secret from the Congress. Franklin would go to France
to reinforce Deane—his name and reputation alone would count
in Europe; Morris was on all the congressional committees concerned, notably the Marine Committee, which was working
toward a navy and was in close contact with William Bingham
on the island of Martinique.[1] Jefferson, it was at some point
decided, would be asked to accompany Franklin, apparently to
make the commission more representative; but Jefferson himself
was of another mind and Arthur Lee, who was still in London

---

[1] Committee of Secret Correspondence, Statement, Oct. 1, 1776, and a
separate communication signed by Franklin and Morris; also Morris to
Horatio Gates, Oct. 27, 1776. Burnett, II, pp. 110–111, 135–136; *Jefferson
Papers*, I, pp. 520–524.

and somewhat in the background, was given the opportunity instead. The Lee family was extremely influential in Virginia, but the choice turned out a mixed blessing, Arthur being temperamentally unsuited to collaborate with his older colleagues.

The immediate object of the mission was to get a large, fresh supply of arms and stores: 20,000 to 30,000 muskets and bayonets, ammunition and brass field pieces, 10,000 blankets, 30,000 yards of broadcloth, and other goods, to be paid for by shipments of rice, indigo, tobacco, and so forth. Again, private merchants as well as the French government were to be approached. An order sent direct to John Ross, one of the purchasing agents stationed in France, graphically described the need for blankets. Ross was to do his utmost to get these goods, which were "extremely wanted," and to find the ships to carry them. If the shipment could not be made direct, the goods were to be consigned to designated agents stationed on the islands of Martinique, St. Eustatia, and Curacao, and at Cape Francois in Santo Domingo, where they would be reconsigned. It was hoped that France would agree to send the arms and ammunition under convoy.

Beyond these pressing requirements, fresh temptations to join in the war were to be set before the French. Eventually France must come in, if the war was to be won, and the French *must* be left under no illusions that "we are able to support the War on our own Strength and Resources longer than, in fact, we can do. . . ." If France waited too long, it might be faced with a reunited British Empire. But as an inducement and as a way of underscoring the importance of naval support, the Americans offered help in reconquering the West Indian islands France had lost to Britain in 1763. Finally, Spain was to be favored with "the strongest Assurances" that it need have no fear of American designs on its possessions.[2]

Two letters dated the same day, December 21, showed that the Americans were still determined but anxious about the

---

[2] *Journals of the Continental Congress*, Washington, D.C., 1906, V, pp. 813–817: Instructions to the Commissioners to France, Sept. 24, 1776; The order to John Ross, dated Sept. 27, 1776, is among the manuscripts of the Franklin Collection in the American Philosophical Society, Philadelphia.

future. On the bright side, the Committee of Secret Correspondence could point to the military stalemate: the British in
Canada had not taken the offensive, as feared, nor had General
Howe penetrated up the Hudson River. Only a few days later
the committee learned of Washington's victory at Trenton,
New Jersey, and promptly sent the word off to Paris. But the
members were aware that France was deterred by fear of a
reconciliation and that somehow this fear had to be overcome.
France's help and Spain's were "indispensably necessary," and
had to be soon; it was especially important that the French send
ships of the line which, if they came in sufficient numbers, could
defeat Lord Howe's small fleet in New York and finish the contest
at one stroke. To overcome French reluctance, the committee
reiterated that the Declaration of Independence was irrevocable
and painted a glowing picture of the new army the Congress
was raising and the new warships that were either launched or
in the process of being built; and, since Deane had reported
wistfully on the resources of the Dutch money market, the
committee authorized him to negotiate a six per cent loan of at
least £2,000,000 sterling.

Robert Morris wrote a separate, almost defeatist, letter
describing the rapid depreciation of the currency, which meant
"total ruin" unless checked. The letter expressed dissatisfaction
with the lack of progress with the navy and emphasized the low
morale then prevalent among the public. Morris's letter makes
one think that the committee, of which he himself was a member,
was whistling in the dark. Somehow France had to be persuaded
to go in for its own sake: it had a "golden opportunity."
But it "must do it soon; our situation is critical, and does
not admit of delay. . . . Should time be lost in tedious
negotiations and succors withheld, America must sue for
peace. . . ." [3] But Morris was never the man to neglect his own
opportunities. Two months later he complained that, with prices
of European goods "enormously high," he could sell any
quantity at a five hundred to seven hundred per cent advance, if
he could only get them. So he urged Deane to try the London
underwriters again; an offer of high premiums, he felt, would

---

[3] Wharton, II, pp. 226–231, 231–238, 240–241.

get results. Besides, at the most, the Americans lost not more than a third of their inbound vessels. But he had less confidence in the ability of tobacco-laden ships to elude capture; Chesapeake Bay was a bottleneck effectively patrolled by two or three British cruisers. Tobacco was the great staple which provided the Americans with foreign exchange, if they could get it to the European market, and therefore the British found it worthwhile to block its main outlet.[4]

Meanwhile, late in November Franklin arrived off the coast of Brittany after a fast, but rough, voyage of only thirty days. An old man of seventy, feeling weak from the trip, he was cheered by the hearty reception given him in Nantes, to which he made his way by land. The sight of several vessels laden with arms and ready to sail for America, and the news of the sailing of the Spanish fleet with land forces aboard for action against the Portuguese in Brazil were both encouraging signs of the pending war in Europe, and Franklin lost little time in writing home of the prospects. His arrival created something of a sensation, both friend and foe divining his purpose. Deane was overjoyed and passed the word to Vergennes. Walpole, Franklin's former business associate, in Paris at the time, commented on the prestige value of his mission, calculated to encourage an alliance, while Lord Rockingham mingled admiration for Franklin's courage and energy in making the journey with fear that he would succeed in inducing France and Spain to administer a deadly blow to Britain. Not sharing the confidence of the government in the peace that would follow suppression of the rebellion, Rockingham was in despair. "There is no man," he wrote his friend Sir George Savile, who had brought him the intelligence about Franklin, "who has access to his Majesty, who has integrity and magnanimity of mind sufficient, to enable him to go and say to his Majesty, the measures and the policy of the measures toward America are erroneous, the adherence to them is destruction." Lord Stormont, the ambassador, was pessimistic too, writing his opinion of Franklin as "a very dangerous engine"

---

[4] Morris to Deane, Feb. 27, 1777, *Deane Papers*, II, pp. 14–15; Committee of Secret Correspondence to commissioners, Feb. 19, 1777, Wharton, II, pp. 273–275.

who would lure the French into open support of the rebellion. Such were some of the impressions of Franklin's arrival recorded on the minds of representative men at the time.[5]

The British ministry, having no intention of provoking a showdown with France, studiously took no notice of Franklin. But how controversial was the subject of the war and its outcome, even among the Opposition Whigs, may be seen by comparing the views of Edmund Burke and Matthew Robinson-Morris. Burke, a party regular (to employ an American expression), was really close to the ministry in his attitude, expecting the rebellion to be suppressed and relations restored on "a footing of dependency." Like his chief, Lord Rockingham, Burke was a Parliament man to whom the Declaratory Act was still the Ark of the Covenant. He chose to ignore the American Declaration of Independence, and was ill-informed on the dangers from France. He was correct, however, in thinking that Franklin would not get the definite commitment for which he had come to Paris, and he hoped "that the Whig party might be made a sort of Mediatours of the Peace" in a way that would "revive the Cause of our Liberties in England, and . . . give the Colonies some sort of mooring and anchorage in this Country." Having an acquaintance with Franklin, he "had for a Moment a strong desire of taking a Turn to Paris," but gave up the idea although, as Rockingham said to him, this was the "time to *attempt in earnest* a reconciliation." [6]

Matthew Robinson-Morris, an independent, was much better informed on the international dangers facing Britain, more clear-headed on the tragic results certain to ensue from attempted military conquest of the Colonies, and explosive in his insistence on an immediate settlement. Robinson-Morris's pamphlet, written in December 1776 and enjoying two editions

---

[5] Franklin to Hancock, Dec. 8, 1776, Wharton, II, pp. 221–222; and my article, "Europe, the Rockingham Whigs, and the War for American Independence: Some Documents," *Hunt. Lib. Quart.*, XXV (1961), pp. 1–28, lists the British manuscript sources on which the remainder of this paragraph rests.

[6] Burke to Richard Champion, Dec. 22, 1776; to Rockingham, Jan. 6, 1777 and Rockingham to Burke same day, *Burke Corresp.*, III, pp. 305–306, 308–317. The italics are Rockingham's.

the next year, described in detail and with considerable accuracy the damage inflicted on the country by the French and the Spanish, and outlined the peril of being surrounded and even invaded. American historians, notably Samuel Flagg Bemis, have erected a built-in legend of the machinations of certain "British spies" in furnishing the ministry with "secret information" about French diplomacy. Robinson-Morris's pamphlet alone explodes this myth: its author, having no contacts with the government, could hardly have derived his information from alleged "spies." On the contrary, he got his facts from merchants who were suffering from French and Spanish depredations and put this knowledge to work in an intelligent and comprehensive manner. What Robinson-Morris knew the reading British public also knew. But unhappily Robinson-Morris was ahead of his time. Few of his countrymen would accept his conclusions:

Why do we not ourselves make peace with the Colonies; why do we by that means not come between them and the French; while there is yet an opportunity or possibility of doing it? . . . . Let us on the terms of an amicable separation make with them the most advantageous peace that we shall be able. . . . Our American war is the rock on which we are running with all our sails set; where the public ship is in instant danger of dashing and of breaking into a thousand pieces; where we risque being wrecked (as it were) before we sleep. . . .[7]

Coincidentally, Robert Morris in Philadelphia, in spite of his ardent wooing of the French, felt the same way. "Nothing do I wish for more than a peace on terms honorable and beneficial to both Country's," he told General Gates, "and I am convinced it is more Consistent with the Interest of Great Britain to acknowledge our Independency and enter into Commercial Treatys with us than to persist in attempting to reduce us to

---

[7] *Peace the Best Policy, or Reflections upon the Appearance of a Foreign War. The Present State of Affairs at Home and the Commission for Granting Pardons in America.* In a Letter to a Friend by Matthew Robinson-Morris, London: printed for J. Almon, Picadilly, 1777. Cf. S. F. Bemis, "British Secret Service and the French-American Alliance," *Amer. Hist. Rev.*, XXIX (1923–1924), pp. 474–495, and his *Diplomacy of the American Revolution*, New York, 1935, p. 66.

unconditional submission."[8] Events did not take this turn, however, and the Americans redoubled their efforts to entice France into the war. Flanked by Deane and Arthur Lee, Franklin lost no time in visiting both Vergennes and the Spanish ambassador, the Count d'Aranda, who on his part had been trying, without success, to persuade the French to endorse Spain's designs on Portugal. This too meant a general European war, on which the Americans counted heavily. In other words, France held the key to the peace: whether she followed the wishes of Spain or of the United States, the event would lead to war, but if she withheld her full support from either one, a general war would not occur and the British would have some chance of "containing" the American rebellion. This, to put it broadly, was Vergennes' problem.

The French foreign minister gave a polite refusal to the American request for a loan of eight ships of the line and for an armed convoy to accompany the vessels carrying war matèriel across the Atlantic. Implying that of course the Americans did not want the war to spread—a masterpiece of diplomatic finesse —he told them that the king would like to give them the ships, but needed them to protect his own dominions. A few ships, moreover, would hardly determine the outcome, but would merely incite the English to make war. On the other hand, in proof of his good will, the king opened his ports to American vessels and furnished the credit necessary for the purchase of arms and supplies. *"Que pourrait on exiger de plus d'elles?"* Vergennes demanded rhetorically.[9]

Suiting the action to the word, the Ministry of Marine soon after permitted the four armed French vessels, whose sailing had been held up in December, to depart. All four were heavily laden with cannon and other firearms for the American Army. The *Amphitrite* was a frigate wearing the legal disguise of a privately owned vessel, and carried the ranking engineer du Coudray and other officers of the French Army to whom Deane had given commissions. The *Amphitrite* and the *Seine* sailed

[8] Oct. 27, 1776. Burnett, II, p. 136.
[9] Vergennes to the American commissioners, Jan., 1777. AAE, Etats Unis II, Corresp. 1777 (Jan.–Dec.).

from Le Havre, the *Mercure* and the *Thérèse* from Nantes. The *Mercure* and the *Amphitrite* sailed direct for Portsmouth, New Hampshire; the *Mercure* arrived first in late April and the *Amphitrite* trailed in early May. The *Seine* and the *Thérèse* used the more circuitous, but safer route via Martinique. The cargo of the *Thérèse* was considered so valuable that it was broken up at Martinique for forwarding in smaller vessels, but the *Seine* was captured by a British warship after leaving Martinique.[10] The departure of these ships, which the British government allowed to go unprotested, marks a milestone in French policy: it was a victory for the war party at court, and virtually committed France to the American cause.

Yet the British government, kept informed by its ambassador in Paris, resolved to keep up the pretence of peace, relying on France's unreadiness for war, on the counsels of the moderates at Versailles, and on the chances of its own ultimate victory in America. It would have been an act of war to have interfered with these ships, as Lord Weymouth recognized, and in its determination to be unprovocative the British government consistently refused to authorize its naval vessels to challenge French ships in European waters. Since the chances for capture on the farther side of the Atlantic were much slimmer, this meant that the French enjoyed a virtual immunity in putting arms into the hands of the Americans.

But the pretence could not be kept up for long. Without a speedy and decisive British victory in America, Stormont warned in March 1777, peace in Europe would not last beyond the year. More French ships laden with field pieces for the rebels had sailed. He had daily proof of the court's duplicity: the ministers put nothing in writing, he said; they sign no treaty with the rebel emissaries, but they give verbal assurances they will not suffer the Americans to lose.

Franklin's arrival had had a great effect in stimulating the war feeling in France. For the first time the young marquis de

---

[10] Franklin, Deane and Lee to Committee of Secret Correspondence., Feb. 6, 1777, Wharton, II, p. 261; Deane to Beaumarchais, Feb. 24, 1777, *Deane Papers*, II, p. 12; Committee of Foreign Affairs to commissioners, May 30, 1777, Wharton, II, pp. 327–328.

Lafayette appears on the scene. Lafayette's name had political value for the Americans because of the prominence of his family at court. Stormont kept track of Lafayette's movements: he had been on a visit to England, but instead of returning to his young wife, who was pregnant, in Paris, he had gone direct to one of the seaports, "I believe to Bordeaux, to embark for the Rebel army: He is a passionate enthusiast to their cause." Just a week later Stormont reported that Lafayette had sailed, taking with him twelve officers, nine of whom were in his own service. "I did not think it proper to raise the point," with Vergennes, remarked the ambassador, and Weymouth did not comment.[11]

The capture of the *Seine* somewhere off the American coast shows that munitions-laden French vessels could be intercepted. British naval vigilance on the American side of the Atlantic was greater than on the European, necessarily so under the policy of side-stepping any possible collision with French and Spanish warships. It was difficult to capture even American vessels in European waters, since the Admiralty did not allow its captains to watch the ports. In patrolling the Bay of Biscay British frigates stood out to sea, well out of sight of land, so that ships both in-bound and out-bound had more than a sporting chance of eluding detection. Dispersion of the fleet was in itself a fatal weakness, making nonexistent the supposed British control of the seas. But because of the nature of the war, the Admiralty had no choice; there were those, like Lord Sandwich, who preferred to keep the fleet at home. With French and Spanish rearmament developing so rapidly, the British felt compelled to keep increasing numbers of their own vessels in reserve for home defense; but at the same time the weakness of the home fleet was such that it was of no value as a deterrent against the two Bourbon powers. Then there was a separate command maintained in West Indian waters.

Lord Howe's fleet, based on New York, had the insuperable task of patrolling the entire American coast. A lengthy report which Howe wrote to the Admiralty in December 1777 discusses the many difficult problems which his officers were obliged to

---

[11] Stormont to Weymouth, Mar. 19 and 26, 1777, SP 78/301.

face; and it becomes clear that effective naval action was limited to a few localities. The purpose of Lord Howe's fleet was not to blockade the American coast—an impossible assignment in any event—but to cooperate with the army and thus to subordinate itself to that branch of the service. Moreover, since the extent of country occupied by the army was at all times limited during the war, the navy could do little; the ships which could not put into shore for fresh water and provisions were under the constant handicap of being forced to return periodically to their distant base.[12]

A startling description of the naval situation in America, written by an anonymous officer returned from the service, appeared in print in London in 1777. With strong Whig sympathies, this officer let his readers know even on the title page of his book that Britain had no chance to win over the Americans and that it was folly to continue the contest. The Americans traded freely with the West Indies and with France, Spain, and Holland in Europe. The French enjoyed all the advantages of war without any of its inconveniences. "If their vessels are detected, . . . they immediately plead distress; they are all bound to Miquelon, but contrary winds and bad weather have reduced them to the necessity" of seeking refuge in an American port. So America "is abundantly supplied with ammunition and clothing, notwithstanding the positive assertions to the contrary." And then, with pardonable indignation becoming a professional serviceman, the officer charged:

Our navy, however, would not have observed much delicacy with them, if the commanders of our ships had not been *privately* instructed to be extremely cautious in their conduct towards the French; and it is owing to the unpardonable timidity of Administration, that France has dared to assist America, and that a little despicable island, rendered inaccessible half the year by ice, should pretend to more commerce, in the depth of winter, than the first trading port in Europe.[13]

---

[12] Howe to Stephen, Dec. 10, 1777. Admiralty Papers I In-Letters, vol. 487, PRO.

[13] *A Letter to the English Nation, on the Present War with America; with a Review of our Military Operations in that Country; and a Series of Facts never before published, from which the absolute impossibility*

Obviously this officer took his professional career in his hands; armed with facts and figures, he was unsparing toward the ministry and even toward his superiors in the service. His book, published well before the news of Burgoyne's defeat at Saratoga, furnished a rich mine of evidence for the use of the Whig Opposition; and, like Robinson-Morris's work, it proves the myth of secret intelligence conveyed from France by "British spies" to be utterly groundless. A union with America, resting on a grant of independence, concluded this writer, was to be advised from every standpoint. Were the Colonies to be subdued, which he held impossible, the final destruction of constitutional freedom at home would begin.

Meanwhile in Paris, Franklin and Deane redoubled their efforts to maneuver France into the war. With authority from the Congress to back them, they sent a formal proposal to Vergennes on the eighteenth of March, 1777 repeating Deane's offer of the preceding November. In a lofty tone, they declared that, while of course the Congress "for the sake of humanity" wanted universal peace, it "would not for the Advantage of America only desire to kindle a War in Europe," yet if France "should think it right to improve the present occasion" for war against Britain, they could offer, in addition to their commerce, certain other advantages based on a division of the spoils: for France, half the fishery and all the sugar islands, in the conquest of which the United States would aid by furnishing provisions and six frigates; for the United States, all the rest—Canada, Newfoundland, Nova Scotia, St. Johns, the Floridas, Bermuda, and the Bahamas. Then if Spain would come in too, the United States would declare war on Portugal "and will continue the said war for the total Conquest of that Kingdom, to be added to the Dominion of Spain." Concluding with a pledge of no separate peace, the two commissioners wound up with an elaborate expression of confidence in the "Goodness and Wisdom" of the King of France, with a request for his advice on making offers to other powers, and with an assurance that on none of

---

*of reducing the Colonies will sufficiently appear, and the Folly of continuing the Contest demonstrated. By an Officer returned from that* Service. This is no Season for Compliments. London, 1777.

these questions "would the Congress take a step without consulting His Majesty's Ministers." In a separate memoir they stated their need for a loan of £2,000,000 sterling, to be secured by a tract of 300 square miles on the banks of the Ohio.[14]

The French making no response to these proposals, Silas Deane during April sent no less than five notes to Vergennes and Gérard, trying various arguments to induce at least some affirmative action. Sometimes he played on their ambitions, at other times on their fears. If only France would embark a few thousand men on transports at Brest and send four or five ships of the line to New York, it would make a great haul; but the United States was distressed to the last degree and would be ruined unless soon relieved.[15] None of these pleas, however, had any noticeable effect on French policy. Vergennes's attention at this time was drawn to India, where he feared Britain would establish its hegemony at the expense of France; and Deane was quick to sense a new method of stirring the foreign minister to action. With India at Britain's disposal, and with alliances concluded with America and Russia, Great Britain would be the mistress of the world:

Russia, like America, is a new state, and rises with the most astonishing rapidity. Its demand for British manufactures and its supplies of raw materials increase nearly as fast as the American, and when both come to centre in Great Britain, the riches as well as power of that Kingdom will be unparalleled in the annals of Europe, or perhaps of the world. . . .[16]

While Deane was thus pushing the French hard, Franklin remained discreetly in the background and cultivated his great popularity with the French public. Arthur Lee agreed somewhat reluctantly to try his hand with Spain. He undertook this mission, he told his brother, because Franklin could not stand the trip, while Deane found an excuse for visiting Holland. Lee's personal relations with Deane were very tense, and with Frank-

[14] *Deane Papers*, II, pp. 25–27; Wharton, II, pp. 296–298.
[15] Deane to Vergennes, Apr. 5 and 7, and to Gérard, Apr. 8, 12 and 17, 1777, *Deane Papers*, II, pp. 38–44.
[16] Deane to Dumas, June 7, 1777, *ibid.*, p. 69.

lin only less so. He hoped that Franklin would move on to Vienna and Deane to The Hague, leaving Paris, the center of political activity, to him. Moreover, he had misgivings regarding the social effects of the conflict, as he confided to his brother:

I do most cordially wish the war were at an end. I consider it as a state of danger, desperation and corruption of manners. The citizen is as yet not quite lost in the soldier, but this will happen if the war continue. Next to entire slavery, a standing army is the greatest evil that can exist in a young state, and the continuance of a civil war with its probable events may kindle the fatal ambition of some Cromwell that would have otherwise slept guiltless of his country's ruin.[17]

Lee crossed the Pyrenees in March 1777 in expectation of visiting the Spanish court in Madrid. His brother, Richard Henry, agreed with him that an alliance with Spain as well as with France was indispensable. This was his prime object, but he did not get past Burgos. He had an influential ally in Sr. Gardoqui, the Bilbao merchant, who had been trading with Willing, Morris & Company. Gardoqui had gone on to Madrid and brought back the Count de Grimaldi, the Spanish foreign minister, for a secret conference. As a result Lee got a contract for the shipment of much needed army blankets, to be paid for by the Spanish government, an assurance that American vessels calling at Havana and New Orleans would be furnished powder and arms *gratis*, and a line of credit with Spain's bankers in Amsterdam on which the American commissioners could draw when making purchases in Holland and France. This last was no mean achievement because, without a steady flow of produce from America, the commissioners were in perennial trouble over their payments. Holland was the center of money and credit. Not a power in Europe, as Deane reported, could go to war without borrowing from the Dutch. And if all the debts, he remarked cynically, "were paid at once to this Republick of Mammon, it would as effectually ruin it, as the breaking in of the sea through their dykes."

All of Lee's persuasive powers availed him nought, however,

<hr>

[17] To R. H. Lee, Oct. 4, 1777, Lee Collection, Alderman Library, University of Virginia.

when the subject of a political agreement with Spain arose. "You have considered your own situation not ours," replied Grimaldi, although he held out the hope that the situation might change within a year. At first disappointed, Lee decided to look on the bright side; the American position was at the moment so vulnerable that concessions might be given that would be repented at leisure. "We shall have to depend more on ourselves," he reflected. "It was in this manner the Roman Republic was so deeply rooted. . . . The liberties and benefits which are hardly earned will be highly prized and long preserved." [18] After returning to Paris, he agreed to go on a mission to Berlin, whose good will was viewed as important because of the advantages of having access to a port on the North Sea whence raiding operations could be extended against British commerce. Lee tried the same arguments used on the French and Spanish to arouse Prussian jealousy toward the British, but got no encouragement; saying in so many words that Prussia could not afford to antagonize Britain, Baron de Schulenburg, the foreign minister, rebuffed his several overtures.[19]

But commercial warfare against Great Britain in as many areas as possible—the West Indies, the English Channel, the Irish Sea, and the North Sea—was viewed as of prime importance. Franklin and Deane argued that "the burning or plundering of Liverpool or Glasgow would do us more essential service than a million of treasure. . . . It would raise our reputation to the highest pitch." [20] And if the French were cold to proposals for a political alliance, they were not at all backward in participating in this type of warfare.

Dark clouds gathered around British shipping in European waters during the summer of 1777. Insurance rates were so high

---

[18] Wharton, II, pp. 271–275, 280–283, 292–295; R. H. Lee to A. Lee, Apr. 20, 1777, Burnett, II, pp. 335–336. Deane to Committee, Dec. 1, 1776, Deane Papers, I, p. 386.

[19] Franklin and Deane to Committee of Foreign Affairs, May 25, 1777; Lee to Schulenburg, June 10, Sept. 21, to the Committee Sept. 9; Schulenburg to Lee, Oct. 8, Wharton, II, pp. 322–325, 334–335, 351, 391–393, 407, 423–424.

[20] Committee of Foreign Affairs, May 26, 1777, Wharton, II, pp. 325–327; Deane to Morris, Aug. 23, 1777, *Deane Papers*, II, pp. 106–111.

that British shippers actually used *French* bottoms in getting their goods to foreign markets. French and Spanish ports were wide open to American privateers, the privateers arriving with tobacco and then being refitted for raids on British commerce in the Bay of Biscay. With profits good and port officials ready to close their eyes with the connivance of the authorities in Paris, French merchants and captains scrambled for a share in this plunder. Even *bas officiers* from the French Navy were used as crew, and various ruses were devised to keep up the pretense of "neutrality" and good faith. Many of the "American" privateers were really French. The British government remonstrated—without threatening to retaliate—and Vergennes and Sartine went through elaborate motions to stop the abuses, but the deception was too thin to be convincing.

In the West Indies, French, Dutch, and Danish ports gave shelter to American privateers. British boarding parties were helpless against these raiders for, as the anonymous naval officer pointed out in his pamphlet, if they intercepted a privateer, its captain was able to show French papers and they had no authority to seize French vessels. From the governor of Martinique especially the Americans could get anything they wanted. The comte d'Argout worked hand in glove with William Bingham, who handed out commissions in blank, bought and sold on his own private account and for his principals Willing, Morris & Company, and handled the business in arms and stores for the Congress.

Complaints from British merchants became so insistent by June 1777 that Weymouth finally ordered Stormont to protest. The British State Papers contain numerous memorials and petitions from chambers of commerce and individual merchants, all of whom tell the same story. Arthur Pigott, a West Indian merchant who spent more than two weeks, from April 21 to May 6, 1777, on the island of Martinique, wrote a particularly graphic account of what he saw: of various ships arriving from France, heavily laden with military stores; of a large vessel from Nantes in particular, which unloaded a small part of its cargo as a ruse and then sailed out of the harbor for Philadelphia; of the open collusion between Bingham and d'Argout; of French ships laden with American tobacco bound for Bordeaux and Marseilles; of the incredible number of privateers, many of them converted from captured prize vessels, most of them owned and operated by Frenchmen. Slaving vessels—Guineamen—were particularly favorite objects of capture. At £21 per slave, Bingham could turn a quick profit and obtain badly needed sterling.[21]

The war spirit in Paris, observed Lord Stormont in July, had reached the point of madness. Clearly the crucial time was not far off. The *Mercure* and the *Amphitrite*, it was now known, had safely delivered their valuable cargoes in America, and the intelligence made a powerful impression. "The arrival of these great succours," commented the ambassador, "greater I believe than ever were furnished by a nation pretending to be at Peace, has raised the Spirits of the Rebels and of their numerous Well-Wishers here."[22] Franklin and Deane, with Beaumarchais's support, had now persuaded Sartine to back them at court in getting the alliance they had long desired. But Vergennes still held his hand, and the king disliked the partiality shown the rebels.[23]

None of this intelligence, however, produced on the British government the effect that was made by the knowledge of French intentions to strengthen their land and sea forces in the West Indies. On August 9 Stormont reported that the French Council of State had held a secret meeting at which it had been decided to send 4,000 troops and five or six ships of the line to West Indian waters. This, the Council recognized, would precipitate war, an eventuality also seen by Lord Weymouth. Weymouth wrote two dispatches on the twenty-ninth in the hope of dissuading the French court from taking so drastic a step. "It must be viewed by us," he wrote, "as the first step toward some hostile designs on the part of His Christian Majesty," and once taken Britain would have no choice but to follow suit. But,

---

[21] These paragraphs on privateering and commercial warfare are condensed from my documented article, "Great Britain, the War for Independence, and the 'Gathering Storm' in Europe, 1775–1778," *Hunt. Lib. Quart.*, XXVII (1964), pp. 311–346.

[22] Weymouth to Stormont, July 4, 1777; Stormont to Weymouth, July 9, Aug. 6 and 30, Sept. 3 and 19, all marked "most secret" or "confidential," SP 78/303–305.

[23] AAE, ff. 228–229, Aug. 23, 1777: a paper read by Vergennes before the king.

Stormont having been told that the French had resolved to go through with the plan, Weymouth sent word on September 17 that the Admiralty was commissioning six additional ships of the line.[24]

Comparatively speaking, the ministers and, to an extent, even the opposition in Britain tended to be complacent toward the munitions and supplies the French sent the rebels. The ministers gambled on winning a decisive military victory in America, disrupting the rebel army and encouraging the forces of moderation and loyalism to come forth. They were confident of the latent strength and numerical superiority of these forces. The opposition did not share this confidence at all, and went so far as to express its abhorrence of a victory over fellow subjects. But it regarded the dangers of an international war as primary, and kept hammering away at the government for fighting the wrong war in the wrong place. The Earl of Chatham returned to this line of attack in a speech he gave in the House of Lords, on May 30, 1777. Depicting *the gathering storm* already breaking in Europe, he accused the ministers of giving away everything to France. "If you conquer," he declared, which he asserted was impossible, "you conquer under the cannon of France; under a masked battery then ready to open. The moment a treaty appears, you must declare war, though you had only five ships of the line in England." In the House of Commons Hartley gave the best speech, filling in with details descriptive of the commercial warfare being waged against Britain. "The American cause gives a mask," he said, "for all the nations in the world, under American colours, to plunder the British trade, which we experience every day, to our severe cost. . . ." [25]

Implacably opposed to outright independence—he would, he told Lord Shelburne, "as soon *subscribe* to *Transubstantiation*, as to Sovereignty by *Right*, in the Colonies"—Chatham held stubbornly to his position of 1775: an offer to redress grievances and return to the *status quo* of 1763.[26] Always more imaginative and flexible, Hartley proposed a "federal alliance" with America,

[24] SP 78/304.

[25] *PH*, XIX, cols. 253–262, 316–318.

[26] To Shelburne, Dec. 3, 1777, the Shelburne Manuscript at Bowood.

a system of legislative independence for the Colonies based on a trade union with Britain. In the following September the Earl of Abingdon, in a closely reasoned pamphlet, went a step further, admitting that America by declaring itself independent had followed the teachings of John Locke and had accordingly established a new civil society over which Parliament had no jurisdiction.[27] But none of these three positions won enough support, and therefore no point of departure for peace talks with the Americans emerged. To the opposition in Britain the war was a terrible tragedy, with the country surrounded and increasingly at a disadvantage; but much as they yearned for peace, they found no means for obtaining it.

The increasing tempo and severity of the commercial warfare and the alarming expansion of French and Spanish naval armament forced the ministers to pay heed to the French danger. Never willing to face this issue squarely, Lord North understood the meaning of the French expedition to the West Indies and thought an attack might come by October. As he wrote to the king:

Whether from an intention to deceive, or from weakness, or from instability, the conduct of the French Ministry is so fluctuating, and so inconsistent with their declarations, that it is impossible to depend upon them any longer, and to defer putting this country, and its dependencies in a better posture of defence.[28]

A cabinet meeting on the subject followed. Lord Sandwich, the First Lord of the Admiralty, had always disliked the dispersion of the fleet and had been sensitive to the French danger, but Lord George Germain, the Secretary of War, was committed to the land war in America. Germain was relying on Burgoyne, in his march south through the forests of New Hampshire, and on Howe, in his expedition by sea from New York to Philadelphia, to break the back of the American revolt; and on August 23, the day of the cabinet meeting, he received a timely report that

---

[27] *Thoughts on the Letter of Edmund Burke, Esq., to the Sheriffs of Bristol, on the Affairs of America,* Oxford, 1777. And see my article, "Europe, the Rockingham Whigs, and the War for American Independence: Some Documents," *Hunt. Lib. Quart.* XXV (1961), pp. 1–28.

[28] Aug. 22, 1777. *The Correspondence of King George the Third* John Fortescue, ed., London, 1928, III, no. 2049.

Burgoyne had taken Ticonderoga, the key to the invasion of the Hudson River from the north. With the king and the ministry so firmly wedded to the idea of victory in America, Germain's view of the war prevailed. At this advance stage there was hardly an alternative: Britain's eggs were all in the American basket and so, aside from meeting the naval threat as best it could, the government continued to gamble on division of opinion and vacillation at Versailles.

Accordingly, in the Speech from the Throne at the opening of the fall session of Parliament, the government reiterated its professions of confidence in French and Spanish friendship, although guardedly admitting that it had been obliged to augment its naval force. In both houses the opposition challenged this position vigorously, insisting in the words of Fox that France was "the directress of our motions." Moreover, the opposition was contemptuous of the government's claims of victory in America, criticized the mistaken strategy of Burgoyne's campaign, and spoke openly of his defeat. On the day on which this debate took place, November 18, 1777, no one in Britain knew that Burgoyne and his whole army had capitulated at Saratoga; but before that, in August, Burgoyne had received a bad setback at the hands of the New Hampshire militia under Colonel Stark, and the Parliamentary opposition seized on its knowledge of this episode to train its guns on the government's conduct of the war. Burgoyne marched deeper into enemy country separating himself from his base in Canada, while Howe, lacking explicit orders to cooperate with him by an advance up the Hudson, had chosen instead to take his army to Philadelphia with the intent of scattering Washington's forces in Pennsylvania. Belatedly Germain realized the fatal weakness of trying to prosecute two widely separated and unrelated campaigns simultaneously, while the Duke of Richmond in the House of Lords, basing his analysis on his knowledge of the failure of Burgoyne's communications with Canada, showed brilliantly that the expedition would come to nothing even if it penetrated to the Hudson. It was only a march and not an invasion, and would therefore not bring about the isolation of the New England provinces.[29]

---

[29] *PH*, XIX, cols. 354, 397–409, 411–445.

Burgoyne surrendered on October 17. Lord Sandwich was the first man in England to learn of the event; a naval officer from Montreal brought the intelligence on the night of December 2. With rumors of the disaster now circulating, Germain was taxed in Commons the very next day with the question. John Almon's *London Evening Post* carried a full account of the surrender in its issue of December 5, and on the eighth stated there were strong suspicions of a treaty of alliance between France and America. This was consistent with the ceaseless effort of the opposition to shift attention away from America and concentrate on the dangers of encirclement by the Bourbon powers; and it now made another, but unsuccessful attempt to force the ministry to resign and to bring hostilities in America to a halt.

The concentration of French, Spanish, and British naval power in the West Indies brought matters to a head. Cumulative factors had reached the point in the summer of 1777 where France had either to go forward to war or else face a humiliating retreat. The principals in all three camps—British, French, American—were fully alive to this. On the very day in September when Stormont learned of the French intention to dispatch a force to the West Indies, he was informed that Vergennes had told the American envoys of the French decision in favor of war. The ambassador had reason to doubt this: Vergennes might be feeding the rebels with false hopes in order to keep them fighting; or it could be false information deliberately planted by Franklin. But the French were now in a tight position. Vergennes was no longer master of policy, free to remain uncommitted. He was exposed to the machinations of Franklin, who like Deane played on French fears of a separate peace. "We advise you," the Congress's Committee for Foreign Affairs had written to Franklin, "to be constantly holding up the great advantages which the Crown and commerce would receive by their seizing the West Indies; and you should make all the use possible of the English newspapers as a channel to counteract the tide of folly and falsehood of which you complain." [30] This is precisely what Franklin had been doing and what he continued to do until he was sure that Vergennes would agree to a treaty of alliance.

---

[30] May 2, 1777, Wharton, II, pp. 313–315.

American historians have dogmatically asserted for years that French policy hinged on an American victory over the British Army, that it was the surrender at Saratoga that decided the matter for Vergennes. But this could not have been so. The turning point came early in September, when Burgoyne was still on his fateful march. By that time the signals were set for war in the West Indies. Well before the news of Burgoyne's misfortune had reached Europe, the British had so strengthened their position in that area that the Americans could not, "with any prospect of safety," export vast quantities of tobacco and other produce which they had accumulated to meet their mounting deficits overseas. Expelled by Howe from Philadelphia, although of course knowing of the American triumph at Saratoga, the Committee for Foreign Affairs kept its eyes riveted on the West Indies and prayed for a European war. "A war in Europe," pleaded the committee in a letter addressed to Franklin on December 2, "would greatly and immediately change the scene." And then French and, it was hoped, Spanish naval help on the western side of the Atlantic would break the blockade and make room for reciprocal commerce.[31] This was the determining factor, not Saratoga.

Intelligence of an unusual number of sailings of supply ships from French and Spanish ports—at least eighty-five from French ports, mostly on private account, and twenty or more American vessels to go in convoy formation from Bilbao—caused Weymouth in late October to take a harder line. He advised the Admiralty to fit out a squadron to intercept them, and told Stormont to drop a hint to Vergennes that seizures might result. This was a long way from threatening the French with a blockade, but it was the first time that the British government was willing to admit officially that it knew of, and was concerned with, the stream of supplies flowing from France. Later, in December, Stormont himself furnished additional details on the numbers of ships engaged in the traffic and the nature of their cargo, and his reports were corroborated by personal observations made by the governor of the Isle of Jersey. It was apparent that the French were now aiding the Americans on a big scale.

---

[31] *Ibid.*, pp. 438–441.

"It seems to be agreed on all hands," observed Stormont, "that it is these succours that keep the rebels going." [32]

The suspicions of a secret treaty between France and America which the *London Evening Post* voiced on the eighth of December were well founded.[33] Lord Stormont was convinced that a secret negotiation had at least started, and that the Americans were holding the threat of a separate peace with Britain over Vergennes' head. They must have sensed that this was a major fear of the French foreign minister—they had used it so often, and this time they had a real weapon in their hands: the British ministry actually did make them an overture.

The overture originated with William Eden, the undersecretary of state for the Northern Department who, ever since taking office, had been exploring avenues for reconciliation. Eden was close to Lord North, whose heart was also not in the war; and on first learning of the disaster to Burgoyne, he proposed that the ministers introduce conciliatory bills into Parliament and take other measures to stop the war. Eden's zeal, it would seem, outran his discretion; knowing of Bancroft's close friendship with Franklin and Deane, he paid the former to keep him informed of the activities of the two American commissioners. Because of this arrangement Bancroft occupied an equivocal position—he has been dubbed a "spy" and "double spy" although his importance has been grossly exaggerated by historians. Lord Stormont's sources of intelligence were always better than Bancroft's, and the ambassador had no relations with him. Eden made the mistake, as it were, of opening his own private line to Paris and not going to Lord Weymouth for the intelligence which Stormont regularly and conscientiously furnished the Southern Department.

Eden's well-meaning efforts turned out to be embarrassing in the end, for, in letting the cat out of the bag in a private letter to

---

[32] Stormont to Weymouth, confidential, Dec. 24, 1777, SP 78/305; additional details in my article, "Great Britain, the War for Independence, and the 'Gathering Storm' in Europe, 1775–1778," *Hunt. Lib. Quart.*, XXVII (1964), pp. 311–346.

[33] AAE, cp, Etats Unis I, ff. 287–288, Overtures sur la possibilité de notre union avec les Americains, 7 Dec. 1777.

Bancroft which outlined the ministry's intentions, he made it possible for Franklin to play on French fears of a separate peace. Eden's personal letter, written as he said "by the advice of a person of high rank," asked Dr. Bancroft to sound out Franklin on terms that would be satisfactory; but Franklin, instead of responding, turned the letter over to the French foreign ministry in whose archives it has only recently been discovered.[34] The letter, of course, was just one more lever for Franklin to use on the cautious Vergennes. Probably it had little effect, since the latter had already had a report on British peace plans from his own embassy in London.

The intelligence as a whole, however, did have a strong, perhaps a decisive, influence in edging the French into the alliance which they had for so long wished to avoid. The aged Maurepas, most pacific of the French ministers, told the British ambassador that he had knowledge of secret approaches that British agents were making to Franklin, and Franklin made the most of his opportunity. He and Deane wrote numerous letters to the foreign ministry and went frequently in person to urge their cause. Lord Stormont was well aware of this unusual activity, the reports of it being too widespread for it to escape his attention. "The rebel agents have been very frequently at Versailles of late," he told Weymouth, "and . . . they always go in the night to avoid discovery." Gérard was paying Franklin return visits at Passy. Moreover, Stormont continued, "the Rumour of War was very strong yesterday," and greatly affected the French funds, several of them falling five per cent but recovering a little the next day.[35]

A memorandum drawn up by Gérard near the end of the year establishes the point that the French ministry was now willing to pay the ultimate price to keep the Americans separated from Britain. A treaty, he asserted, would give them the confidence in France essential to keep them from listening to any British peace proposals that did not include recognition of their political and

---

[34] *Ibid.*, f. 310. While unsigned, there can hardly be a question of this letter's authorship. See also Van Alstyne, *op. cit.*, for the documentation on Eden and Bancroft.

[35] Stormont to Weymouth, most secret, Dec. 24, 1777. SP 78/305.

commercial independence. But Gérard was ready to go further: he would, for the sake of enfeebling Britain, guarantee to the United States its territory and any additional conquests it might make on the continent of North America; and he would continue rendering material and financial aid until the war was won. The main French fear at this point seems to have arisen over the reluctance of Spain to join in; Gérard in this memorandum associated Spain with France in the proposed alliance, but the Spanish court refused to follow suit.[36] Accordingly the negotiations were slowed down, greatly to the disappointment of the Americans and of Gérard too, the latter expressing his belief that a treaty should be dispatched directly to the Congress as a means of heading off the British. Doubts had found their way into the French mind when it was learned that the Congress, under the influence of the Lees, had ordered Deane home. Deane's sudden recall was taken as a bad sign, as he had been the most aggressive of the American delegates in trying to win over the French.

As disappointing as the Spanish attitude was, it proved impossible now for Vergennes to halt the negotiations with the Americans. French war preparations had gone so far, and so many persons with influence at court were bent on going to extremities that there was no turning back. Either Britain or France would seize the lead in Europe, and this would depend on which of the two succeeded in binding America to itself. Again the old question of the North ministry's losing power and the Chathamites coming in on the basis of peace and collaboration with the Americans arose to plague the cautious foreign minister. Aware that the British were preparing to launch a fresh peace offensive, Vergennes dared not turn his back on the American commissioners. He shared with other Frenchmen an obsession that Britain meant to attack at the first opportunity and strip France of its remaining colonies.[37]

Talk of the coming war between the two countries, and of the alliance the Americans were making with France, was now out in the open. Almon's *London Evening Post* on January 8, 1778,

---

[36] AAE, cp, Etats Unis II, f. 344; Meng, *op. cit.*, pp. 80–82.
[37] AAE, MD, Etats Unis II, ff. 228–235, 236–242, 250–253: three memoirs arguing intervention, nos. 17, 18 and 19, Dec. 1777.

viewed the alliance as concluded and warned that Britain was no match for a union between France and America. The Netherlands and Prussia would follow the French lead, and France benefiting from American commerce would become the richest and strongest nation in Europe. Meanwhile Lord Stormont in Paris was trying to ascertain whether a treaty really had been concluded. He did not doubt that negotiations were proceeding, and when on January 22 he taxed the French ministers with his suspicions he got a virtual confession of the fact. Vergennes "seemed more embarrassed than ever I remember him, plaid with his fingers and remained quite silent. . . . His silence is too clear to need a comment." Maurepas said: *"il n'y a rien de conclu encore,"* and admitted the Americans had made repeated offers. Stormont suggested he be authorized to make a formal demand on the French court that it deny negotiating with the Americans, but since this was virtually an ultimatum Weymouth refused permission.[38]

Equally, if not more important in Stormont's mind, was the intelligence of accelerated preparations at the ports. Five thousand men had been assembled at Brest, where three ships of the line and a frigate were being held in readiness; Franklin and several of his friends had dined with the comte d'Estaing of the Navy, who was eager for war and willing to bet on one coming by the end of March; and orders had been sent to all the sea officers to be ready for duty, and to the fleet at Toulon in the Mediterranean to put to sea as soon as possible. This last piece of intelligence seemed so important to Stormont that he dispatched a special messenger to London. He thought it might portend a sudden French and Spanish attack on Gibraltar. Weymouth replied that he too thought war likely, but he had no special instruction for the ambassador save to continue his vigilance.[39]

On Friday, February 6, 1778, the French and Americans signed two treaties—one of amity and commerce, the other of alliance. France acknowledged the "liberty, sovereignty, and

---

[38] *London Evening Post*, Jan. 1, 8 and 10, 1778; Stormont to Weymouth, Jan. 22 and 25, Weymouth to Stormont, Jan. 30, 1778, SP 78/305.
[39] *Ibid.*

Independence absolute, and unlimited" of the United States, and agreed to give the United States a free hand in conquering the Bermudas and all the British colonies on the mainland of North America in return for a free hand in taking the British colonies in the West Indies. The alliance, moreover, was also to be "forever," a unique requirement for a wartime alliance. No scholar has been able to show how it got into the text of the treaty, or to say whether it originated with the French or the Americans. But it seems to have been in accord with the ideas of both: Silas Deane had been hammering away on the theme of mutual profit, politically and commercially, at the expense of Great Britain, while the French were impressed in similar manner by the long-range advantages of a tieup with a power possessing unlimited economic potential.[40] If America was the source of British strength and wealth, it might now become so for France.

At least one other historical puzzle obtrudes itself: these treaties were supposed to be secret, but knowledge of their existence quickly became general. Lord Stormont reported them to Whitehall on the very day they were signed, although he did not learn of them through Bancroft as has been erroneously alleged. He did not see the actual texts, and his knowledge was imperfect, but he understood their general importance. Charles James Fox stated positively in Commons on the nineteenth of February that there was a treaty, that he derived his information "from no contemptible authority." Stormont, viewing the crisis as something that could no longer be ignored, urged the government to take a stand against France. "Her whole system with reference to the rebels," he commented, was "so knavish, so mean, and so paltry as well as odious that, when revealed in its true colors, it will form a striking contrast with the dignity of our course." But Weymouth preferred to temporize, remaining passive although he was warned that an armed convoy of eighteen to twenty vessels had been ordered to sail from Brest. The ministry kept up the pretense of good relations with France, although it knew about the treaties.

---

[40] For the texts of the treaties and notes see Hunter Miller, *Treaties and other International Acts of the United States of America*, 7 vols., Washington, D. C., 1931–1942, II, pp. 3–47.

Stormont was disgusted. He had lost patience and stopped seeing the French ministers. He was ready to pawn his honor and his reputation on the existence of the treaties, he declared, and this was ground enough for war. A delay would only make matters worse. If the armed convoy was allowed to sail unchallenged, it would deal a hard blow to British prospects in America, and France would add insult to perfidy, whenever it chose to publish the treaty.[41]

It seems likely, in the absence of documentation to the contrary, that the French intended not to show their hand and remain silent about the treaties at least until they heard of their acceptance on the farther side of the Atlantic. They had the final word, therefore they had no motive for haste in making the alliance known. The pressure of events drove them into it; they feared a separate peace, heartily desired by strong vocal interests in Britain, and a return of Chatham to power. To Vergennes Chatham was a dreaded spectre, a magic name that might still bind up the wounds of the British Empire.

The French acted probably sooner than they had intended. Saying nothing of the alliance which was the subject of the second treaty, they chose to have their ambassador, the comte de Noailles, deliver a paper at Whitehall announcing their recognition of the United States on the basis of the treaty of friendship and commerce. The paper hinted at more aggressive measures, but did not specify what they would be. So the British again sacrificed the initiative to their rival, having now no choice but to break relations. Stormont guessed the reason why the French acted prematurely: aware of the plans for a special British peace mission to America, they hoped by a *fait accompli* to head it off and, by promoting the internal dissension in England, to render Britain still more helpless.[42] Probably he guessed correctly.

---

[41] Stormont to Weymouth, Feb. 25, Mar. 5, 11 and 12, 1778; Weymouth to Stormont, Feb. 27, 1778, SP 78/306.
[42] Stormont to Weymouth, Mar. 14, 1778, *ibid.*

# CHAPTER VI

## The British Try and Fail to Make Peace

The United States of America are willing to be the friends, but will never submit to be the slaves of the parent country. They are by consanguinity, by commerce, by language, and by the affection which naturally spring from these, more attach'd to England than to any country under the sun; therefore, spurn not the blessing which yet remains; instantly withdraw your Fleets and Armies; cultivate the Friendship and Commerce of America. Thus, and thus only can England hope to be great and happy: seek that, in commercial alliance, seek it e're it be too late; for there alone, you must expect to find it.—*General Horatio Gates to Lord Rockingham, October 26, 1777*

G ENERAL GATES, THE VICTOR AT SARATOGA, wanted the war to end and wrote his friend, Lord Rockingham, to say so. Gates wrote only a few days after his victory, and entrusted his letter to General Burgoyne, who delivered it in person on his return to England. Rockingham read the letter to the House of Lords on February 16, 1778 just as that body was about to debate a set of peace proposals which Lord North's government had prepared for submission to the Americans. French aid had made Gates's victory possible, but Gates was no friend to the alliance with France which was now beginning to be discussed publicly. Like the English Whigs, among whom he had been reared, Gates viewed the war as "unjust, impolitic, and unnatural," and hoped that "some state Physician" would appear in Britain to confirm the independence of America and heal the wounds between the two countries. Such ideas had been expressed publicly in Britain many times, and were common currency again in speeches heard in Parliament *before* anyone in the country had heard of the disaster at Saratoga.[1] Abingdon's pamphlet of September 1777 had made a real impression. Its arguments were "bold, spirited, and severe," as one famous commentator, Horace Walpole, put it. And on two occasions before the news of Saratoga, clear-headed and courageous speakers in both houses of Parliament spelled out these ideas.

It was Britain's evil fortune, however, that it had no "state Physician." Chatham and Rockingham, the two leaders of the opposition, could not team together. They were long-standing political rivals, temperamentally they clashed, and both of them suffered from ill health. Enjoying the friendship and loyalty of his immediate followers like Edmund Burke, Rockingham cut a poor figure before the public and would not take the strong position that friends like the Duke of Richmond urged on him. Chatham was forthright enough, but he entangled himself in a mass of inconsistencies. He demanded a cease fire in America, a recall of the army, and a repeal of all the Acts of Parliament since 1763, but, he roundly declared, he would *never* recognize American independence—"as if men whom you could not conquer were not and would not be independent," to borrow the caustic words of Horace Walpole. Chatham's trouble was, of course, that he was old and infirm: the chief architect of the triumphant empire of 1763, he was ever watchful of France and ever ready to conciliate the Americans, except for the one short step needed to make American friendship cool toward France—a grant of independence. The barrier arose at this point. Few minds in Britain were conditioned to look past it, nor did Saratoga make any difference.

On their part, the king and Lord North were equally ready for peace but equally unready for independence. Learning of Howe's victory over Washington at Brandywine and expecting Burgoyne to win likewise, North confided to a friend his idea that Britain should "take advantage of the flourishing state of our affairs to get out of that d--d war, and hold a moderate language. . . . If our success is as great as the most sanguine politician wishes or believes, the best use we can make of it is

---

[1] Van Alstyne, *The Rockingham Whigs, op. cit.,* pp. 17–26.

to get out of the dispute as soon as possible." [2] As a parliamentarian able to hold his own in the House of Commons, Lord North had few equals. And if Edward Gibbon, the great historian, who also sat in the house on the government's side, is to be believed, he was "one of the best companions in the kingdom." But this did not give him the stern qualities of a statesman, much less those of a war leader. Against his own inclinations and in spite of chronic ill health, he remained in office out of personal loyalty to the king, but even so there was no one in Parliament who could step into his shoes.

Very close to Lord North and ever hopeful of finding a successful road to peace was William Eden, the under-secretary in the Northern Department. Through his agents on the Continent, notably Paul Wentworth, the New Hampshire loyalist, Eden tried to keep up to date on French war preparations and relations with the Americans; but his agents failed him completely on the thing the British needed to know most of all. This was the preparation of a fleet under the comte d'Estaing to sail in the spring from Toulon to America with the object of breaking British sea power in the western Atlantic. Aware that the outcome of Burgoyne's expedition was still unknown, Eden assisted in the writing of the king's speech to be delivered November 18, 1777 at the opening of the fall session of Parliament; but the speech and the debates that immediately followed took place in ignorance of the event that had occurred at Saratoga the preceding month. When the news did arrive on the night of December 2, it shattered the ministry's hopes for an early termination of the war.

Eden was the first to recover sufficiently from the shock to sketch out a plan for conducting peace negotiations with the Americans, which he did in a private letter to Lord North four days after.[3] Thinking in terms of a negotiated peace rather than of a simple stoppage of the war and grant of independence, Eden posed a number of practical questions. The government, he suggested, should assume the lead in sponsoring a compre-

---

[2] North to Eden, Nov. 4, 1777, Auckland Papers, III, British Museum Add. Mss. 34, 414.

[3] Eden to North, Nov. 9 and Dec. 7, 1777, *ibid.*

hensive act of legislation repealing previous measures which
had led to rebellion, and authorizing peace commissioners to
proceed whenever they found the Colonies receptive. But
whether hostilities should continue in the meantime, whether
the armed forces should not retain their grip on certain strategic
positions such as New York, whether the commissioners should
deal directly with the Congress, and other questions that did
not lend themselves to easy answers—these were matters that
Eden raised but did not try to resolve. In short, he concluded,
peacemaking was no simple matter; there was an immense
amount of detail to be settled before the peace talks were even
opened. The government was in no position to move hastily.
When it moved for adjournment of Parliament over the Christmas holidays, Burke protested that a delay would only spell
further defeat. It would mean the entry of France into the
war. The ministry, however, got its way by a wide margin:
Parliament adjourned on December 10 for a period of six weeks,
and another six weeks were to pass before the debate opened
on the peace overture.

Meanwhile Eden, using Wentworth as his intermediary, tried
to get the three American envoys in Paris to commit themselves.
Wentworth made no progress, however. Franklin, speaking for
the group, pointed with pride to the support he was now getting
from France and demanded an immediate cessation of hostilities
and an evacuation of all thirteen provinces. Wentworth guessed
correctly that Franklin was using his overture mainly to excite
the French, and that it was dangerous to continue the conversations. Withdrawal of the troops included those in Canada
and Florida, leaving those strategic provinces without benefit
of even a paper guarantee. Franklin built his hopes on a
European war: such an event would give the United States
freedom of action in its own sphere. "War has grown again to
be the general topic," Wentworth reported just before Christmas; "everyone from Versailles whispers it in the French
way. . . ." So Wentworth advised stopping the talks and letting
the Americans reflect on the advantages of reconciliation before
committing themselves irrevocably to the Bourbon powers.[4]

---

[4] Wentworth to Eden, Dec. 17 and 22 (two dispatches), 1777, *ibid.*

Wentworth felt that Britain had more to offer than France, and that in the long run the Americans would realize this. But he gambled against the growing spirit of independence, fostered by the successes the Americans were having with the French; and, moreover, reconciliation with Britain meant submission to the Navigation Laws, a retrogressive step to the American mind considering the opportunities for trade with Europe which the war had opened up.

Nor was the question to be decided by cold reason, as the British seemed to expect. Even the cool mentality of Franklin was not free from the passions of war. His letters to his several English friends, especially to David Hartley who was nearest to him in sympathy, show that he was having difficulty distinguishing between the ministry, against whom he had long nourished a bias, and the whole British nation. Formerly he had blamed the British government; now he was in a mood to indict the British people. The war, he wrote in one of his more temperate letters, was not merely ministerial; the majority in Parliament were against us, and the populace rejoiced "on occasion of any news of the slaughter of an innocent and virtuous people, fighting only in defence of their just rights. . . ." [5]

Hartley's several attempts to explore the road back, made solely on his own volition, met with the same negative results as Eden's. Moreover, Franklin used them as sparks for lighting up the war between France and Britain: he turned these letters over to Gérard and Vergennes. But, he finally told Hartley, if "wise and honest men," such as Hartley himself, were to come to Paris at once armed with powers to treat, they might not only obtain peace with America, but also prevent a war with France. This was indeed grasping at a straw, if Franklin really meant it. He was in the midst of a great vogue of personal popularity in Paris, but was made to pay a price for it. "How I am harrass'd," he complained. "Great Officers of all Ranks, . . . Ladies, great and small, besides professed Sollicitors, worry me from Morning to Night, . . . I am afraid to accept an Invitation to dine abroad, being almost sure of meeting with some Offi-

---

[5] Franklin to Hartley, Oct. 14, 1777, Smyth, VII, No. 855.

cer . . . who, as soon as I am put in good Humour by a Glass or two of Champaign, begins his Attack upon me. . . ." [6]

By New Year's Day of 1778, Wentworth had lost any illusions he might have had of reaching an agreement with the American envoys in Paris. Franklin seemed agreeable to friendly talks and Silas Deane, whom Wentworth disliked, participated, but with Arthur Lee it was impossible to say a word. Lee was already on bad terms with his associates, and to Wentworth he was "suspicious and insolent." But minds did not meet. To the Americans, by now in the advanced stage of negotiation with the French, independence was everything; to the British it was impracticable. Wentworth knew of the negotiation and of the American effort to draw France into the war. Imbued himself with the idea of a reunited Empire, his verdict on their course of action could only be adverse. "They see plainly," he said, "their independence (the goal they sacrifice every other consideration to) declared by such a step, and they are careless of the consequences, destructive as they must be to America in the most favorable events." Moreover, Wentworth knew that Deane's brother Simeon had left Paris for Bordeaux, to take ship in company with Jean Holker, who was to be the first French consul in America. Through them advance intelligence would reach America of the French intention to recognize independence. [7]

Several sources besides Wentworth kept Whitehall well informed of what was happening in France. Lord Stormont's information was even better than Wentworth's. The letters he received from Paris, Lord North told Eden privately, "put an approaching rupture with France almost out of doubt." There was but one factor which might distract French attention: the Elector of Bavaria died in January, and there was a succession question which might keep both France and Prussia preoccupied. [8] With this slim hope, and with full knowledge that the

---

[6] To a Friend, Dec. 1777, *ibid.* No. 862.

[7] Wentworth to Eden, Jan. 1 (two dispatches), 4, 6 and 7, 1778, Auckland Papers, IV, British Museum Add. Mss. 34, 415.

[8] North to Eden, Sunday night (no other date, but placed in the collection following Jan. 28, 1778), *ibid.*

Americans in Paris were uncompromising, the ministry resolved nevertheless to go ahead with plans for enacting conciliatory legislation.

What foundation did it have for believing that its proposals would succeed in Philadelphia when they had failed in Paris? The intelligence it received from America was scanty and not to be compared with the quality of the reporting from the Continent. What little it got came from army and navy sources, otherwise there seems to have been almost a vacuum. Sir George Collier, in command at Halifax, wrote two letters describing the situation in New England. Quantities of goods from Britain were being smuggled through Nova Scotia on their way to the small ports to the south. The customs-house books at Halifax showed imports ten times more than could be sold locally. Great numbers of people in New England were discontented, traditionally against the Southern Colonies, and ready to return to their allegiance. Eden himself received a letter from a friend serving with the army in America which may have given him some hope. Unfortunately we do not know the identity of the letter writer because his signature has been obliterated, nor do we know the date other than that it was written sometime early in the year. The vast majority of the population, the letter said, were tired of the war, were "totally averse" to independence, and would gladly return to their allegiance if they were told the terms. But the leaders of the rebellion were intransigent, and had staked their whole future on it. They would keep the power they had got by any means whatever, and "will dragoon and compel the deluded multitude to support them as long as possible." [9]

Eden was perhaps the moving spirit in the conciliation movement. He was predisposed to go ahead in spite of the discouraging reports he had had from Wentworth in Paris. His friend and patron, the Duke of Marlborough, who thought the use of force against the Americans futile, agreed that it was worth a try. Britain could not be expected to do more than make a fair Parliamentary offer of terms, he wrote. The first attempt would

---

[9] Collier to Sandwich, Dec. 6, 1777 and Jan. 23, 1778, Sandwich Mss., National Maritime Museum, Greenwich, Eng.; Auckland Papers, IV, *ibid.*

probably fail, "but it seems to me that the opening any treaty of that nature may produce peace in the end by its operations on the different feelings and mind of the Rebels; for the bulk of the people there cannot but be tired of this war and will probably be soon clamorous for peace, unless the terms we offer are very hard and indigestible indeed." [10]

Eden, his friend Alexander Wedderburn, the solicitor-general, and others drafted three conciliatory bills, which the government introduced into both Houses of Parliament on February 17, 1778. These bills repealed the Massachusetts Government Act of 1774, stipulated that Parliament would not impose any duty, tax, or assessment on any of the Colonies, and empowered the government to appoint commissioners with authority to treat with any body or assembly in America, to order a cease fire, to suspend all or any of the acts passed since 1763, and to take other steps calculated to result in peace and reconciliation. The bills were debated, given their third reading, and passed without a division on March 9, 1778. Eight days later the French formally announced their recognition of the United States, but the announcement contained no information regarding the alliance which by now was pretty much an open secret. The timing of the announcement and the method suggest that it was a tactical move, made in response to the conciliatory bills. The treaties signed with the Americans the previous month were secret, nor was provision made for their going into operation at any specific time.

Let us pay attention for a moment to the debates in Parliament over the conciliatory bills. The taxation issue, which was supposed to have caused the rebellion in the first instance, was not even raised. "I always wish'd to declare that we would not exercise the right of taxation upon America," said Lord George Germain privately to Eden.[11] Such a statement is arresting coming from the man whom the opposition delighted in making the scapegoat for the war. But actually it was consistent with Lord North's conciliatory resolution of February 20, 1775. Although French aid to the Americans and participation in privateering

---

[10] Marlborough to Eden, Jan. 8, 1778, Auckland Papers, IV, *ibid.*
[11] Feb. 10, 1778, *ibid.*

operations against British commerce were public knowledge, and although the probability of a war with France was freely mentioned, the debates were conducted in a kind of false atmosphere that France was really "neutral." With virtually positive knowledge to the contrary, the ministry refused to admit that anything was amiss in Anglo-French relations. Its reputation rested on this illusion, and the outcome of its peace offensive depended on preserving it. Once the Americans were quieted, the French danger would evaporate.

A few prominent speakers in both houses expressed dissatisfaction with the bills and declared forthrightly that only a grant of independence would bring results. Rockingham at last came out on this side, joining with the Duke of Richmond in saying that it was necessary to head off the French. The most outspoken opponent of independence was the Earl of Shelburne, Chatham's closest disciple, who took the ministry's view that the bills went far enough. But Shelburne also gave a masterly analysis of the poor strategy the government had employed against the Americans, and seemed to say that competent management and reform of military strategy, combined with the peace proposals, would bring the Americans around.

There was much sense in Shelburne's plan for a successful campaign: he favored the retention of the leading ports in North America from Halifax south to Philadelphia, the effective use of sea power based on these ports, and the capture of the interior posts to control the inland water system resulting in a gradual forcing of the Americans toward the sea. In contrast to this systematic program of encirclement, the ministry had carried on an aimless war of raids and depredations, making it possible for Washington to avoid a decisive encounter, and employing mercenaries and savages. The general outcome was to enrage the local population and drive it into the arms of the extremists who demanded independence. Shelburne's main object was to force the government to resign, but with only a handful of supporters he stood no chance of success.[12]

Eden had been giving his unbroken attention, meanwhile, to the proposed peace commission: who was to go and how best

---

[12] *PH*, XIX, cols, 850–856.

they might succeed. Men of family, influence, and consideration should be on it, he thought. The commission should have one lawyer, and Eden's choice was his close friend, Sir William Blackstone; Scotland should be represented, and here he had a list of names; the Parliamentary opposition should have a member; the peers one, and somebody from the friends of the administration. His colleague in the Northern Department, William Fraser, in a prepared memorandum tried to anticipate the conditions which the commission would encounter. The independence party in America, Fraser assumed, would oppose every overture made it, hence it was important to find a way of going beyond it and winning the people to the commission's side. The indispensable first step was to offer to return to the *status quo* of 1763. But beyond that it was difficult to know what to do. Eden was warned of the danger of a cease-fire order: it would give the Americans time to gather fresh supplies to strengthen their positions and to keep the British forces immobilized. Hence it was decided to maintain hostilities while negotiations were in progress.

On the internal situation in America and the leadership in the several Colonies and the Congress, Eden received the benefit of a lengthy analysis by Paul Wentworth, based on Wentworth's knowledge of conditions in 1774–1776. Wentworth was not sanguine of the commission's success; he felt that political control in America had passed into the hands of men who would not compromise. But Eden felt strongly that, to avoid any appearance of duplicity or intrigue, the commission should start with the Congress and the commander-in-chief of the American Army. "Their Confederacy," he wrote, "is certainly a State for the purpose of Treaty," and if they call themselves the representatives of free and independent states, "it does not seem necessary to make any objections. . . ." A long list of other questions arose in Eden's mind, but he thought the commission should say positively at the outset that it had no power to consent to independence, to relinquish the right to control and regulate commerce, or to infringe on the king's right to appoint governors, military officers, and other officials connected with the central government.[13]

---

[13] Stevens, nos. 374, 375, 379, 487.

After all of the pains he had taken, Eden encountered a series of disappointments. He hoped the commission would be appointed and take its departure as soon as the bills had passed Parliament. But a whole month was lost, and the commission when finally constituted was by no means the distinguished delegation he had originally envisaged. Other than himself — he apparently had had no personal desire to go — the only other members who sailed were George Johnstone, a former governor of West Florida who shared the views of the Rockingham Whigs, and the Earl of Carlisle, who turned out to be more level-headed and responsible than could be assumed from his previous career. So serious an undertaking called for careful briefing at the top, yet this factor was conspicuously lacking. Eden's interest alone seems to have carried the project along. Lord North was his customary casual self. He "finished all his Conferences on this side of the Atlantic with me, very much in the stile of a common Acquaintance who is stepping from your room to the water closet and means to return in five minutes." The king was indifferent, an attitude shared generally by the public. Eden himself was beset with doubts.[14]

In sharp contrast to this easygoing, almost equivocal attitude toward the peace commission were the military preparations which followed hard on the French announcement respecting their recognition of American independence. The contrast is best shown by comparing two secret orders which Germain dispatched to Sir Henry Clinton, who was now in command in America. The first order was dated March 8, 1778, a week before the French announcement; the second was dated March 21, only five days after the announcement. In the first order Germain took it almost for granted that the Americans would accept the peace offer but, if they refused, he proposed sending a large new expeditionary force and embarking on a comprehensive plan of war that would separate the northern Colonies from the less rebellious southern Colonies. The second order instructed Clinton to detach 5,000 men from his command for service in the West Indies where, in conjunction with the navy, they were to be used for an attack on St. Lucia. The capture

---

[14] Eden to Germain, Mar. 3, to Wedderburn, Apr. 12, 1778, Stevens, nos. 385 and 441.

of this small island with its fine harbor would neutralize French power in Martinique and Guadeloupe. Clinton was told to execute this order immediately. Next he was to detach 3,000 for service in the Floridas, and with the remaining troops he was to evacuate Philadelphia and go to New York to await the outcome of the peace negotiation. In a word, offensive warfare was to be launched against France in the West Indies on the theory that a decisive campaign there would bring victory, operations against the Americans in the meantime to be sharply curtailed.[15]

Clinton received this important order on May 8, but was unable to carry it out in the manner directed; he lacked the ships required for so large an operation. So he decided to move his army to New York, where the main British fleet was stationed. The West Indian expedition, he believed, could be more efficiently organized from New York.[16] He began preparations very promptly for evacuating Philadelphia, of which the Americans soon learned; and when the peace commission reached the Delaware River, bound upstream for Philadelphia, it met British transports carrying baggage and equipment going in the opposite direction. Naturally, having been kept in ignorance of the secret order of March 21, the sight of the army abandoning the American capital just as they were arriving threw the commissioners into the greatest consternation. All three of them vented their anger on Germain, but the answers they ultimately received are a commentary on the extraordinary lack of communication among the ministers at Whitehall. If any one minister was negligent, Lord North was the man: Germain had not been consulted on the peace commission, and he expressed surprise that the commissioners had not been told of the order to Clinton.[17] The commission itself was partly responsible for the blunder through its decision, while on the high seas, to alter course for Philadelphia in place of New York,

---

[15] Germain to Clinton, most secret, March 8 and 21; George III to Clinton, secret instructions, Mar. 21, 1778, Stevens, nos. 1062, 1068, 1069.

[16] Clinton to Germain, May 10 and 23, June 5, 1778, Stevens, nos. 1082, 1084, 1093.

[17] Commissioners to Germain, June 15; Germain to Eden, July 31; Wedderburn to Eden, Aug. 1778, Stevens, nos. 511, 514, 1107.

its original intended destination. But this was a minor factor in
a sum total of misconceptions, misunderstandings, and incredi-
bly poor administration that had put the odds against it ever
since Eden had begun to think about it. Crossing the Atlantic
took seven weeks, yet when it arrived off Philadelphia the
commission had little to show for all its efforts beyond its
good intentions.

The commissioners' own judgment was that they would have
met with success except for the military exodus from Philadelphia "at a time the most critical . . . and with a tendency the
most prejudicial to the Conduct of our Negotiation." And they
cited evidence that at least sounded plausible: Chesapeake Bay
was now entirely open for American communication with
France. Jefferson in Williamsburg observed this very thing,
reporting on June 6 that a French ship had just come in with
a vast cargo of woolens, stockings, shoes, and other articles
for the army, and 50,000 pounds of powder. The commissioners
said that the Pennsylvania Assembly had just enacted a law
requiring all persons in the state to take the oath of allegiance
to the Confederated States on pain of forfeiting all their property; deprived suddenly of British protection many of the citizens now had no choice but to conform. The commissioners
further said that Washington's Army was sickly and poorly
supplied, in contrast to the British forces who were in fine
shape. Both Jefferson and Richard Henry Lee expressed their
anxiety over Washington's Army, and agreed that a vigorous
recruitment campaign was necessary. The timely arrival of
the news from France stimulated the volunteering. Finally, the
commissioners concluded that it was the British military withdrawal coupled with the intelligence of the French alliance that
caused the collapse of their plans.[18]

When the commissioners arrived in the Delaware, the French
alliance had been ratified for more than a month. Washington
greeted "with heartfelt joy" the first word of the success of the
American envoys in Paris, which he learned through the arrival

---

[18] Commissioners to Germain, June 15, 1778, Stevens, no. 1107; Jefferson
to R. H. Lee, June 6, Lee to Jefferson, May 2 and 3, 1778, *Jefferson Papers*,
II, pp. 175–177.

of Simeon Deane who brought the text of the agreement. The
Continental Congress convened on May 4 and promptly ratified
the alliance without dissent. It is not surprising therefore that
the British conciliatory bills, knowledge of which became
general in America during the month of May, fell on stony
ground. Sir Henry Clinton, trying to be conciliatory and going
forward with his evacuation plans, asked Washington for an
interview, but met with a rebuff on the thirtieth of May.
Washington administered a second rebuff ten days later when
he refused a passport to the commissioners' secretary, who was
to carry a letter to the Congress. Finally, however, the letter
did reach Henry Laurens, the president of the Congress, asking
for a meeting and a negotiation within the framework of the
conciliatory bills. Richard Henry Lee, who had consistently
linked independence with an alliance with France, described
this letter as "a combination of fraud, falsehood, insidious
offers, and abuse of France"; and Laurens rejected it on the
same grounds that Franklin had in Paris: an outright grant of
independence and a withdrawal of the troops.[19] The British
forces had by this time already evacuated Philadelphia, but a
complete evacuation of the continent was something different.

Just after Eden had sailed for America, North had written
him a letter cautioning him against surrendering Canada. Although Eden apparently did not know about it, there was a
plan afoot in the Congress for a second attempt on Canada,
and, of course, France in the treaty of alliance had accorded
the United States freedom to make such an attempt. A single
grant of independence, in other words, did not end the matter,
especially since when the British commissioners finally arrived,
the Americans had already bound themselves to the French.
It is hard to see, therefore, how even in more auspicious circumstances the British peace mission could have succeeded.

Retiring to New York with Clinton's forces, the British commissioners admitted the awkwardness of their position. But
they did raise a question or two not capable of facile reply.
The French treaty, reported Lord Carlisle, "was not relished by

---

[19] Lee to Jefferson, June 16, 1778; D. S. Freeman, *George Washington*, V,
p. 6.

the people at large," and had Clinton remained in Philadelphia
and kept the advantage over Washington the effect would have
been to destroy the power of the Congress; so many people
would have defied it. With the army gone, however, that power
was fixed, "and no motive but necessity can make them accede
to terms which would shake their power." Clinton supported
this view. Most bitterly disappointed of all were loyalists like
Joseph Galloway, who were now compelled to leave their homes
and accompany Clinton to New York. Galloway insisted that
the people of the Middle Colonies were tired of the rebellion
and ready to offer their services in suppressing it, if encouraged
by the British commanders. Like the others, he regarded the
retreat from Philadelphia as a great strategic blunder. If the
city were retained, the retention would lead to a peace through
a treaty; if it were given up, this would prolong the war. On
his part Germain, who had issued the order to concentrate on
the West Indies, showed that he still underestimated the power
of the rebellion in America. He still took it for granted that the
peace mission would succeed because, among other things, "We
understand several of the General Officers in Mr. Washington's
Army, and the People of the Country, were disposed to
Peace. . . ."[20]

Meanwhile, dating from the time when the finishing touches
were being put to the Franco-American alliance, the French
Navy began hasty preparations for a fleet of twelve ships of
the line and five frigates under the command of the comte
d'Estaing. The fleet was assembled at Toulon, and its objective
was the Delaware River in anticipation of wresting control of
American waters from Admiral Lord Howe. Lord Stormont
knew of this fleet at the time and reported it, but he did not
know its objective. This remained a well-kept secret; and after
the break in relations with France, which came in March, the
embassy was no longer a source of intelligence. Paul Wentworth
was the first to send positive information from Paris. Learning

---

[20] Carlisle to Lady Carlisle, June 21, 1778, Hist. Mss. Comm., 15th Rept.,
App., London, 1897; Joseph Galloway, "Reasons against abandoning
Philadelphia and the Province of Pennsylvania," Clinton Papers, W. L.
Clements Library; Germain to Clinton, July 1, 1778, *ibid.*

on April 9 that Gérard and Silas Deane were leaving to join d'Estaing at Toulon, Wentworth advised Eden that he had no doubt of the fleet's destination. Deane had been recalled by the Congress and Gérard was going as ambassador to Philadelphia. But whether Eden, preoccupied with his peace plans, passed on this important piece of intelligence is in doubt: there is nothing on record to show that he shared the secret. D'Estaing sailed on April 13, but was becalmed in the Mediterranean and did not pass Gibraltar until May 16. His voyage from Toulon to the Delaware took eighty-seven days.

Intelligence of the Toulon fleet and speculation concerning its destination overshadowed the British peace mission. Actually Eden and his fellow commissioners did not get away from England until the twenty-third, ten days after d'Estaing had left Toulon. North and others, including the king, shared the opinion that d'Estaing was bound for America, but the Admiralty faced the dilemma that if it attempted to match d'Estaing in American waters, it would so weaken the British home fleet as to be incapable of meeting a French challenge in the Channel. D'Estaing, objected Admiral Keppel, might actually be bound for Brest to combine forces with d'Orvilliers for an attack on Britain itself. Spain too was hardly to be ignored. In its refusal to take chances, the admiralty lost an opportunity to intercept the French fleet at Gibraltar, a piece of timidity which subsequently drew bitter criticism in Parliament. But the most Lord Sandwich would do was to send a single frigate to Gibraltar to observe and report on the French commander's course when he emerged into the open Atlantic. Having sighted d'Estaing and ascertained his direction, the frigate returned to England on June 3. Six days later a strong fleet left England to reinforce Howe at New York.[21]

D'Estaing entered the Delaware on July 7 but, with the British Army gone and with no prospect of refreshing his men after the long voyage, he sailed immediately for New York,

---

[21] North to Sandwich, Apr. 23 and 29; the king to Sandwich, Apr. 29; Sandwich to Stephens, May 1, 1778, Sandwich Papers, II, pp. 41–43; J. J. Meng, *D'Estaing's American Expedition 1778–1779*, N. Y., Amer. Soc. of the French Legion of Honor, 1936.

after letting off his two passengers, Gérard and Deane. On the American side it was assumed that the French commander would soon overpower Lord Howe's smaller force and capture both New York and Rhode Island. Richard Henry Lee, so long an enthusiast for the French alliance, met Gérard whom he found "a sensible well-bred Man, and perfectly well acquainted with the politics of Europe." Gérard's coming, he was positive, foreshadowed the establishment of relations with other countries in Europe, particularly with Prussia. King Frederick had said as much, so Lee believed, although he was due for a disappointment. But another and more immediate disappointment was also in store for him. D'Estaing, he told Jefferson, would "check the British insolence on the Sea as we have already done on the land." As yet war had not broken out in Europe, but that no longer mattered, "since we so powerfully experience the aid of France. For it is certain this Squadron is to Act with and for us so long as the enemy by continuing here renders it necessary. . . ." [22]

D'Estaing, however, was fated to find himself in the midst of quarrels and mutual recriminations between the new-found allies, while in Philadelphia Gérard found himself up against fierce rivalries and factional struggles in the Congress. First, d'Estaing met with disappointment at New York; his American pilots, insisting that his ships were too large to get past the bar at Sandy Hook, would not take him into the harbor where lay the inferior British fleet. Then, still without fresh water and food, he retired to Rhode Island where he enraged the American General Sullivan by refusing to cooperate in surrounding and capturing the British garrison at Newport. Sullivan vented his wrath publicly, jeopardizing the alliance which his superiors recognized was their one key to victory. D'Estaing finally, near the end of August, took haven in Boston's harbor where he spent an uncomfortable two months among armed clashes between his men and the local inhabitants. In the meantime the new British fleet reached New York and quickly re-established naval ascendancy in American waters, leaving

---

[22] Lee to Jefferson, July 10, Aug. 10, 1778, *Jefferson Papers*, II, pp. 204–205, 208–209.

the French no choice but to retreat to the West Indies. Here too the British gained the lead by the capture of St. Lucia, as originally ordered by the king in the preceding March.[23]

D'Estaing's disappointing performance caused Jefferson and Lee to reflect on the possibility of an advantageous peace with Britain. The pamphleteer Israel Mauduit, who had previously expressed his sympathies with the Americans, came out boldly in March 1778 in favor of a full grant of independence, and both Jefferson and Lee seized on the chance that Mauduit was really speaking for the British government. Focusing on the necessity of outbidding the French, Mauduit implied—or so Jefferson thought—that America should have a free hand in writing its own terms of independence; and since Mauduit wrote his piece as a handbill only three pages long, it got wide circulation in America and led to the guess, which proved wrong, that it was designed as a trial balloon. Ambitions dampened by d'Estaing's fiasco quickly revived. Gains for which France had been looked to for help were now thought possible through negotiation with Britain. The conciliatory bills and Eden's peace mission were scorned, but now there was an opportunity to play France off against Britain. Mauduit himself said as much: "All hope of conquest is over," he had written. "America stands on high ground; France and England must now court her. . . ."

Noting this, Jefferson thought first of the Newfoundland fisheries, "a nursery for seamen for the nation that has them." Then, "in our present prosperous state of affairs, we should have regular access in every court of Europe," but especially in the Mediterranean countries, the major markets for great commodities like fish, wheat, tobacco, and rice. Turkey was an excellent market for the last two products and, moreover, "this power . . . is likely to be in our scale in the event of a general war." Lee responded, concurring in the desirability of the fisheries but reminding Jefferson of the importance of having Canada too. Rueful over the British regaining the ascendancy

---

[23] Meng, op. cit.; Freeman, Washington, V, pp. 47–56, Alexander Hamilton to Elias Boudinot, Sept. 8, 1778, The Papers of Alexander Hamilton, I, pp. 545–546.

at sea, Lee added the consoling thought that, with so much British power assembled in American waters, France would have an opportunity for attack in the English Channel.[24]

Meanwhile, in Paris, Franklin put up a trial balloon of his own. Occasionally voices were heard in Parliament suggesting the repeal of the Quebec Act. The importance of this measure in keeping Canada apart from the United States was not infrequently overlooked. When proposals were made to return to the *status quo* of 1763, the Quebec Act generally went unmentioned. Eden, meditating on the agenda for his peace mission, left it out of account, and Lord North had to be briefed on it. Eden and his colleagues had already boarded ship when the minister wrote to warn him on the subject. And North continued:

The eagerness shown by the revolted Provinces for [repeal of this Act] is very suspicious. They certainly consider it as a step favourable to the uniting Canada to themselves as a fourteenth State, and till that is accomplish'd, they will be always obliged to pay attention to Great Britain. If we have recovered and preserved that province by arms, we must take care not to lose it by Treaty . . . .

Hartley, always searching for peace, in a long speech in Parliament just a few days previously had specifically advised repealing the Act. Undoubtedly it was this speech which aroused alarm against making so vital a concession, and induced North to send Eden a reminder. But Franklin, observing the stalemate that followed the French alliance in 1778, suavely argued with Hartley that the cession of Canada would be a generous gesture which would bring peace and pay rich dividends in the future. Obviously Franklin, like Jefferson and Lee, flirted with the idea of using the diplomatic arts to obtain something important that could not be gained through conquest. But the gesture was futile. Hartley spoke only for himself. Neither the British nor the French contemplated such a move. Gérard had come to Philadelphia to make it clear that, notwith-

---

[24] Israel Mauduit's *Proposal for Colonial Independence*, Broadside Collection, Rare Book Room, Library of Congress; Jefferson to Lee, Aug. 30, Lee to Jefferson, Oct. 5, 1778, *Jefferson Papers*, II, pp. 210–211, 214–216.

standing the text of the alliance, France would not support American territorial aggrandizement. In his eyes the territorial limits of the United States should be those of 1775.[25] So, in spite of the exhilaration of having France in the war, the year 1778 passed in frustration for the Americans.

---

[25] North to Eden, Apr. 23, 1778, Stevens, no. 447; Van Alstyne, *Rising American Empire*, pp. 51–57; Meng, *Despatches and Instructions of Conrad Alexandre Gérard, 1778–1780*, pp. 125–130.

# CHAPTER VII

## France to the Rescue

I know of no better rule than this: when two nations have the same interests in general they are natural allies; when they have opposite interests, they are natural enemies. . . . But . . . the habits of affection or enmity between nations are easily changed, as circumstances vary and as essential interests alter.—*John Adams, May 17, 1780*

T O THOSE DETERMINED OPTIMISTS, the leaders of the American Revolution, France in 1778 was the natural ally, Britain the natural enemy. With the French, it was felt, interests harmonized to the point of perfection; with the British they clashed so that compromise or reconciliation was impossible. The alliance with France was viewed as a marriage. The Congress performed the final rites willingly and gladly on the fourth of May. Consummation, it was assumed, would follow the ceremony as a matter of course; the alliance would endure "forever."

A statement issued by the Committee of Foreign Affairs in Philadelphia only ten days after the formal vote nicely illustrates this confidence. Independence, asserted the committee, is now firmly adopted. "Nova Scotia has long ago expressed its wishes to be adopted by us, and afresh solicits. Canada will be greatly affected by the news of our alliance with its former parent State. In short, Sir, everything which could be added to our own determination of being free and independent is insured by this *eclaircissement* of the court of Versailles. . . ." [1] Richard Henry Lee, Robert Morris, and James Lovell, a resident of Massachu-

---

[1] Burnett, III, pp. 236–237. *Jefferson Papers*, II, pp. 176–178, 204–205, 208–209.

setts—all zealous suitors of France for upward of two years—
were the authors of this statement.

But there were others who expressed themselves just as
hopefully. Even the reticent George Washington voiced his
pleasure and began laying his plans, with the enthusiastic support
of Lafayette, for another invasion of Canada. William Ellery of
Rhode Island advised his friend William Whipple of New
Hampshire of his conviction that the alliance would lead to
"the divesting of Britain of every foot upon this Continent. I
think it absolutely necessary to a future, lasting peace," he
added, "that we should be possessed of Canada, Nova Scotia
and the Floridas, which we cannot so well effect without the
open assistance of France." [2] William Henry Drayton of South
Carolina, a one-time loyalist converted to ardent patriotism,
saw both France and Spain throwing in their entire lot with
America and declaring war on Britain, thereby enabling "these
United States to continue the war and with the blessing of God
to establish their independence." Drayton was so sure of this
that he actually proposed a motion that the Congress "demand"
of the Bourbon powers that they commit themselves to act
forthwith.[3]

It remained for John Adams to erect these ideas of the differences between natural allies and natural enemies to the level
of a system. "As long as Great Britain shall have Canada, Nova
Scotia, and the Floridas, or any of them," declared Adams, "so
long will Great Britain be the enemy of the United States, let
her disguise it as much as she will." Adams's discourse is worth
quoting in full:

It is not much to the honor of human nature, but the fact is certain
that neighboring nations are never friends in reality. In the times
of the most perfect peace between them their hearts and their passions are hostile, and this will certainly be the case forever between
the thirteen United States and the English colonies. France and
England, as neighbors and rivals, never have been and never will
be friends. The hatred and jealousy between the nations are eternal
and ineradicable. As we therefore, on the one hand, have the surest

---

[2] May 31, 1778, Burnett, III, p. 269.
[3] May 1, 1778, *ibid.*, p. 213.

ground to expect the jealousy and hatred of Great Britain, so on the other we have the strongest reasons to depend upon the friendship and alliance of France, and no reason in the world to expect her enmity or jealousy, as she has given up every pretension to any spot of ground on the continent. The United States, therefore, will be for ages the natural bulwark of France against the hostile designs of England against her, and France is the natural defense of the United States against the rapacious spirit of Great Britain against them. France is a nation so vastly eminent, having been for so many centuries what they call the dominant power of Europe, being incomparably the most powerful at land, that united in a close alliance with our States, and enjoying the benefit of our trade, there is not the smallest reason to doubt but both will be a sufficient curb upon the naval power of Great Britain.[4]

Adams in fact had executed an about face since 1776. Originally a skeptic on the subject of a tie-up with France, he was now all enthusiasm. "The longer I live in Europe, and the more I consider our affairs, the more important our alliance with France appears to me," he wrote his old friend Joseph Warren. "It is a rock upon which we may safely build. . . ."[5] By this time Adams had been in France for approximately five months, having been sent over as the third commissioner when Silas Deane was recalled. Apparently the sectional conflict in the Congress was such that three commissioners (or ambassadors) of equal rank were required in place of one.

Adams was at first pleased and flattered by the attention he received in France, but his attitude toward his two colleagues soon became something less than cordial. Franklin, thirty years his senior, got too much attention from the ladies of Paris. The old doctor, he observed, was "so fond of the fair sex that one was not enough for him, but he must have one on each side, and all the ladies both old and young were ready to eat him up." Franklin's proficiency in the French language must have pleased them, but not Adams: he was critical of the old gentleman's grammar and pronunciation. More seriously, he disliked Franklin's friendliness for David Hartley, who came over often

---

[4] To Samuel Adams, July 28, 1778, Wharton, II, pp. 667–668.
[5] Aug. 4, 1778, *ibid.*, pp. 675–677.

from London on his quest for peace and reconciliation. And when Silas Deane, who had drawn the bitter enmity of the Lee brothers, issued a public statement in his own defense, Adams argued heatedly over it with Franklin and threatened to go to Vergennes with the quarrel. Toward Arthur Lee, who was hardly on speaking terms with Franklin, Adams felt more gracious. Lee at least was "honest and faithful" to America, although Adams admitted that the French had no confidence in him. He had given offense through his indiscreet speeches. Unfortunately Adams had to confess that only Franklin had the qualities that appealed to the French, and that he knew how to keep his reputation both in society and with the statesmen at Versailles. Back home in Massachusetts, after more than a year in Paris, Adams relieved himself of some of his feelings on the subject. Franklin, he observed, was a wit and humorist.

He may be a philosopher for what I know. But he is not a sufficient statesman for all the business he is in. He knows too little of American affairs, of the politics of Europe, and takes too little pains to inform himself of either to be sufficient for all these things—to be ambassador, secretary, admiral, consular agent, etc. Yet such is his name on both sides of the water, that it is best, perhaps, that he should be left there. . . .[6]

Meanwhile the Committee of Foreign Affairs realized that the French alliance did not, after all, swing open the door to victory. Gérard's cautious admonitions and d'Estaing's disappointing retreat could not be ignored. In October 1778 the committee decided on a fresh and more comprehensive approach to the French. Lifting the veil a little higher on American inability to win the war alone, the committee set out to convince the French how much France would gain if it sent decisive help and how much it would lose if it permitted Great Britain to win. High on the list of steps to be taken were the conquest of the Newfoundland fisheries and the reduction of Quebec and Halifax. But instead of assuming, as previously, that these prizes would go exclusively to the Americans, the committee offered to share

---

[6] *Adams Papers*, II, pp. 309, 323, 345–346; Wharton, III, pp. 331–333.

them with the French. Its proposal almost suggested a willingness to see France seated again in North America somewhat as it had been before 1763. Possibly the committee had submitted to the skillful diplomacy of the French minister.

With the fisheries in French and American hands, the combined commerce and shipping of the two countries would be strengthened, the frontier in the interior secured, and a portion of the fur trade restored to France. But if they remained under the enemy, small British armed ships could continue raiding French and American coastal commerce to the south. Moreover, argued the committee, the British drew their strength in the West Indies from Nova Scotia and the fisheries: the islands of the British Caribbean were nourished on the bread, fish, and lumber which came from the north. Once this source of supply was cut off, the British West Indies would be open to conquest. The committee hoped that the French would agree to initiate an attack on Quebec to be followed, if successful, by an attempt on Halifax. France, it proposed, should dispatch from two to five thousand troops from Brest in May, to be convoyed by four ships of the line and four frigates. Quebec was now defenseless, and could easily be taken in July. But, the committee warned, the French should bring their own provisions; memories of the fate of the American expeditionary force of two years previously were perhaps still fresh. An American force might join the French at the mouth of the St. Francis, although the committee was strangely reticent about promising such help. After Quebec the capture of Montreal would come as a matter of course, and Canada would be so far subjugated by August as to enable the vessels to return downstream to lay siege to Halifax. With the aid of land forces from Massachusetts and New Hampshire, this key naval base might be taken by the middle of October and time would still be left for an invasion of Newfoundland. If not, the troops could be put into winter quarters to await the arrival of good weather in the spring of 1780.

The committee took pains to silence any doubts His Christian Majesty might have respecting American intentions to stay in the war. It pointed to the adverse conditions under which the Declaration of Independence had been issued in the first in-

stance, and to the perseverance since then although no victory
was in sight. Then it dwelt on the demoralized state of American
finance—the resort to paper money both by the Congress
and by the individual states, and the resulting alarming depreciation
of the currency. Although America was rich, it was
impossible either to levy taxes or to float internal loans. Only
the alliance with France had kept America from drowning in
its own sea of paper, the committee admitted. Clearly the French
were expected to open their purses, if they wanted their American
ally to be effective. A very substantial loan or an outright
subsidy would be necessary. The committee's figure was
£5,000,000 sterling, plus two other loans of twenty million and
ten million dollars respectively.

Finally, the committee remarked on the possibility of Spain
entering into an alliance with the United States and uniting its
forces with France. Accordingly it felt the time had come to
outline the terms of peace considered essential to secure the
independence of the United States. The committee showed great
interest in having Nova Scotia, although it conceded that claims
to this province might be yielded in favor of a share in the
Newfoundland fisheries. Canada was to be restricted to its
"ancient limits," meaning a small, close-in area confined to the
banks of the St. Lawrence and back from the Great Lakes, both
shores of which were to go to the United States. To the west
the committee stipulated the Mississippi as the boundary; but,
evidently realizing that Spain would want to recover the
Floridas, which included the lower portion of the river, it
specified that Americans should have a free commerce through
one or more ports situated inside the Spanish domain.[7]

All of this was contained in a long communication addressed
to the three American commissioners in Paris, who concentrated
on persuading Vergennes of the desirability of a powerful
fleet operating in American waters. Acting in concert with
American armies, such a fleet would destroy the whole of
British power in North America and reward France by winning
for it a monopoly of the West Indian trade. The British, declared

[7] Draft of instructions to Franklin, Oct. 21, 1778, Papers of the Continental Congress, Reports of Committees, no. 25, vol. I, NA.

the commissioners, had nearly four hundred transports in the American service constantly passing from New York and Rhode Island to the home country, to Nova Scotia, and to the West Indies. If any one link in this chain was broken, their forces could not subsist. French naval superiority would lead to a rich trade between America and the French West Indies, American currency troubles would be cured, and the Americans would be able to buy more goods directly from the French. In short, the commissioners concluded, "it is obvious to all Europe that nothing less is at stake than the dominion of the sea, at least the superiority of naval power, and we can not expect Great Britain will ever give it up, without some decisive effort on the part of France." [8]

Vergennes not responding to this argument, Franklin nearly two months later tried his hand with a private letter. Apologizing for a severe attack of the gout and a fever that had left him so ill that he could "neither write nor think of anything," the elderly doctor reopened the case for reducing first Rhode Island and then Halifax. Four or five thousand French troops could be used profitably for this purpose, and then be sent to the West Indies for the winter. The Congress, Franklin added, had considered another attack on Canada but did not have the necessary resources. If France would help, the fur trade would again be open to the French, and if they decided in favor of joint operations, care should be exercised in appointing officers who could cooperate with their American opposites. [9] Here then was the first American bid for a French army, to be employed as auxiliaries to a sea force whose objective was the expulsion of the British from all of North America, with the exception of their remote posts on Hudson Bay, and from the West Indies. John Adams, writing to Lafayette, who was again in Paris, made substantially the same proposal. [10]

Vergennes's indifference to these overtures is easily understandable, although the Americans in Paris were completely in the dark about it. Anxious for Spanish support and ready to

---

[8] Jan. 1, 1779, Wharton, III, pp. 3–7.
[9] Feb. 25, 1779, Smyth, VIII, nos. 954 and 955.
[10] Feb. 21, 1779, Wharton, III, pp. 55–56.

pay the price Spain demanded, the French foreign minister was about to reach an agreement with Floridablanca for a combined fleet operation and invasion of Britain itself. Floridablanca, bent on retrieving Gibraltar, insisted on this move; Vergennes, mindful of the coalition which France under Louis XIV had brought on itself, lacked conviction. He "always laid down the principle," Vergennes pointed out, "that while devoting our efforts to humbling England, we must carefully avoid giving any impression that we are seeking her destruction. She is necessary to the balance of Europe, wherein she occupies a considerable place. . . ." [11] Nevertheless, in March 1779 he agreed to a plan of campaign by a combined fleet of thirty French sail of the line and twenty Spanish against Portsmouth and Plymouth, the two principal naval bases on the south coast of England. The destruction of these bases was to be followed by an army of invasion intended to frighten the British government into making peace on terms dictated by the two Bourbon powers.

Belatedly the French fleet sailed from Brest in early June, to rendezvous with the Spanish off Corunna. But the Spanish were even more tardy, and the armada, sixty-six sail of the line strong, did not sight Plymouth, its second objective, until the middle of August. Against it was a British fleet of thirty sail of the line, which was blown off course by a gale carrying it far to the west. The two fleets failed to meet, nor did the projected attack on Plymouth and Portsmouth ever take place. On the Spanish and French vessels a raging epidemic of putrid fever and smallpox broke out and, suffering too from a scarcity of fresh water and provisions, the armada limped back to Brest in September. Meanwhile an invasion force of 31,000 combat troops had been assembled under the command of the experienced comte de Rochambeau at the ports between Le Havre and St. Malo, and five hundred vessels brought together awaiting intelligence of the expected successes of the armada. Practice landings were made repeatedly through the hot summer months, while food supplies rotted and cannon and ammunition had to

---

[11] A. Temple Patterson, *The Other Armada. The Franco-Spanish Attempt to Invade Britain in 1779*, Manchester, Eng., 1960, p. 227 and passim.

be put ashore for storage. The whole project collapsed in disgrace, to the great good fortune of Britain who was ill-prepared to meet the onslaught.

It is surprising how little the Americans in France knew of this elaborate expedition and how indifferently they behaved toward it both before and after the event. Vergennes's secret was well kept; even the ardent Lafayette who volunteered for the invasion withheld the information from his American friends. John Adams sailed for home on a French frigate from Brest in June, but appears to have been unaware of what was going on. Adams had as his traveling companions the Chevalier de la Luzerne, who was going out to replace Gérard, and Barbé Marbois, who was serving as Luzerne's secretary. Marbois, "one of the best informed, and most reflecting men I have known in France," partially revealed the secret after the ship had left port; but, characteristically, Adams felt jealous because the Bourbon allies omitted from their plans all reference to American independence.[12] Luzerne, who had drafted the plan for attacking Plymouth, told Adams nothing about it during the entire voyage.

Even the usually observant Franklin suspected little. In May he was still hoping for a French expedition against Halifax and Quebec, but it was only two weeks later that he heard vague rumors of something important about to happen in Europe during the summer. In spite of disagreeable relations with Arthur Lee and his friends, the old gentleman was thoroughly enjoying himself in Paris. The French, he told Josiah Quincy, were "a most amiable nation to live with" and were free of any national vice. "This is the civilest nation upon earth," he exclaimed and then proceeded to go overboard for the French ladies, who were all kindness and affection: they disliked being kissed, he told his niece, but they had "a thousand other ways of rendering themselves agreeable; by their various attentions and civilities and their sensible conversation. 'Tis a delightful people to live with." [13] In spite of the fiasco of the attempt on

---

[12] *Adams Papers*, II, pp. 387–388.
[13] Smyth, VII, nos. 993 and 1045.

Britain, Franklin by now was leaning heavily on France and looking to Spain for additional assistance. Meanwhile the Congress had learned of the invasion plans from Gérard, Vergennes telling the minister to warn the Americans against accepting any new peace offers from the British. But the intelligence aroused little interest, and later advices of the expedition's failure drew no reaction.

How is such lack of concern explained? The armada was comparable to the famous one of 1588; and had it achieved its objective, it would have altered the whole international complex. France and Spain would have been the controlling powers. Since they had ignored the Americans in making and executing their plans, it is a foregone conclusion that they would not have brought them to the peace table in the event of a Bourbon victory. The alliance with France which the Americans prized so highly would have become a nullity. While these great events in Europe were occurring, the situation in America was going from bad to worse. Affected by the depreciating currency and other problems, Washington privately confessed he feared collapse. Letters to Thomas Jefferson, the governor of Virginia, reflect the same sort of pessimism. Anti-French feeling was building up in the country, committees on peace were springing up, and opposition to the New England fishery interest was becoming vocal in the other colonies. Rumors reached Jefferson of an insurrection pending on the Virginia frontier, and he issued orders for drastic action at the first sign of an outbreak.[14] These several anxieties preying on the minds of the patriot leaders furnish at least a partial explanation of their neglect of the European theater.

But paradoxical as it undoubtedly was, a swelling sense of national pride coupled with a feeling of satisfaction over the prestige of being allied with France buoyed up the American leaders. Preoccupied with their own ambitions, they remained

---

[14] Washington to Jay, May 10, 1779, and Holker to Luzerne, Jan. 10, 1780, Wharton, III, pp. 163, 455–456, Jefferson to Fleming, May 22, Fleming to Jefferson, May 22, June 22, and July 13, 1779, Cyrus to Jefferson, July 13, 1779, P. Henry to Jefferson, Feb. 15 and Jefferson to G. R. Clark, Mar. 19, 1780, *Jefferson Papers*, II, pp. 267–269, 288–289; III, pp. 10–11, 32–35, 316–317.

inattentive to the armada and its significance. Whether it won or lost does not seem to have mattered to them, and when the armada did break up, neither France nor Spain lost prestige in the eyes of the Americans. John Adams, who arrived home after enjoying the company of Luzerne across the Atlantic, was positive in his belief that America would soon hold a great position among the powers of the world. Evidently Luzerne exerted considerable influence on Adams during the voyage, convincing him that France, "our august ally," put great stress on winning American independence, and that the French again occupied, to the advantage of America, a central position of power and influence in Europe. Adams was certain that the United States would have Canada, Nova Scotia, and the Floridas, although he could not have gotten such ideas from the very adroit French minister who took pains, shortly after his arrival, to discourage the Americans from dreams of conquest. Adams believed that Prussia would follow the French lead and, with King Frederick taking us by the hand, as he put it, Holland, the rich usurer of Europe, could be induced to make loans. In a long communication addressed to the Congress, Adams got so lost in his own logic that he saw the whole European constellation changed as a result of the American war. He wrote off Britain as "a great wide, spreading tree that has been girdled at the root"; Austria would "seize with eagerness" the advantages of close relations with America; while Russia and the Scandinavian powers showed signs of hostility toward Britain.[15] In short, it seemed to Adams that America would fall heir to the wealth and maritime trade that Britain had enjoyed formerly.

When, at the beginning of 1780, he found himself again in Europe armed with power to negotiate peace with the British government, Adams held to the same view. America would rise to greatness through the aid that France and Spain, in their own interest, would send. Spending some weeks in the northwest part of Spain, where he landed first, he enjoyed the attentions and curiosity the Spaniards showed him although, incredible as it may seem, his papers indicate that he had not

[15] To the president of congress, Aug. 4, 1779, Wharton, III, pp. 278–286.

even heard of the armada and its fate. When asked when the war would end, he replied when the French and Spanish kings sent a fleet of twenty or thirty sail of the line to reinforce d'Estaing and enable him to take all the British forces and possessions in America. To the president of the Congress he expressed his hope for a solid treaty of alliance with Spain; and from Paris he reported his satisfaction that a fleet of seventeen sail of the line under Admiral Guichen had already left for the West Indies and that a convoy with clothing and arms for 15,000 men was about to sail for America.[16] Adams's instructions and the tone he now assumed in France betrayed his belief that he would supersede Franklin at the court of Versailles, Franklin's enemies, particularly the Lees and Ralph Izard, were intriguing against him in Philadelphia, and the old gentleman was beginning to feel the effects. Arthur Lee, he confided to a younger acquaintance, who kept him informed, was "the most malicious enemy I ever had"; and as for John Adams, Franklin observed that:

We live upon good terms with each other, but he had never communicated anything of his business to me and I have made no inquiries of him, nor have I any letter from Congress explaining it, so that I am in utter ignorance. Indeed, the Congress seems very backward in writing to me.[17]

Franklin, however, kept the favor of the French court; he was prudent and tactful in his relations with Vergennes. Knowing that everything depended on France, he was sensible about the danger of riding a free horse to death, as he told a Boston friend who was writing pro-French articles for the benefit of the American public. Amidst the war's stalemate and the uncontrollable inflation that had now set in in America, Franklin feared that expressions of impatience and even of hostility toward the French would bring on a sharp reaction in France. The king, he told Samuel Huntington, takes pleasure in reflect-

---

[16] *Adams Papers*, II, pp. 408, 411–434; and to president of congress, Feb. 15 and 19, 1780, Wharton, III, pp. 494–495, 504–506.
[17] To Carmichael, Mar. 31, 1780, Wharton, III, pp. 585–587.

ing on his benevolence toward an oppressed people. The court should be treated with decency and delicacy. But this was not Adams's way. When Congress devalued the dollar at the rate of forty for one and French merchants complained over the losses they faced accordingly, Adams informed Vergennes that they would have to take their medicine. This angered the foreign minister, whose complaints Franklin answered with soothing language; and at the end of June 1780 Vergennes told Adams he was bored with his arguments and would deal thereafter exclusively with Franklin. The king, he told the latter, expected the Congress to reconsider its decision, for it should "know how to prize those marks of favor" he had constantly shown the Americans.[18]

Adams now left for Amsterdam to see whether he could pry a loan from the Dutch bankers: he fancied the prospect of more trade with America would appeal to them and that, with a Dutch loan secured, the Americans would not be so dependent on France. The Committee of Foreign Affairs had already dispatched John Laurens for this purpose; the United States was now hopelessly in arrears in its payments and a foreign loan offered the only possible escape from bankruptcy. Meanwhile Franklin, much relieved by Adams's departure from Paris, complied with Vergennes's request, although his act could be no more than a gesture. The Congress had long since resorted to the practice of drawing bills on him for payment to the merchants and for meeting the expenses and salaries of its other agents in Europe; and Franklin's only recourse in turn was to get the money from his wealthy French friends, notably from Le Ray Chaumont, and from the French Treasury direct.

Added to these many embarrassments were recurrent attacks of the gout, which sometimes kept him confined to the house for as much as six weeks at a time. Franklin's supreme gift was his sense of humor, which he could on occasion turn on himself, as a satirical dialogue between himself and the Gout

---

[18] Franklin to S. Cooper, Mar. 16, to J. Ross, Apr. 22, to S. Huntington, Aug. 9, 1780, Smyth, VIII, nos. 1091, 1103, 1139 and 1144; Vergennes to Adams, June 21 and 30, Adams to Vergennes, June 22, 1780, Wharton, III, pp. 805–816, 824–828.

which he wrote for his own amusement will testify.[19] These troubles, whatever their cause, gave Arthur Lee, whom Vergennes had barred from court, a fresh opportunity to report on the old gentleman's morals. "The truth is," Lee told the Congress, "that Dr. Franklin is now much advanced in years, more devoted to pleasure than would become even a young man in his station, and neglectful of the public business."[20] John Adams assumed an equally lofty view of Franklin's private life, but ironically Vergennes was not similarly impressed. The minister seems to have had a special regard for Franklin; for the other American agents, he had none at all.

Basically, however, Franklin no longer possessed the initiative. Conrad Alexandre Gérard had it when he boarded d'Estaing's flagship for Philadelphia in April 1778. As undersecretary of foreign affairs, Gérard had been influential in steering France toward intervention in the war. Now, as the king's first minister to the United States, he dealt directly with the Congress and its committees, his prime object being to guide that body in such a way as to insure that it keep in step with France. Gérard was the welcome ally of the militant leaders of the Revolution, who rejected out of hand the British peace offer and reiterated their determination to see the war through to victory. To men like Washington, Jefferson, Lee, and Henry Laurens, who had slammed the door in the faces of the British peace commissioners, the boost that the French minister was able to give to the faltering morale of the Americans was most helpful.

In spite of d'Estaing's failures, Gérard convinced the doubting that France would sustain the cause of independence. This was a rudiment of French policy: if the British efforts at reconciliation succeeded, or if the Americans became so fainthearted and divided among themselves as to negotiate a separate peace, France would suffer a disastrous setback. Gérard stiffened the Congress to render void the generous terms that Gates had granted Burgoyne's army at Saratoga; and he launched a

---

[19] Vergennes to Adams, July 29, and to Franklin, July 31; Franklin to president of congress and Adams to same, Aug. 9, 1780, Wharton, IV, pp. 16–19, 21–25, 29–32. See also Smyth, VIII, no. 1159.
[20] Lee to president of congress, Dec. 7, 1780, Wharton, IV, pp. 182–186.

propaganda program, which his successor extended, of hiring certain American writers to publish articles favorable to France and the French alliance. The Reverend Dr. Samuel Cooper of the important Brattle Street Congregational Church of Boston accepted a stipend of £200 sterling per year and, according to Franklin, did yeoman service in promoting the alliance. Tom Paine was subsequently rewarded with cash payments too, although his contribution seems to have been of little value.[21]

Gérard proved himself a most effective diplomat. He was personally committed to American independence, although he skillfully avoided entanglement in the factional quarrels in the Congress and gave no encouragement to the schemes of conquest that emanated chiefly from New England. The American position deteriorated steadily during his mission, currency depreciation becoming so bad by May 1779 that it was feared that the dollar would lose all value and the army would consequently break up. A rumor that Gérard was giving up and going home caused deep alarm. Washington thought it would have a most serious effect, and Jefferson deplored the possibility as a "most dreadful calamity."[22] A law passed in Virginia at Jefferson's instigation, confiscating and providing for the sale of British-owned property, helped temporarily to relieve the financial crisis in that state; but the only ultimate recourse was a large French loan, which Gérard was unable to promise. On the contrary, he twice warned the Congress against a separate peace and against expecting from France more than the treaty required. Aware of Vergennes's anxiety for a Spanish alliance, he told the Congress it must come to terms with Spain which would attract that power into the war; otherwise the Americans would get no further French naval support.[23]

---

[21] Franklin to Cooper, Mar. 16, 1780, Smyth, VIII, no. 1091; Meng. *op. cit.*, pp. 91–122; William Emmett O'Donnell, *The Chevalier de La Luzerne, French Minister to the United States 1779–1784*, Bruges et Louvain, 1938, ch. II.

[22] Washington to Jay, May 10, 1779, Wharton, III, p. 163; Jefferson to Fleming, June 8, 1779, *Jefferson Papers*, II, pp. 288–289.

[23] May 22 and 27, and Lovell to J. Adams, June 13, 1779, Wharton, III, pp. 175–178, 194–195, 220–221.

Gérard's success was matched by that of Luzerne, who came over to replace him in August 1779, just as the Franco-Spanish armada was making its bootless attempt on England. In spite of their jealousies toward one another, all three of the American commissioners in Paris sang praises to the new French envoy, who had an impressive military, but comparatively slight diplomatic background in Europe. Both in Boston and at West Point, where he interviewed Washington, Luzerne learned from the Americans of their impatience for another attempt on Canada and Nova Scotia, but he turned the subject in favor of a Spanish alliance. Arthur Lee, with his customary enthusiasm, had already urged this step on Congress and, under Gérard's prodding, that body decided on making Spain an offer just about the time that Luzerne arrived in Philadelphia.[24]

The possibility of a Spanish alliance, however, raised questions on which the French had not had to commit themselves. One party in the Congress, led by John Dickinson, proposed that both France and Spain pledge their support in the acquisition of Canada, Nova Scotia, the Bermudas, and the Floridas, although it signified its willingness to concede the Floridas and the navigation of the Mississippi, if the Spanish insisted, in exchange for the other conquests. Another party, readier to bargain realistically, moved that the United States offer to aid in recovering the Floridas for Spain. The final decision, which appeared in the instructions to John Jay who agreed to undertake the mission, showed a disposition to ask more from Spain than to give. The Spaniards might take the Floridas on their own, provided they promised free navigation of the Mississippi; Jay was to try especially for a port or ports on the river below the thirty-first parallel; and he was to solicit a subsidy, or at least a loan, so that the United States could carry on the war.[25] Franklin in Paris shared this optimism; in spite of the costly failure of the armada, he was asking the French for a new and a very large shipment of supplies and the ministers, he said, were extremely well disposed. Moreover, he hoped for Spanish assistance, which French influence would succeed in extracting.

---

[24] *Ibid.*, pp. 171–173, 318–322.
[25] *Ibid.*, pp. 310–312, 332, 352–353.

"My sole dependence now," he confessed, "is upon this Court. . . ." [26]

Meanwhile the new French diplomat, the Chevalier de la Luzerne, was expertly taking over the job left by Gérard in Philadelphia. France and Spain meant to carry on, he informed a secret committee of the Congress, and to maintain a superiority at sea. It was up to the Americans to strengthen their army and to get ready for the spring campaign. If the stalemate was not broken and the British were not dislodged from their positions on American soil, it would be extremely difficult to win independence from them. Luzerne was already familiar with the sectional divergencies among the states, and when the members from the northeast raised the question of using a French fleet against Nova Scotia, he avoided an answer by suggesting that the Americans would do better to expel the British from their own soil first. France, he hinted, would send supplies and some ships, but what force, he asked, could the Americans assemble in the field? The Congress pledged 25,000 effectives in addition to the militia, but warned that practically all the supplies and stores would have to come from France.[27]

Then Luzerne advised the Congress of the need to conclude an alliance with Spain and, without saying so directly, he implied that France endorsed the terms the Spanish would impose, namely, the United States to be confined to the seaboard east of the Alleghenies and to have no access to the Mississippi, and Spain to have a free hand in reconquering the Floridas.[28] This brought an immediate reaction from the members representing the southern and middle states, with some support from the northeast. Tempers rose high, one delegate declaring that France, in making the alliance, committed itself to the United States' having everything that was formerly British. At this point Luzerne thought it discreet to terminate the meeting with a recommendation that the delegates practice moderation. Fiscal

---

[26] To John Jay, Oct. 4, 1779, Smyth, VII, no. 1044.
[27] Luzerne to Vergennes, Jan. 25, Feb. 7 and 11, 1780, AAE cp Etats Unis 11, no. 33, ff. 88–113 and no. 53, ff. 184–206.
[28] Luzerne to president of congress, Jan. 25 and Feb. 2; answer of congress, Jan. 31, 1780, Wharton, III, pp. 469, 483–486, 488–490.

weakness, a military stalemate, unrest, and threats of mutiny in Washington's dwindling army, all fostered a sense of helplessness and frustration in this country; and if the United States collapsed, France too would suffer a decisive setback.[29]

American envoys abroad in the meantime kept sending encouraging reports. De Guichen's departure for the West Indies was noted. John Adams was certain the French court meant business: it would supply arms and clothing to equip 15,000 men and would extend the war at sea. William Carmichael, who had gone out with John Jay to Spain, reported on the cordial support the French ambassador was giving him in Madrid. Franklin wrote of French fidelity to the alliance, reinvigorated by Lafayette who had again returned to Paris and who was very popular and influential.

The war too showed signs of spreading in Europe, to Britain's increasing disadvantage: the Dutch were restive over British interference with their prosperous carrying trade with the Baltic countries; and in March 1780 the Empress Catherine of Russia, whose favor the British government had been courting, decided that Russian interests lay more with the other shipping nations of northern Europe. By endorsing the legal principle of "free ships free goods," which the Americans had also been pushing for the advantage of their commercial contacts with Britain's rivals, Catherine dealt a blow at British warfare at sea. But of most immediate importance to the Americans was the intelligence first sent by John Adams on February 27 of a new French armament in preparation at Brest, consisting of eight or ten ships of the line with land forces of six or eight thousand men commanded by the comte de Rochambeau. The expedition was intended for overseas, but whether for the West Indies or for service on the mainland Adams did not know and, he added, "at present it ought not to be known." [30]

---

[29] See D. S. Freeman, *Washington*, V, pp. 132–167.
[30] Adams to president of congress, Feb. 15 and 27, to S. Adams, Feb. 23; Carmichael to president of congress, Feb. 19; Franklin to Huntington, Mar. 4, 1780, Wharton, III, pp. 494–495, 507, 513–514, 524–527; and see Isabel de Madariaga, *Britain, Russia and the Armed Neutrality of 1780*, London, 1962, passim.

Actually the French ministry was planning just such an expedition for America, giving it thought even before Luzerne had left on his mission. Lafayette's personal influence, seconded by Gérard, may have decided the matter; Lafayette was still in Paris and was having talks with Vergennes on the subject. The French had failed miserably in their war plans of the preceding summer, they were aware of the dangers of an American collapse, and, prompted by Lafayette's admiration for Washington and zeal for war against England, the ministry may have concluded that America was the one theater which held out some hope of success. Whatever the origins of the project—no record is apparently to be found—Vergennes dispatched a message to Luzerne on the fifth of February, telling of the preparations and saying that the expedition would sail as soon as possible. As the minister put it, the intention was to encourage the Americans and bind them closely to the alliance. The troops were to be employed as auxiliaries to Washington's force, and Lafayette was to go ahead to make the necessary arrangements. The expedition was to be limited to six ships of the line and five thousand troops, and its destination was to be Rhode Island which the British had by now evacuated. Luzerne was given the discretion of revealing the secret if he thought it wise, and of emphasizing that the purpose was to stimulate the Americans to redouble their own efforts to win the war, but not to pursue dreams of conquering Canada or Nova Scotia. The French force, moreover, was not large enough to embolden schemes of aggression.[31]

The expedition sailed from Brest on May 2, trailing a Spanish armament twice its size ordered for action in the West Indies. From Madrid Carmichael sent a warning that Spain meant to exclude every other nation from the Mississippi and indeed from the Gulf of Mexico. This meant that the Spaniards intended to recapture the Floridas.[32] John Adams, still in Paris, com-

---

[31] Lafayette to Vergennes, Feb. 2; Vergennes to Luzerne, Feb. 5, and to Lafayette, Feb. 24 and Mar. 5, 1780. AAE cp Etats Unis no. 46, ff. 163–170; no. 62, ff. 219–222, 234–238, and BN, NA, ff. 157–168, 256–277. See also: William B. Wilcox, "Rhode Island in British Strategy, 1780–1781," *Journ. Mod. Hist.*, XVII (1945), pp. 304–331, and *Hamilton Papers*, II, p. 179.
[32] To Committee of Foreign Affairs, May 28, 1780, Wharton, III, pp. 736–739.

plained privately that both the French and the Spanish were missing their opportunities. Their "true" interests were to furnish the Americans with a handsome loan or even a subsidy, and to send a fleet into American waters that would "lay the axe at the British tree."

Adams was nothing if not sure of himself, and since he was reading the debates in Parliament and taking note of the desires of Hartley and others for a cease fire and a truce, he enjoyed setting them up as straw men whom he could knock down with his logic. Britain was "that little island" who would be "our natural and habitual enemy." America, according to Adams, had only sought the alliance with France "reluctantly," but it was "natural" and "perpetual," and the Spanish and French should join hands in punishing the English. Portugal, that "little impotent morsel of a state," should be punished too for being helpful to its British ally; and, asked Adams, why were the Bourbon powers so lethargic in allowing the annual homeward bound British convoys from the West Indies to pass? This trade "is every year exposed, yet every year escapes; by which means they [the English] get spirits to indulge their passions, money to raise millions, and men to man their ships."

To Esmé Jacques Genet, who was writing propaganda articles in London, Adams addressed long communications intended to convince the English public that there was no possibility of compromise. And "independence" to Adams meant the incorporation of all British territory in North America and American commercial ascendancy at sea. America, he declared pompously in spite of his admission that success rested with France, "has taken her equal station, and she will behave with as much honor as any of the nations of the earth. . . . The Americans at this day have higher notions of themselves than ever. They think they have gone through the greatest revolution that ever took place among men; that this revolution is as much for the generality of mankind in Europe as for their own. . . ." [33] By

---

[33] Adams to Carmichael, Apr. 8 and May 12; to Jay, May 13 and 15; to Genet, Apr. 29, May 9 and 17; to Digges, May 13; and to president of congress, May 20, 1780. *Ibid.*, pp. 603–604, 666–667, 672–674, 676–677, 685–688, 693–695, 752–758.

this time Adams was making himself obnoxious to Vergennes, whose abrupt note of dismissal forced him to leave Paris for Amsterdam.

Meanwhile Luzerne and Lafayette, who had returned to America at the end of April, were able to give the Americans advance intelligence of the relief expedition coming from France. Apparently, however, they did not stress the relative smallness of the French force, since Washington, his own army now literally at starvation's door, immediately began to think of the superiority at sea that the French might obtain all the way from the West Indies to Nova Scotia. The American leader was especially concerned with the destruction of Halifax—" a matter of infinite importance" which, once accomplished, would render "the support of the enemy's marine in those seas and in the West Indies exceedingly difficult and precarious." The exuberant Lafayette may even have led his friend astray, for Washington went on to say: "Our very good friends and allies have it much at heart and view the reduction of Halifax as a matter of great consequence, as being the arsenal of support to the enemy's fleet in these seas and in the West Indies." [34] This was precisely what Vergennes had taken pains to discourage; and Luzerne, who dealt with the Congress, was properly cautious, advising that body merely to lay its plans for the spring campaign and to name a committee to act with Washington in arranging a reception of the French force. Lafayette, it is plain to see, was prone to let his enthusiasm and pride outrun his discretion. In a warm letter to Governor Reed of Pennsylvania, he admitted that he had not told the French court and the French generals how poorly manned and equipped the American Army really was.[35]

The French, when they arrived at Newport on July 11, were not alone in their surprise at the realities. At the insistence of both Luzerne and Washington, the Congress dispatched a small

---

[34] Washington to General Heath, May 15; to James Bowdoin, May 15; to Luzerne, May 14; Washington Papers. Washington to Jefferson, May 15, *Jefferson Papers*, III, pp. 375–376. Luzerne to president of congress, May 16, 1780, Wharton, III, p. 683.

[35] May 31, 1780, Wharton, III, pp. 746–747.

committee to army headquarters to concert measures for cooperation with the expected expedition. Although Washington had informed the Congress of the situation, the committee was not prepared for what it found. Food supplies depended entirely on contributions from the separate states, from Pennsylvania and Virginia in particular; and both Washington and other responsible men in Congress and in the state governments feared disgrace in the eyes of the French when they should arrive. The country was generally prosperous, but the small army was ill-clad and without bread and meat for often five or six days at a time. America really possessed the means to expel the enemy, commented the committee on June 12, but the situation demanded "a display of that virtue which distinguished the Citizens of Rome when their State was, as ours now is, on the brink of ruin. . . ." [36]

By this time Sir Henry Clinton's important victory over the Americans at Charleston, South Carolina, was known. It took twenty-four days for the news to travel north to Virginia, almost as long as it took to reach Paris. The way was now open for the British to end the war by means of a pincer movement between Charleston and New York, relying primarily on the Royal Navy to dominate the coast and focusing on Chesapeake Bay where, the distance between the mountains and the sea being the narrowest, they might "clamp a tourniquet on the artery of American supplies." [37] The arrival of Rochambeau and the small French fleet at Rhode Island, which the British had shortsightedly evacuated the year before, softened the blow to American morale and somewhat damaged British prospects for controlling the sea. At least Sir Henry Clinton feared so, although Admiral Sir Thomas Graves with six ships of the line reached New York on the thirteenth of July and easily cancelled out the advantage temporarily gained by the French. Personal

---

[36] Washington to Reed, May 28 and June 5; to his brother, July 6, Washington Papers. Huntington to Jefferson, May 19; Madison to Jefferson, June 2; the committee to Jefferson, June 12, 1780, *Jefferson Papers*, III, pp. 378, 411, 434–436. See also Freeman, *op. cit.*, V, pp. 143–167.

[37] Jefferson to Huntington, June 9, 1780, *Jefferson Papers*, III, pp. 425–427. The quoted phrase is William B. Willcox's, "The British Road to Yorktown: a study in divided command," *Amer. Hist. Rev.*, LII (Oct., 1946), pp. 1–35.

friction inside the British command, tardiness in establishing dominance over Chesapeake Bay, and finally the rash action of Cornwallis in taking his army inland from Charleston and losing contact with his base of supplies led ultimately to the surrender at Yorktown instead of to the quick suppression of the rebellion as Clinton had hoped.[38]

The fall of Charleston created a tremendous impression in Europe, sobered in London, however, by the outrages committed by mobs in the Lord George Gordon riots of June 1780. Franklin in Paris showed his glee over the destruction wrought by these lawless mobs, and looked to the new league of neutrals in northern Europe, initiated by the Empress Catherine of Russia, to make more trouble for Britain. Everything in Europe, Franklin commented, wore a new face, with all the powers raising naval forces for use against British interference with their trade. Catherine conceived of the league as an instrument for extending Russian trade and influence in Europe, an objective which she accomplished. But whereas her action was a diplomatic defeat for Britain, it resulted in no benefits for the Americans. Meanwhile, temporarily upset by the news of Charleston, John Adams soon became as cocksure as ever. To separate America from Britain was an object of more importance to France and Spain than any concessions they might extract from Britain. Hence, America need stand in no fear of being deserted.[39]

But John Jay and William Carmichael in Madrid had a different story. Floridablanca had stopped payment on Jay's bills until the American envoy submitted to Spanish demands regarding the Mississippi, and Jay was reduced to writing Vergennes personally begging for financial relief. News of the American surrender of Charleston had an effect "as visible the next day as that of a hard night's frost on young leaves." Jay wanted to buy clothing to supply ten American regiments, and

---

[38] Washington to Jefferson, July 18 and Aug. 14, 1780, *Jefferson Papers*, III, pp. 489–490, 547–549; Willcox, *op. cit.*

[39] Philip Mazzei to Jefferson, June 22, *Jefferson Papers,* III, p. 458; Franklin to Jay, June 13, to Carmichael, June 17, to Dumas, June 22, Smyth, VIII, nos. 1123, 1126, 1129; Adams to president of congress, Aug. 23, 1780, Wharton, IV, pp. 41–42.

needed a loan of £100,000, but neither the Spanish foreign minister nor the merchant Gardoqui was responsive. Not a single nail would drive. Both of the Spaniards made exclusive possession of the Gulf of Mexico and navigation of the Mississippi their conditions before they would negotiate.[40]

France was the one power to whom the Americans could look with some hope, but Rochambeau's expedition was too small to be of much use, and the Americans in September fell back on fresh appeals to Versailles for a larger and stronger force. Through Luzerne Washington pleaded with Admiral de Guichen at Martinique to send more ships. A land force, he said, might help if it came with the fleet. It would boost morale at a time when his own army was being starved for lack of recruits. Then, addressing the French minister, Washington wrote:

I need use no arguments to convince your excellency of the extremity to which our affairs are tending and the necessity of support. You are an eye witness to all our perplexities and all our wants. You know the dangerous consequences of leaving the enemy in quiet possession of their southern conquests, either for negotiation this winter or a continuance of the war. You know our inability to expel them, or perhaps even to stop their career.

The Congress made a similar confession in an address to the king of France, and accompanied it with an appeal for another loan.[41]

By this time Franklin's enemies in Philadelphia had mustered so much strength that they were able to dispatch a new minister to Versailles, but Vergennes, burdened with financial embarrassments and his patience wearing thin, sent back a rebuke through Luzerne, flatly declaring that Franklin alone would be given attention. The Congress must absolutely refrain from its exorbitant demands, he said, "you must speak in a peremptory manner." But Franklin was able in March 1781 to get from

---

[40] Jay to Vergennes, Sept. 22; to Franklin, Oct. 30; to president of congress, Nov. 6; Carmichael to Committee of Foreign Affairs, Sept. 25 and Nov. 28, 1780. Wharton, IV, pp. 63–66, 69–72, 108–109, 112–150, 164–168.

[41] Sept. 12, Nov. 22, 1780, *ibid.*, pp. 54–55, 157–160; and see also Hamilton to Duane, Sept. 3, and to J. Laurens, Sept. 12, Washington to Franklin, Oct. 9, 1780, *Hamilton Papers*, II, pp. 411, 428, 457.

the king a free gift of six million livres, in addition to a previous subsidy of three million. Even John Adams was impressed.
The Dutch had been cold to his bid for a loan, and he believed
they were holding back waiting for Spain to act. "If only
America could dissemble enough to threaten other nations with
a return to Great Britain," he complained, "they would be
ready to hang themselves to prevent it. But America is too
honest and sincere to play this game. England would have all
the mountains of Mexico and Peru in a few years if America
should join her. . . ." Then Adams characteristically thought of
something better: after receiving this "noble aid" from France,
America would soon have the power to tax all Europe whenever it pleased by imposing export duties large enough to pay
the interest on foreign loans.[42]

This myopic view of "national interest," central to Adams's
mentality, drew from Franklin a cool reply. But Adams was
hardly the man to keep a check on his own egoism. Snubbed
by the Dutch, he taunted them with lack of courage. "The
military character," he affirmed, "is lost out of this nation. The
love of fame, the desire of glory, the love of country, the regard
for posterity, in short all the brilliant and sublime passions are
lost, and succeeded by nothing but the love of ease and money.
. . ." Soon after this outburst he was praising the British
merchants for their wisdom in keeping up their trade with the
Americans in spite of the war. Vast quantities of British goods
were reaching America via the Netherlands, France, and even
Sweden, and, in contrast to the Germans, the Dutch, the French,
and the Spaniards, the British merchants were still ready to sell
on credit. "Any American merchant by going over to London
obtains a credit," Adams reported. "The language of the London
merchants to the American merchants is 'Let us understand one
another and let the governments squabble'." [43]

Adams, however, saw no inconsistency between this sentiment and his desire for a grand coalition of the powers against

---

[42] To Luzerne, Feb. 14; Franklin to president of congress, Mar. 12; Adams
to Franklin, Apr. 16 and May 8, 1781. Wharton, IV, 256, 281, 363–364,
403–404.
[43] Adams to president of congress, June 26, 1781. *Ibid.*, pp. 450, 520–522.

Britain, out of which America would extract the maximum advantage. Grasping the significance of the Empress Catherine's move in putting Russia at the head of the European neutrals, the Congress had commissioned Adams's secretary, Francis Dana, to seek recognition and membership in the Armed Neutrality. Under Adams's prodding, Dana finally started from Holland on a long circuitous journey to St. Petersburg. Diplomatic support from France was much to be desired, but Vergennes would not give it. Dana reached the Russian capital at the end of August, and found himself treated hospitably. "This is the finest city I have seen in Europe," he observed, "and far surpassess all my expectations. Alone, it is sufficient to immortalize the memory of Peter the First." But Catherine had calculated her move of the previous year to advance Russian prestige. She had no intention of giving the Dutch armed assistance, and Dana stood no chance of being received at court.[44]

In America meanwhile hopes were riveted to the interests of the two Bourbon powers. Austrian and Russian mediation, basically preferential toward Britain, rested on the assumption that the British might retain possession of the ports on the Atlantic seaboard then under their control. But a peace based on the principle of *uti possidetis* did not suit the minimum requirements of France and Spain: it left their major enemy in the dominant position in North America. Under pressure from Robert Morris, who judged that France could no longer carry the financial load, the Congress showed a disposition to turn to Spain. Relinquishment of the claim to the navigation of the Mississippi, it was felt, would induce the Spanish to agree to an alliance and furnish badly needed specie to bolster American credit. Morris, having been made superintendent of finance, in July 1781, outlined his plans for a national bank for the benefit of the governor of Havana and appealed to him to send four hundred thousand Mexican dollars immediately for deposit. America presented the curious spectacle of an affluent society

---

[44] Instructions to Dana, Dec. 19, 1780; Adams to Dana, Apr. 18; Dana to president of congress, Apr. 4 and July 28, and to Adams, Aug. 28, 1781. *Ibid.*, pp. 201–203, 349–351, 368–370, 610–613, 679–681; Madariaga, *op. cit.*

which depended on foreign loans and credits to support the war, but its currency situation had again become so chaotic that only reasons of state could motivate foreign governments in extending further favors. The devaluation of 1780 had had only a temporary effect in arresting the decline of the dollar.[45]

Morris still harbored the illusion that Spain, whose reserves in specie were greater than those of any other European state, could be lured into an alliance with promises of conquest. With a cash subsidy direct from Havana, America could help the Spaniards to take the Floridas, the Bahamas, and perhaps even Jamaica. The Americans themselves could take Nova Scotia, which would give them control of the supply of masts and ship's timber which the Spaniards would be eager to buy. The Americans could then expel the British from the fisheries, and the Spaniards could oust them from the Gulf of Mexico. A New Order could then be erected on the basis of a close trading alliance between Spain and the United States.[46] Spain, however, having previously made known her opposition to American expansion, remained unresponsive, and Morris never received his hoped-for deposit from Havana.

France was the only hope, but the French like the Spanish were unmoved by repetitious American arguments for conquest. Rochambeau's force had been kept purposely small, so small as to raise questions about its utility value. Rochambeau himself reported to Versailles that, when he first arrived at Newport, he awoke little enthusiasm until he told the Americans he would be followed by a larger force. They wanted 20,000 men and twenty ships of the line, and he concurred that such a force would be required to evict the British from New York. He admitted, however, that France would have to bear all of the expense, the Americans not possessing the means to provision or arm the troops. This intelligence frightened Versailles and was at least partly responsible for the decision against sending any more troops.[47] Nor would the French grant any more

---

[45] Huntington to Jay, May 28; Morris to Huntington, July 9, and to governor of Havana, July 17, 1781. *Ibid.*, pp. 451–453, 555–556, 578.

[46] Morris to Jay, July 4, 1781. *Ibid.*, pp. 531–539.

[47] BN NA, ff. 171–181.

credits. The six million livres advanced to Franklin in March were gone before John Laurens reached Paris, and Vergennes "exclaimed vehemently against the exorbitance of our demands. Argument and expostulation on our part were fruitless." France's own credit was strained to the breaking point, and the French had no confidence in the way the Americans had managed their finances. "I used every argument of national interest," reported Laurens, but to no avail.[48]

Meanwhile Vergennes had committed himself to obtaining naval superiority over the British in the West Indies; and in sending Admiral de Grasse with a fleet of twenty sail of the line to reinforce Guichen, discretionary power was given to extend operations northward into American waters if desirable. In May Washington, having been disappointed in not receiving the necessary strength from France with which to take the offensive against New York, begged Luzerne to persuade de Grasse to come to his assistance. De Grasse agreed, since active campaigning in West Indian waters during the summer months was out of the question. By the middle of October, the Admiral stipulated, he would return to his base at Martinique to look after French interests in conjunction with the Spanish.

With this encouragement, Washington put in a second plea for French land forces to supplement Rochambeau's men; and Luzerne, alert to the political opportunity and to the strategic advantage of occupying Chesapeake Bay before the British got it, urged the admiral of the squadron at Newport to move his ships to the great bay. Taking the British admirals by surprise, de Grasse moved his entire fleet, twenty-eight sail of the line, with four thousand troops on board, thereby exposing the French West Indies. This massive force, joined by the smaller one from Rhode Island, occupied the Chesapeake on August 30, and the British found themselves outnumbered and outmaneuvered both on land and sea. Cornwallis, aware of the enemy in the bay, made no effort to retreat through Virginia but remained passive behind his trenches at Yorktown while the four thousand French from the West Indies disembarked to join the combined army brought south from the Hudson

---

[48] Laurens to president of congress, Sept. 2, 1781. Wharton, IV, pp. 685–688.

River by Washington and Lafayette. Robert Morris in Philadelphia took in the situation by the seventh of September, and wrote Franklin his belief that a victory was near. Down to this point the war seemed to be hopelessly deadlocked.

The smaller British fleet under Admiral Graves from New York could not attempt to save Cornwallis without running the risk of itself being trapped inside the bay and losing control of the entire coast and the West Indies as well to the enemy. It chose the lesser of these evils, and Cornwallis surrendered his army of five thousand on October 19. France in the persons of de Grasse, Rochambeau, Lafayette, and the Chevalier de la Luzerne at last came decisively, although somewhat fortuitously, to the rescue of the Americans.[49]

---

[49] Vergennes to Laurens, May 16; Washington to Luzerne, May 23 and June 13; Luzerne to Destouches, May 7; Morris to Franklin, Aug. 28 and Sept. 7, 1781. *Ibid.*, pp. 400–401, 418–419, 428–429, 501–502; Freeman, V, p. 295; Willcox, *op. cit.*; Piers Mackesy, *The War for America, 1775–1783* (Cambridge, Mass., 1964), pp. 413–430.

# CHAPTER VIII

## Maneuvering for Peace

If America is to become substantially independent of Great Britain, let them be independent of France and of all the world.—*David Hartley, M.P., October 29, 1778*

In spite of the disappointments encountered in America, the British peace commission had returned home in October 1778 in good spirits. Rebuffed by the rebel leaders, the commission had nevertheless remained in the country long enough to enable it to size up the situation; and all three of its members felt that, with patience and better management on the British side, the resistance could be overcome. This did not necessarily mean, however, an early end to the war. With France there could be no compromise: the French could never be permitted to dictate the terms between Great Britain and the Americans. William Eden, the undersecretary whose efforts had brought about the commission in the first instance, recounted his experiences and reiterated his faith for the benefit of Parliament during its fall session. While in America, he had talked with a great many persons and he firmly believed that, despite the intransigence of the minority, reconciliation would eventually come about. "We desire you as brothers," he had told the Americans. "We insist only on one king, one friend and one enemy, a free union of force and friendship." But the rebel leaders had replied: "We will have a total and eternal separation from you; we have attached ourselves to your inveterate enemy and to that we adhere." To this Eden had given the only answer: "We must consider you then as Frenchmen; the contest has changed; and so we must prosecute the war." [1]

George Johnstone, Eden's Whig colleague whose experience in America went back many years before the war, furnished details bearing out his own conviction that the majority of Americans were tired of the war, preferred Britain to France, and felt oppressed at the hands of a revolutionary Congress that was itself divided into factions. Johnstone convinced Burke, who was otherwise rather cool toward him, that such was the case. "I do believe," said Burke, "that violent animosities and very ill blood subsist among them [the Americans]." Johnstone, he added, was "the talk of the town." He planned an attack on the ministers and a demand for the impeachment of the Howe brothers for their mismanagement of the war; and he "declares his opinion that the forces now in America, in the present divided and distracted state of that country, are sufficient to subdue them to the acceptance of what he calls 'reasonable terms'." [2]

Johnstone also convinced his brother William Pulteney (they *were* brothers despite the difference in name). Pulteney was both wealthy and independent on the Whig side, and had familiarized himself with Franklin's point of view at the time Parliament was debating the Conciliatory Bills. The bills had at least united public opinion in Britain, he argued. Pulteney envisaged the broadest possible liberties for the Americans reunited with Britain under the same king. Mutual rights of citizenship should be stipulated—a condition on which Hartley had already put great stress—but with the Americans' operating under their own constitutions, they might even escape involvement in Britain's wars. However, peace at the present moment was out of the question: not only had the rebels tied themselves to France, but also in rejecting the British offer, they had revealed ambitions which could not be tolerated. If the war stopped now, the Americans in alliance with the French, would impose the terms. They would not be content with a simple grant of indepen-

---

[1] *PH*, XX, col. 850; William Eden, *Four Letters to the Earl of Carlisle*, Edinburgh, 1779.
[2] Burke to R. Burke, Nov. 20, 1778. *Burke Corresp.*, IV, pp. 28–30.

dence, but would seek to make inroads on Britain's remaining position. They would want Canada, Nova Scotia, the fisheries, the Floridas, even the West Indies. Its enemies thus threatening in so serious a manner, Britain had no choice but to proceed with the utmost vigor.[3]

Influential American loyalists, encouraged by their talks with Eden and Johnstone and discomfited by the failure of Sir William Howe to capture or disperse the rebel army, succeeded in putting their case before the British reading public. Pulteney, writing very early in the year 1779, felt strongly that Britain could not desert these people. Joseph Galloway, the energetic Philadelphian who had seen his plan for reunion scrapped by the radicals at the First Continental Congress five years previously, was their principal mouthpiece in London. Galloway had joined the British Army in 1776, but had lost patience with Howe for not making an attempt to mobilize the loyalists who, Galloway felt, greatly outnumbered the rebels and who, if asked, would have lent a hand in suppressing the revolt.

Losing all of his property to the rebels in 1778, Galloway made his way to New York and then to London, where he used all of his influence, including that of an able pen, to convince the British public that with proper leadership, the war could still be won. From fellow exiles whom he had left behind in New York he received a stream of letters documenting their grievances, describing their mistreatment at the hands of the rebels, and calling on the mother country to come to their rescue. James Humphrey wrote about the persecution he and his family had endured for having been a printer for the Crown. "I am now a second time an exile, separated from my wife and all my effects, the fruits of hard work valued at £2700 seized," he complained. A lengthy and very eloquent letter from Charles Inglis, the scholarly rector of Trinity Church in New York, narrated in detail the discriminations and methods of intimidation practiced by the Patriot party, and how the minority had got control of the vote even in local elections. "A man might as well attempt to write against the Pope or Inquisition in Spain

---

[3] Pulteney, *Considerations on the present state of public affairs, and the means of raising the necessary supplies*, London, 1779.

or Portugal, as to write against the Rebellion in America," Inglis declared. But the rebellion was also weak, and the rebels were divided among themselves. "The conclusion . . . is obvious," he continued. "The Rebellion be assured is on the decline . . . ; and nothing but a little perseverance and a moderate share of prudence and exertion on the part of Britain is necessary to suppress it totally." "The Rebellion hangs by a slender thread," wrote Isaac Ogden. "The majority of the inhabitants are dissatisfied with their present tyrannical government, their money depreciating, the French alliance detested. One vigorous campaign, properly conducted, will crush the rebellion." [4]

From these reports and from his own experiences, Galloway published early in 1779 a hundred-page pamphlet of his own recounting how the rebellion had been organized by "the violent few," how in all of the new states the revolutionary governments had been elected by less than one-tenth of the people, and how three-fourths of the men in the rebel army were English, Scotch, or Irish. Only a minority of native Americans, according to him, had taken arms against the king. In Pennsylvania, he insisted, fewer than two hundred voters out of a total electorate exceeding 30,000 chose the assembly. "The Congress are usurpers of despotic power," he exclaimed; and if the British under the new leadership of Sir Henry Clinton would seize the initiative and show that they could protect the large segment of the population wanting peace, they would have nine-tenths of the people on their side. [5]

Galloway's counsels were the epitome of perfection: he oversimplified the situation, of course, and no British commander, no matter how well schooled in statecraft, could have made good on them. But he carried conviction, avoided diatribe and personal abuse of the men who had wronged him, and backed up the statements of men like Eden and Johnstone. He brought welcome support to the government for a policy it had previously resolved to pursue. His influence on the government was

---

[4] "Letters to Joseph Galloway from leading Tories in America," *The Historical Magazine*, V (1861), pp. 271–273, 295–301, 335–338, 356–364.
[5] Galloway, *Letters to a Nobleman, on the conduct of the War in the Middle Colonies*, London, 1779.

both direct and decisive, naturally so because what he reported was what most wanted to believe. The king, Lord North, Lord George Germain, and Lord Amherst whose experience in America dated back to the previous war, all read Galloway's pamphlet and talked with him personally. "Lord North has had a long conversation with Dr. Galloway and some others about the present state of America," reported the prime minister on January 29, "and has every reason to believe that a campaign conducted with vigour and ability promises the most happy success in this moment." Two months later Germain followed through with a directive to Sir Henry Clinton, saying that loyalist support was indispensable to victory and promising to send agents to help Clinton recruit it.[6]

The return of Howe and Burgoyne from America brought a lengthy inquiry in Parliament. Both of these unsuccessful generals had seats in Commons and both sat on the Whig side of the house; hence the opposition had a fine opportunity to bring down the government. Hartley restated his conviction that the Americans were in fact independent and that Britain was fighting the wrong war: it should make peace with America and put all its strength into the war against France. With Spain about to come into the war—the armada was actually beginning to assemble when this debate took place—this was all the more necessary. As Fox put it: the ministry should not be allowed to make peace with France, "either upon the condition of ratifying her treaty with America, suffering her to continue her connections with the United States, or giving up any part of the British dominions." Hartley added the idea of a ten years' truce, the immediate withdrawal of all British forces from America, and the negotiation of a federal alliance, and Fox agreed. Curiously, Hartley used Galloway's evidence as justification for doing the opposite of what Galloway himself projected. Hartley was very friendly with Franklin, and in his anxiety for reconciliation he pictured the Americans as dupes of the French, a relationship which was not in accord with the facts.

---

[6] Fortescue, nos. 2492–2494, 2510; Paul H. Smith, *Loyalists and Redcoats, A Study in British Revolutionary Policy*, Chapel Hill, 1964, pp. 118 ff.

Burke, looking at Hartley with the eye of a practical politician, expressed himself as astonished at Hartley's perseverance under so many disappointments and concluded that Hartley's proposals would lead nowhere. And, although Burke was himself opposed to the war in America, he and Fox adopted a partisan technique, attacking the ministry for its past mistakes, but leaving it to Hartley to say what should be done. As the latter differed from the government only on the means and not the end—all parties wanting reconciliation on the basis of union under the king—Hartley's peace proposal failed to win favor. In Commons two motions for a cease fire and peace with the Americans were offered in June 1779, the very month when Bourbon plans to invade became known; but neither of these motions got sufficient support to be brought to a vote.[7]

Opinion was virtually unanimous that Galloway was right: the rebels in America were a small minority and were near the end of their rope. Major General Robertson, who had also left the country in the preceding fall, was the government's star witness. "More than two-thirds of the people would prefer the King's government to the Congress's tyranny," he testified, and backed up his contention with statements of fact. Robertson's conclusion received general support. "The subduing the rebellion," he declared, "depends more on our management than our force," although he did not expect an immediate collapse.[8] The king, watching the debate, put a clear interpretation on the war as he saw it. "The present contest with America," he wrote, "I cannot help seeing as the most serious in which any country was ever engaged. It contains such a train of consequences that they must be examined to feel its real weight. . . . Step by step the demands of America have risen—independence is their object, that certainly is one which every man not willing to sacrifice every object to a *momentary and inglorious* peace must concur with me in thinking that this country can never submit

---

[7] David Hartley, *Letters on the American War*, London, 1779; *PH*, XX, cols. 836–854, 901–915; Burke to Mrs. William Dowdeswell, Nov. 14, 1778, *Burke Corresp.*, IV, pp. 27–28.

[8] *PR*, 1779, XIII, pp. 274, 324; Burke to R. Champion, June 15, 1779, *Burke Corresp.*, IV, pp. 89–90; *A View of the evidence relative to the conduct of the American War*, London, 1779; P. H. Smith, *op. cit.*

to; should America succeed in that, the West Indies must follow them. . . ." Eventually "this Island would be reduced to itself, and soon would be a poor Island indeed, for reduced in her trade merchants would retire with their wealth to climates more to their advantage, and shoals of manufacturers would leave this country for the New Empire. . . . Consequently this country has but one sensible, one great line to follow, the being ever ready to make peace when to be obtained without submitting to terms that in their consequences must annihilate this Empire, and with firmness to make every effort to deserve success." [9]

Intelligence continued to flow in from America substantiating these views. Sir George Collier, in command of the naval forces in New York, wrote a vigorous dispatch giving his opinion that the "rebellion is at last thrown on its back, . . . the rebel Congress no longer possessing the least confidence. . . ." Admiral Arbuthnot reported the repulse of a combined French-American force at Savannah, and announced his intention of making an inroad into Virginia in order to cut off the export of tobacco, the one staple the Americans possessed for meeting their bills in France. Friction between the French and the Americans was now out in the open, and the rebellion would never have lasted so long except for General Howe's inertia. Clinton would do better. The people of the Middle Colonies were basically loyal and thoroughly tired of the war; moreover, they were the key to success, since they furnished the provisions for the rebel army. A firm hold on any two of them would break the back of the rebellion, and this could be accomplished in the next spring by an army of ten thousand men and by a liberal policy calculated to win the active support of the loyal element which, if properly aroused and led, was numerous enough to overthrow the revolutionary regimes.[10]

At home the threat of a Bourbon invasion aroused the British fighting spirit, and when the armada turned out to be a fiasco, the British were in a mood to launch a counterattack. The Ad-

---

[9] Fortescue, no. 2649.
[10] *A Letter to the Rt. Hon. the Earl of Sandwich on the present situation of affairs. By a Sailor,* London, 1779; Franklin to Jay, Oct. 4, 1779, Smyth, VII, no. 1044; *Sandwich Papers,* III, pp. 131–140; Fortescue, no. 2904.

miralty favored an offensive in the West Indies, with Martinique the chief target, and in December it was resolved to dispatch additional ships to the aid of Parker and Rodney in those waters. The British West Indian fleet had been neglected—many of the ships needed to be sent home for refitting—but once the vessels were copper-bottomed (an important improvement in which the British had the lead over their enemies), they might defy the whole power of France and Spain. The king, a genuinely pious man who gave Providence full credit for Britain's success in standing off its enemies on these several widely scattered fronts, summed up the new spirit succinctly in a letter to Lord North a few days before Christmas. "I do believe," he declared, "that America is nearer coming into temper to treat than perhaps at any other period, and if we arrive in time at Gibraltar Spain will not succeed in that attack which will very probably allay the fury of the Spanish monarch and make him more willing to end the war. . . ." [11]

There was some dissent. Hartley again held out for a long truce. A thoughtful writer in an *Essay on the Interests of Britain* revived the prewar arguments of Arthur Young that "the very conception that an isle can preserve, for any length of time, an influence by force over a vast continent beyond the Atlantic is absurd." Josiah Tucker, the outspoken dean of Gloucester, with Galloway's writings especially in mind, vigorously denied the possibility of subjugating the Colonies and argued that, if they were left to themselves, they would soon tire of their French allies, "the general incendiaries of the world," and return to the fold of their own accord. [12] But the irony of these arguments lay in the fact that the proponents of the war did not themselves rely on force alone. The king, Lord North, and Lord George Germain were emphatic on this point. With two-thirds or more of the Americans against the rebellion, they anticipated its suppression and the road opened to reconciliation.

---

[11] Adm. Papers, Adm. II, 1336: to Parker, Secret, Dec. 3, 1779, and to Rodney, most secret, Dec. 8 and 9, 1779; *Sandwich Papers*, III, 164–189; Fortescue, no. 2886.

[12] *An Essay on the Interests of Britain, in regard to America*, London, 1780; Tucker, *Dispassionate Thoughts on the American War*, London, 1780; *PH*, XX, cols. 1187–1196.

Independence, however, was inadmissible. On this point all parties agreed. It meant to the British mind the eventual disappearance of Great Britain itself as an independent power. France would be supreme in Europe and remain in league with the Americans. In due time the Americans would throw off the connection and build their own territorial and commercial empire. Of this there could be no doubt: the revolutionary leaders themselves had many times said as much, and had attracted France into an alliance with them as a necessary step in the advancement of their own interests. Wearing his heart on his sleeve, Hartley tried to talk Franklin into the advantages of peace and reconciliation. Aware of this eagerness, Franklin used British overtures as a means for prodding Vergennes. But he also set a trap for his English friends: if Britain really wanted peace, it should offer Canada and Nova Scotia. Even Hartley turned a deaf ear to this proposal.

Better, perhaps, than any British writer Galloway put the case against independence: through its American alliance, France would realize its historic ambition of becoming *la monarchie universelle*. America, recovering swiftly from the war's distresses, would regard the politics of Europe with indifference. This attitude would benefit the French, since Britain without American support, could not put a checkrein on French ambitions. Then Galloway formulated the classic doctrine of American isolationism, anticipating the very words used later by Washington and Jefferson. Of America he wrote:

Her distance, and the safety arising from it, will render her regardless of the fate of nations on this side of the Atlantic, as soon as her own strength shall be established. The prosperity or ruin of kingdoms, from whose power she can have nothing to fear, and whose assistance she can never want, will be matters of equal indifference. She can wish for no other connection with Europe, than that of commerce. . . .

Once the political union with America was dissolved, Britain would fall victim to a series of misfortunes. Its sugar islands and its fisheries would go first. Beholden to foreign countries for the vital supply of naval stores, its merchant marine and navy would be reduced to contempt, he said, and Britain would find itself in a "forlorn and wretched state," a mere pawn between a French-ruled Europe on one side and an American hegemony on the other. In bowing before the rebel faction in America, Galloway charged, Britain was guilty of "inhumanity and treachery"; it was deserting its own friends in America. A helping hand held out to them would reverse the trend and reunite the Empire.[13]

British opinion now was more united on the objects of the war, and more confident of winning it, than at any previous time. Bourbon muddling in the Channel showed there was little reason for fear in home waters; the time had come for offensive warfare in North American and West Indian waters. Clinton's capture of Charleston in May 1780 pointed in the right direction. It remained to secure control of the sea from New York to the West Indies and to restore civil government in the Southern and Middle Colonies, protecting the loyally inclined and holding out the prospect of amnesty for the rebels. But these were tasks more easily put down on paper than carried into execution. French and Spanish naval armament in the West Indies showed unexpected strength and skill, and a complex situation in the Carolinas, centering around Lord Cornwallis, nullified Clinton's achievement and turned victory into the surrender at Yorktown in October 1781.[14]

Robert Livingston, who assumed office as secretary for foreign affairs on the very day following this spectacular Franco-American victory, wrote of it that it "must fix our independence not beyond all doubt, but even beyond all controversy." But Livingston was premature, as he himself soon ruefully confessed. Without France the Americans were completely helpless. Conscious of this and anxious to capitalize his advantage over the British, Washington appealed at once to de Grasse to take part in a combined operation against

---

[13] Galloway, *Cool Thoughts on the Consequences to Great Britain of American Independence*, London, 1780.

[14] Adm. I, vols. 486, 489; *Sandwich Papers*, III, pp. 119–274, IV, pp. 125–214; James, *British Navy in Adversity*, pp. 269–300; Piers Mackesy, *The War for America 1775–1783*, Cambridge, Mass., 1964, pp. 319–352; William B. Willcox, *Portrait of a General. Sir Henry Clinton in the War of Independence*, New York, 1964, pp. 300–444; P. H. Smith, *op. cit.*, pp. 154–161.

Charleston. But de Grasse responded in the negative; his orders were to return to the West Indies and fulfill his commitments to the Spaniards, and he gave the American commander no hope of further help. Washington was deeply chagrined. "I am obliged to submit," he confessed to Governor Rutledge of North Carolina. It was no use laying siege to Charleston unless the French supported him from the sea.[15]

How easy it would be to end the war, mused John Adams in Amsterdam, if Spain and Holland would cooperate with us as France has done. Command of the sea off the American coast and in the West Indies was all that was needed. Adams, however, did not know how near to collapse the United States was at this moment of seeming triumph. Livingston and Morris knew it, and so did Washington. Vergennes had refused further pecuniary aid, and unless he changed his mind and made available additional credits, the benefits of Yorktown would come to nothing.

Franklin was told he must get at least twelve million more livres out of France. "Never was there a time in which money was more necessary to us than at present," Livingston warned. Can the French really mean to cut us off at this critical juncture? "The most serious consequence" may ensue. Franklin had to try to convince them that their own best interests were at stake. But if he failed, if France had other objects which came first, "all we can do is to . . . submit to her determination." Morris on his part had put his case to the state governors, but as usual he met with little response. "The languor of the States," he told Franklin, "had been so fostered by their teeming expectations from France, that it became my duty to prevent, if possible, the ill effects of it." And Morris, shrewd enough to see that Britain would now concede independence if the Americans broke with France, dropped a hint that such an eventuality might arise.[16]

---

[15] Livingston to Dana, Oct. 22, 1781, Wharton, IV, pp. 802–805. Washington to de Grasse, Oct. 20, de Grasse to Washington, Oct. 23, Washington to Rutledge, Oct. 31, 1781; Fitzpatrick, XXII, pp. 248–250, 306.

[16] Morris to State governors, Oct. 19; Adams to Franklin, Nov. 26; Livingston to Franklin, Nov. 26; Morris to Franklin, Nov. 27, 1781. Wharton, IV, pp. 790–794, V, pp. 4–8, 12–29.

American spirits sank to their lowest level during January and February of 1782. The war, it was believed, would go on indefinitely. Hopes of getting Spain and Holland into the alliance with France were dashed with the receipt of a communication from Vergennes. Livingston received fair warning too that French patience had its limits. France, he felt, should assist in getting the fisheries and the trans-Allegheny West for the United States. The French had an interest, he argued, in diminishing Britain's mastery of the seas, and their support of American claims was the best way to accomplish this end. But Vergennes's letter indicated that, in the French mind, America was the chief obstacle to peace. With this chilling bit of intelligence, Livingston learned not to expect French help in negotiating a peace treaty with Britain. Vergennes's letters, he told Franklin, were alarming; still, although mortifying, it was necessary to keep on asking the French for more financial aid. Meanwhile, despite the massing of their fleets in the Caribbean, the French and the Spanish had made little headway. The British had the situation at sea well in hand, and on the twelfth of April, 1782, a superior British fleet under Admiral Rodney defeated de Grasse and took him prisoner.[17]

In terms of sheer military advantage, Rodney's victory wiped out Cornwallis's defeat. Britain, moreover, kept its grip on Gibraltar against the Spanish siege, held a lead over the French in the Indian Ocean, and controlled the waters nearer home. In December 1781 all of its overseas trade routes were open, and fleets of merchant vessels freely arrived and departed from the home ports. It was this strong position which Britain occupied that undoubtedly led men like Washington, Franklin, and Adams to think that the war would continue.[18] But York-

---

[17] Livingston to Franklin, Jan. 7, to president of congress, Jan. 29, and to Greene, Jan. 31, 1782; Morris to president of congress, Feb. 11, 1782. Wharton, V, pp. 87–94, 138–139, 142–143, 152–161; Washington to president of congress, Feb. 21, 1782, Fitzpatrick, XXIV, pp. 16–17. Mackesy, *op. cit.*, pp. 446–459.

[18] Fortescue, no. 3510; Adams to Jay, Nov. 28, and Morris to president of congress, Feb. 11, 1782, Wharton, V, pp. 82, 152–159; Franklin to Morris, Jan. 9, Smyth, VIII, no. 1271; Washington to William Moore, Feb. 21, 1782, Fitzpatrick, XXIV, pp. 16–17.

town had made a deep impression in Britain: it destroyed the government's confidence in its ability to suppress the rebellion, and it caused the opposition to raise demands for a settlement with the Americans which this time could not be ignored. Intelligence of Cornwallis's surrender reached London on November 25. Parliament, opening its fall session two days later, got the news from the king himself in the usual speech from the throne. On the eighth of December the ministers concluded that it was impracticable to send more troops to America, and the king somewhat reluctantly agreed.[19]

Opposition members in both houses of Parliament mingled purely partisan attacks on the government, aimed at shaming it into resigning, with more basic arguments heard many times before which expressed their aversion to the war on their fellow subjects, the Americans. Men primarily concerned with unseating the government attacked it on its war record, making accusations that could as readily have come from Franklin. Words like "treachery," "folly," and "madness" heated up the debate but did not contribute to the difficult problem of how to make peace. Fox and Burke headed the list of partisans, demanding a "total change of system" and blaming the "influence of the Crown" for loss of the war. This was an attempt to return to the language of a famous, although unsuccessful resolution offered by the Whig lawyer, John Dunning, two years previously. Dunning's resolution implied that the king was personally guilty, bending the members of the majority party to his will through corrupt use of the patronage power. But, as Lord North correctly pointed out in response, the Americans had not originally objected to the authority of the Crown; they had protested the right of Parliament to legislate for them. The underlying issue was the supremacy of Parliament, and the ministers, supported by the king, had tried to preserve and uphold this principle.

No better illustration of this paradox is to be found than in a brilliant speech delivered by Lord Camden, one of the Whig peers who was not bound by party loyalties. Camden made sea power the theme of his speech, and he enumerated various

---

[19] *PH*, XXII, cols. 634–637; Fortescue, nos. 3462, 3466.

strategic errors that the navy under Lord Sandwich had committed. But he did not recognize the overwhelming handicaps that the navy had encountered—the multitudinous tasks that it had been called on to perform, the inevitable dispersal of the fleet that the nature of the war had required. And he assumed that the war with America had to go on, but that it should be prosecuted not by the use of land forces but by strengthening the navy in the West Indies for offensive warfare against the French.[20] This was exactly what the government had endeavored to do previously, and what it was now to do with striking success. Rodney's victory was the result.

Opinions on how to stop the war in America bore on two related questions: whether to withdraw the troops and whether to evacuate the seaports—New York, Charleston, and Savannah —that enabled control of the seas from Halifax to the West Indies. The Duke of Richmond, like Camden an independent Whig, stated the case for withdrawing the troops. He felt the French forces in America would become useless, the "unnatural" alliance which the Americans had contracted would begin to break up, and the road would be open to reconciliation. Lord Stormont, no doubt recollecting his wartime experiences in Paris, gave the most concise rebuttal to this point of view. France, the real enemy, depended on America to win. If the British surrendered their footholds in America, they would be unable to check the French in the West Indies. Moreover, the Americans would give their own ambitions free rein and carry out their program of conquering Canada, Nova Scotia, and the fisheries. All the subsequent debates in both houses of Parliament hung on these two questions, which were really one: if the troops were evacuated, the ports could not be held. All sides agreed on the desirability of *reconciliation,* but none pronounced candidly and clearly in favor of *independence.* "Take away America," declared Lord George Germain, "and we should sink into perfect insignificance." This was the nub of the matter.[21]

---

[20] *PH,* XXII, cols. 637–751; Ian R. Christie, *The End of Lord North's Ministry 1780–1782,* London, 1958, pp. 267–283.

[21] *PH,* XXII, cols. 650–751; Christie, *op. cit.,* pp. 283–298.

To the British mind the dilemma appeared insoluble. American independence was repugnant because it meant placing Britain in a helpless position. Reconciliation was quite another matter, axiomatic with all parties. But to withdraw the troops and trust the Americans to return to the fold met with little favor; the risk was too great. How to detach America from France: this was the burning question, to which there was no immediate answer. In December 1781 a new motion to stop the war in America was offered, and the debate on this motion establishes the point. Lord North volunteered not to send armies marching through America but, as he said, to evacuate the ports would mean crippling the government and handing the initiative to France. Dunning, who had been in the forefront against the ministry, now found himself on the same side; he opposed a grant of independence and expressed himself as unready to relinquish the ports.[22] Nevertheless, discontent with the North administration was now too general to be ignored, and in January Fox returned to the attack. Again the issue between the government and the opposition rested on a false premise. The government had no intention of waging *offensive* war in America, and the opposition was, to say the least, ambiguous on the subject of independence. Burke, aligned with Fox, equivocated on the question of the ports—he said they should be occupied by "only a few men"—but he avoided any mention of independence. He did say that reconciliation was out of the question so long as the present ministry remained in office.

Against these thrusts Lord North gave a spirited defense of his administration. But in March 1782 he finally went down before a series of sustained attacks; the opposition drove home the point that without a change in the government a settlement with the Americans was not to be had. This was the chance for which Franklin in Paris had long been waiting: in so many words he had repeatedly told his English friends that, if they wanted peace, they would first have to turn out the North administration. Franklin and Burke now exchanged felicitations; the shrewd American envoy scented victory for himself and the American cause in the fierce partisan debates in Westminster

---

[22] *PH*, XXII, cols. 802–867.

which he observed from the farther side of the Channel. Burke, however, even more than Fox remained in the shadows of party politics, and left it to an independent Member of Parliament, Henry Seymour Conway, to take the responsibility. With forty years of experience behind him, Conway had somehow managed to remain uncommitted to any of the factions in the house. In a series of three resolutions which he drew up Conway declared that *offensive* war against the Americans was impracticable. In the third resolution of March 4, he went so far as to say that those who suggested such a war were to be viewed as enemies of the king and the country. The irony of the situation, however, is obvious: there was no real difference between the defeated Lord North and his enemies; and a new government, headed by Lord Rockingham and the Earl of Shelburne, the deceased Chatham's principal disciple, took office on the same ambiguous position held by its predecessor.[23]

Never a robust man, Rockingham died in July. His position on the American question, and that of his followers like Burke, was rather equivocal. In February, while the North ministry was still in power, Shelburne had publicly said: "He never would consent, under any possible given circumstances, to acknowledge the independency of America." But "the Jesuit in Berkeley Square," a sobriquet which paid tribute to Shelburne's keen intellect, was much more supple than these words would indicate. Sensing the possibility of coming between the Americans and the French, he lost no time in taking up the quest. Sir Guy Carleton, the former military governor of Canada, well known for his sympathetic attitude toward the Americans, was commissioned commander-in-chief of the British forces in North America and told to evacuate all three of the American ports, transferring the troops partly to the West Indies and partly to Halifax. Carleton, moreover, was authorized to inform the Americans of these orders and to open peace talks with them.[24]

---

[23] *PH*, XXII, cols. 878–946, 1028–1109; Burke to Franklin, Feb. 28, 1782, Wharton, V, p. 208; Christie, *op. cit.*, pp. 304–370; Namier and Brooke, *A History of Parliament. The House of Commons, 1754–1790*, II, p. 246.
[24] *PR*, 15th Parl., 2 sess., VIII, p. 103; Fortescue, no. 3613; Mackesy, *op. cit.*, 474.

A friendly letter from Franklin put Shelburne on the alert, and through the king and William Eden the new minister learned that both the Americans and the French were anxious for peace. Adams in Amsterdam was reported to be ready for confidential talks. Most important perhaps was a face-to-face meeting between Shelburne and Henry Laurens of South Carolina. A former president of the Continental Congress, Laurens had been captured at sea and brought to London, where he was confined in the Tower. Laurens was adamant on the subject of independence, but gave Shelburne the impression of being against France and well disposed toward Britain. Laurens was just the person, Shelburne decided, to establish a confidential intercourse with Franklin and Adams on the Continent. The problem, however, proved more intractable than Shelburne perhaps suspected; Laurens returned from Amsterdam with a demand that independence be formally recognized before the talks started, a move which to Shelburne was unthinkable.[25] Laurens made the mistake, so it would seem, of going to Adams first.

An overture to the more flexible Franklin in Paris turned out better. For this contact Shelburne chose Richard Oswald, a Scottish merchant of Franklin's own age whose friendships and business connections in both Britain and America extended back many years. Oswald had properties in Virginia, in the Floridas, and in the West Indies. In his younger days he had engaged in the slave trade, and Laurens had been his agent in Charleston. Oswald had often talked with Lord North during the war; with his knowledge of the American South, he believed that, with prudence on the part of the British government, the great families of the Southern Colonies would break relations with New England. This was precisely what the North administration had hoped would happen, but which did not turn out as expected. Oswald, it should be added, thoroughly appreciated the necessity of separating America from France, and intelligence received in London on the eighteenth of May of the sensational

---

[25] Fortescue, nos. 3613, 3631, 3675, 3686; John Norris, *Shelburne and Reform*, London, 1963, pp. 164–169.

British naval victory in the West Indies made this possible.[26] The victory impressed Fox, who now was second only to Shelburne in British government circles, and the two of them agreed to have two envoys in Paris—Oswald to deal with the Americans and Thomas Grenville, who was much younger, to negotiate with Vergennes. Oswald was a great success with all of the Americans whom he encountered; they liked his rugged honesty and his candor. Grenville's position was rather anomalous; he was in Paris at Fox's insistence, and was made to feel uncomfortable because of his comparative youthfulness and because the Americans did not treat him with the same consideration they showed Oswald.

In the meantime both Franklin and Vergennes anticipated the course that British diplomacy would pursue. His strong protestations to the contrary notwithstanding, Vergennes had yielded to American importunities and obtained another subsidy of six million livres from the French treasury. Franklin's finesse had something to do with this—he assiduously cultivated the *noblesse*, who were the real power in France, but Vergennes himself sensed the risk to France if the Americans were tempted to turn away from the alliance. The French foreign minister took the position that the Americans might properly treat directly with the British envoys, while the French on their part would do the same, provided there was a general peace at the end. Franklin and Shelburne readily agreed to this, and so by the beginning of May the way was open for serious negotiations to start.[27]

Franklin now summoned John Jay from Madrid, and Jay was delighted to make the change. After the cold refusal of the Spanish court to recognize him, Jay warmed to the hospitality shown him in Paris and at first he shared Franklin's enthusiasm for the French. The old gentleman's long residence in Paris, the intimate friendships he had formed, and the unbroken chain of

---

[26] Fortescue, nos. 3687, 3757; *Richard Oswald's Memorandum . . . Written in 1781*, W. Stitt Robinson, Jr., ed., Charlottesville, Va., 1953.

[27] Franklin to Livingston, Mar. 4, 1782, Wharton, V, pp. 214–217; Vergennes to Luzerne, Apr. 9, Franklin to Vergennes, Apr. 15, Vergennes to Luzerne, May 2, 1782, AAE cp Etats Unis, vol. 21, no. 11, ff. 32–35; no. 21, f. 55, ff. 133–134; Luzerne to Livingston, May 28, Wharton, V, pp. 443–445.

political and social successes that had been his over the past four-and-a-half years had naturally tied him sentimentally to France. "This is really a generous nation, fond of glory, and particularly that of protecting the oppressed," he had exclaimed, and Livingston, a close friend of the French minister in America, agreed. Both men had reason to be jubilant as France had come again to the rescue. The French court "stand very high in the esteem of this country," was Livingston's comment, and the name of Lafayette was already working its magic. As for the British, they should be expelled *from this continent*, and the task would not be difficult. But immediately after writing this letter, Livingston learned of Rodney's smashing victory at sea— "a severe blow," he said to Adams, whom he asked to furnish "the most minute details" of any peace move that Britain might take.[28]

Rodney's victory put an end to the hopes of Livingston and others in America that the French would return in force from the West Indies and establish a naval superiority that would oblige the British to retire from North America. But the victory did not, on the other hand, make the Americans more yielding on the matter of their independence. General Carleton on his arrival in New York repeated the attempt of the peace commission of 1778 to win the Americans back to the British side. Reconciliation and reunion was the British object now as it was then. Shelburne's policy was the same as Lord North's, but he was more confident of success: Britain, he knew, was stronger, and his government was the kind of an administration which would naturally appeal to the Americans. Since the latter were near the end of their rope and since, as was said openly in Parliament, their army was fed, clothed, and paid for by France, on whose internal strains the British were also well informed, a peace settlement on British terms seemed entirely possible to Shelburne.

A polite letter from Carleton to Washington was the first overture; it was accompanied by a request for a passport for

---

[28] Franklin to Jay, Apr. 22, Smyth, VIII, nos. 1320–1321; to Livingston, Mar. 4, 1782, Wharton, V, pp. 214–217; Livingston to Franklin and to Adams, May 30, *ibid.*, pp. 459–463; Jay to Livingston, June 25, and to Montmorin, June 26, 1782, *ibid.*, pp. 516–517, 522–524.

his secretary to deal directly with the Congress. But the quick-thinking French minister in Philadelphia stepped in. News of the birth of a prince in Versailles gave Luzerne the opportunity to stage a celebration which led to an official reaffirmation of faith in France. Carleton received a rebuff, whereas Luzerne sent out agents to the state legislatures to arouse them to pass similar resolutions. Rodney's victory, he admitted, heartened those people in America who wanted reconciliation. But Luzerne was not alarmed; he was sure there was no general demand for a separate peace, and the action of the Congress bore him out. A resolution hastily drafted by a committee of three and passed by that body in secret made even an exchange of views with the British generally impossible.[29] The road to a peace between Britain and America ran only through Paris.

There the two British envoys found Franklin more amenable to private talks than perhaps they expected. Franklin's eagerness for Canada and Nova Scotia betrayed him; he wrote a paper for their benefit, repeating all of the old arguments he had used on Hartley to convince the British that it was to their own best interest to give these provinces away. Franklin thought he made a dent on Oswald: "we parted exceedingly good friends," he wrote in his journal. Grenville, who reflected Fox's optimism that a separate peace was obtainable, believed that here was the opening wedge. But the price was too high, Shelburne dodging an answer and allowing the discussion to taper off.[30] The issue of Britain making such a remarkable good-will gesture in favor of the United States did not again arise.

Fears of finding themselves isolated from France continued, however, to haunt the Americans; and in August signs that the alliance might loosen began to appear. Franklin regarded it as the keystone of success, and twice warned Morris and Livingston, who were perennially short of funds, against making further

[29] Luzerne to Vergennes, May 14 and June 3, 1782, AAE cp Etats Unis, vol. 21, ff. 164–173, 282–289; Livingston to Adams and to Franklin, May 22, Luzerne to Livingston, May 28, Secret Journals of Congress, May 31, 1782, Wharton, V, pp. 433–435, 443–445, 464–465.
[30] Wharton, V, pp. 474–477, 540–542; Smyth, VIII, pp. 541–560; Fortescue, nos. 3757, 3771–3772.

demands for money on the French. Although negotiations were now progressing in Paris in the direction of a general settlement, Franklin was fully appreciative of Britain's strong position as a result of Rodney's victory, and somewhat apprehensive that Carleton's overtures in America might after all take effect. To make matters worse for him he was again in trouble with the gout which, added to the affliction of a painful kidney disease, kept him confined to his bed for more than three months.[31]

Carleton's peace feelers may or may not have had their effect —there is no way of saying. Early in August the British general wrote Washington a second time, informing him of the peace negotiation in Paris and of the king's readiness to recognize independence. Carleton, moreover, made his communication public. Even Livingston, with his strong pro-French feelings, was impressed and thought that Britain would no longer want to hold on to the country west of the Alleghenies. Furthermore, it may have been sheer coincidence, but on August 8 the Congress was led to reconsider the sweeping instructions it had given its commissioners the year before. According to these instructions, the commissioners were obliged to accept the advice of the King of France on the terms of peace.

Richard Henry Lee, one of the earliest advocates of the French alliance, now protested that it jeopardized the independence of the United States. He had learned of Spain's interest in the Western lands, and concluded that France through its long and close connection with that country would identify itself with Spain when it came to a choice. "We shall be so circumscribed in our boundaries," he insisted, "that our independence will be a nugatory independence." Lee and others were so aroused that they envisaged the United States as a future French satellite. Obviously embarrassed, James Madison affirmed his faith in France's respecting its promise to uphold the "independence and sovereignty absolute and unlimited" of the United States, and declared himself against altering the instructions because of the effect the change would have on the British attitude, already flushed with Rodney's success. Madison managed to

---

[31] Smyth, VIII, p. 558 and nos. 1334, 1349, 1352; Wharton, V, pp. 510, 655–657.

shunt the move to change the instructions into a committee of which he was a member, and although this committee ultimately affirmed its complete trust in France, it is evident that serious doubts had arisen.[32]

Similar differences in view emerged among the three commissioners in Europe. Although Franklin was now cognizant of Spanish intentions to confine the United States to the seaboard, his loyalty to France remained undiminished. He recalled the enormous amount of aid the French had provided over the past seven years, in money lent and given, and in stores, arms, ammunition, clothing, and so forth; he pointed to the harmony between France and the Swiss cantons as indicative of what the United States might expect of France in the future; and he expressed his conviction that the union between the two countries would endure. More objectively perhaps, he tied America's future position in the world to the French connection. It was the element which insured the respect of the other powers of Europe and gave weight with England. And he grieved at the criticisms of the French that came to his ears. "If we were to break our faith with this nation, on whatever pretence," he exclaimed, "England would again trample on us, and every other nation despise us . . ."[33]

Having shared none of Franklin's triumphs in France, Adams, still in the Netherlands, indulged in a bit of flag waving, reproaching the other powers of Europe, especially the Armed Neutrality powers, for not coming to the side of the United States and made independence his watchword—"independence of friends and foes," he described it. Suspicious of Lord Shelburne, he thought the time was approaching when a makeweight against the Bourbons would be necessary. The support of the European neutrals, he decided, would be enough to keep America from slipping too much under the direction of France.[34] The Armed Neutrality powers had attracted Adams's

---

[32] Wharton, V, pp. 645–653, 792–796.

[33] To Livingston, Aug. 12, and to Samuel Cooper, Dec. 26, 1782, Wharton, V, pp. 655–657, VI, pp. 168–169.

[34] To Jay, Aug. 10, to Dana, Sept. 17 and to Lafayette, Sept. 29, 1782, ibid., pp. 732–733, 785–786.

interest from the start; he saw in them a successful defiance of British supremacy at sea. But Russia, the leader of the Armed Neutrality, recoiled from issuing a challenge to Britain—Russian commercial interests were too closely identified with the British to make such a program feasible—and the Russian court politely but firmly discouraged American hopes of gaining its recognition.

Since Adams, like Arthur Lee before him, had put great store on winning Prussia to the American side, he could hardly have been pleased had he been privileged to read the communications which passed between King Frederick and the Prussian ambassadors in London, Paris, and Madrid respectively, commenting on the peace negotiations in 1782. Frederick regarded America as a pawn between France and Britain, and coolly decided, even before Rodney's victory, that the odds were in favor of Britain. Once the British overcame their dread of American independence, they would be in a position to recover American good will and the best part of American trade. As for his entering a commercial agreement with the United States, Frederick thought poorly of it: without sea power it would be unenforceable, and Prussia was not ready for such an adventure.[35] The indifference and caution of both Prussia and Russia showed that Adams, in his excess of nationalistic zeal, did not understand the European situation as he fancied he did. Actually he admitted there was no choice, for the present at least, but to stick with France. Acutely aware of the continuing shortage of funds, he joined Robert Morris in praying that the court of Louis XVI would "with their usual goodness" make up the deficit.[36]

Meanwhile John Jay, at first so cordial toward the French, had veered around to the opinion that France would side with Spain and try to keep the United States under its direction. He was annoyed with Vergennes for failing to extract from the British government a formal recognition of American independence before allowing the peace talks to start, and he estimated

---

[35] *American Independence through Prussian Eyes*, Marvin L. Brown, Jr., trans. and ed., Durham, N. C., 1959, pp. 11–24, 131.
[36] To Lafayette, Sept. 29, 1782, Wharton, V, pp. 785–786.

that France would take the Spanish view regarding the Mississippi. When in October Oswald returned to Paris with a new commission so worded as to meet the formality, Jay took credit for winning a diplomatic victory *over the French*: he had decided that Vergennes did not want Britain to recognize the United States. And if Adams was to be taken at his word, Jay had acquired a prejudice against *all* Frenchmen: "He says they are not a moral people. They know not what it is. He don't [sic] like any Frenchman. . . . La Fayette is clever, but he is a Frenchman." And, more seriously:

> Our allies don't play fair. . . . They were endeavoring to deprive us of the fishery, the western lands, and the navigation of the Mississippi. They would even bargain with the English to deprive us of them. They want to play the western lands, Mississippi, and the whole Gulf of Mexico into the hands of Spain.[37]

These were harsh words, although they reflected Adams's own suspicious frame of mind. Adams and Jay came to regard themselves as having performed virtually a rescue operation for America against the wiles of French diplomacy and the pliancy of Franklin who, according to Adams, was "submission itself." Adams had worked himself up into a fine state of wrath toward Vergennes who, he decided, meant "to keep his hand under our chin to prevent us from drowning, but not to lift our heads out of water," and of jealousy toward Franklin who was "puffed up to the top of Jacob's ladder in the clouds." But Adams went to even greater length in claiming credit for himself. He was persuaded that a series of letters he had written, ten of which were published in the English papers during January and February of 1782, had converted Shelburne to the idea of independence. Then, reasoned Adams, our refusal to treat on an unequal footing had clinched the matter: Shelburne issued the new commission to Oswald, by which "Great Britain has got the start and gone to the windward of the other European powers."[38]

---

[37] Jay to Livingston, Sept. 18, and to Gouverneur Morris, Oct. 13; Adams's Journ., Nov. 5, 1782, *ibid.*, pp. 785–786, 810, 849.

[38] Adams to Livingston, Nov. 8, 1782, *ibid.*, pp. 864–866.

Of Shelburne's finesse there can be no doubt; British diplomacy did get to the windward of France and Spain. But Jay and especially Adams were overdrawing on their imagination. Shelburne had always stood for *reconciliation*. Occasionally a voice was raised in Parliament during the war in favor of *independence* but, except for the idea thrown out by Hartley in October 1778 (quoted at the beginning of this chapter), the word remained formless in the English mind or rather, to put it more accurately, it was abhorrent because it spelled an American *dependence* on France. Shelburne's practical, but subtle mind took hold of the idea of independence, as conceived by Hartley, and combined it with the idea of reconciliation. "If America is independent, she must be so of the whole world," he told Oswald in April 1782. "No secret, tacit, or ostensible connection with France." Oswald was instructed to make every effort to satisfy the Americans so that "they can have no justifiable motive to persist in a war which, as to them, will no longer have any object, and it is to be hoped, will not be inclined to lend themselves to the purposes of French ambition."

Oswald's reports of his talks with Franklin convinced the British statesman that he was on the right track. Britain, Shelburne informed Oswald on July 27, "is prepared to make the most unequivocal acknowledgment of American independency." He felt the separation of the two countries most deeply, he went on to say. But "the same motives which made me perhaps the last to give up all hope of re-union, make me most anxious if it is given up, that it shall be done *decidedly*, so as to . . . lay the foundation of a new connection better adapted to the present temper & interests of both countries." And to make this foundation secure, Shelburne was ready "to go further with Dr. Franklin perhaps than he is aware of, and farther perhaps than the professed advocates of independence are prepared to admit." [39]

A face-to-face meeting with Admiral de Grasse, which occurred soon after he had written this to his envoy, further helped Shelburne to see the road ahead. The French admiral was brought to England after his capture in the Caribbean,

---

[39] Shelburne Mss.

216 EMPIRE AND INDEPENDENCE

and Shelburne took an immediate liking to him. He "is like the plainest of our seamen," was the minister's comment. De Grasse wanted peace, and from his orders he deduced that the French court would not be difficult. Its objects were: independence for the Americans, and the return to France of the islands of St. Lucia and St. Domingue. By means of the latter the French position in the West Indies would be restored. Other matters, according to de Grasse, were negotiable.[40]

Shelburne, on his part, wanted a comprehensive settlement involving all the powers, and he was determined not to recognize America before being certain of a peace treaty. He and the king got the impression that Franklin was trying to trick them. But, the point seems important, he could negotiate with the two allies separately. This procedure suited the Americans, including Franklin, who wanted to make their own terms with the British, and Vergennes was also agreeable. French interests embraced many subjects with which the United States was not concerned—India and the East Indian trade for instance. In addition, we may conjecture that Vergennes saw difficulties trying to steer between the Americans and the Spanish. Not only was the Rock of Gibraltar at stake, the Spaniards having in vain tried to capture it; but also there was the Gulf of Mexico, which the Spaniards intended exclusively for themselves. This latter objective was a maxim of Spanish policy, and it involved the Floridas and the Mississippi. The Americans had been eager applicants for a Spanish alliance, but Floridablanca had always given them the cold shoulder. The French knew of Spanish opposition to American independence but they habitually avoided giving the Americans any assistance in settling this matter.[41]

Actually the French had their own ideas on American independence, and it is not surprising that they correlated much

---

[40] Shelburne to the king, Aug. 11, and the king to Shelburne, Aug. 21, Fortescue, nos. 3877, 3894; de Grasse to Vergennes, Aug. 13 and Shelburne to de Grasse, Sept. 3, 1782, AAE cp Angleterre, vol. 538, nos. 26 and 50, ff. 56 and 116.

[41] Jay to president of congress, Oct. 3, 1781, Wharton, IV, pp. 738–765; Montmorin to Vergennes, Mar. 30, and Livingston to Jay, Apr. 27, 1782, ibid., pp. 287–289, 332–335.

better with the Spanish than with the American. The person most qualified to formulate the French concept was Conrad Alexandre Gérard, the undersecretary at the foreign ministry who had backed the policy of intervention from the outset and who had then in 1778 gone to Philadelphia. Gérard in forthright fashion expounded his ideas before a committee of the Congress in January 1779, and sent Vergennes a long report on the subject. He told the committee, at which John Jay was present, that from the French point of view the United States had absolutely no claim to the trans-Allegheny West, that such ambitions were contrary to the principles of the alliance and irreconcilable to French relations with Spain, that France would not support these aspirations which would surely cause future trouble with both Britain and Spain, and that the United States was a commercial republic of thirteen states which would fail if it sought an inland empire. His statement, he reported, made a deep impression: the committee divided on the subject, with the majority, he thought, inclined to his view.[42]

Gérard's younger brother Rayneval, who followed him at Versailles as undersecretary, made another study of the subject in 1782 and reached similar conclusions. The Americans assumed that the early Colonial charters gave them their right to the trans-Allegheny West. Rayneval rejected this argument in favor of Britain, who held this country and the Floridas under the treaties of Paris of 1763. This French view of America as a commercial republic looking out to sea and shut off from the hinterland by a mountain chain was, to be sure, historic; and Gérard's design, moreover, met the basic requirements of French policy, which was to obtain American independence in its restricted sense but not to encourage territorial ambitions which would in the long run prove dangerous to France itself.

Rayneval did not overlook the attempt at conquest which George Rogers Clark made in 1780 at the instigation of Jefferson. Clark's expedition he characterized as merely an "ephemeral journey," and refused to take it seriously. He did anticipate

---

[42] Gérard to Vergennes, Jan. 28, 1779, Wharton, VI, pp. 167–168.

a new division of the Western country, Spain recovering the Floridas and extending them north to the Ohio, and the British and the Americans disputing the Ohio Valley between them. The most the Americans could expect from Spain, he thought, was the use of a port on the Mississippi for the convenience of the people who had migrated westward. With this opinion in hand and with the knowledge of Shelburne's ideas he had obtained from de Grasse, Vergennes early in September 1782 sent Rayneval to London for private conferences with the British statesman. These conferences covered many subjects not involving the United States; and the reports which Rayneval sent back to Versailles were handed on to the Spanish ambassador, but not to the American envoys. Rayneval acquired a high respect for Shelburne, "a man of lofty, as well as of penetrating genius," who "sees things in their large aspects, and detests minutiae." The British minister showed a disregard toward Spain, however, refusing to budge on Gibraltar and telling the French envoy that he intended to share use of the Mississippi with the Americans. To this, Rayneval objected but without effect.[43]

Shelburne on his part had a good opinion of Rayneval, learning from him of Vergennes's anxiety for peace and discovering a certain jealously toward America. As de Grasse had said, France would insist on "independence," but beyond that there was room for maneuver. So with this in mind Shelburne authorized Oswald to treat with the representatives of the "Thirteen United States"; this was the face-saving formula which satisfied the pride of both parties. A definitive recognition of independence could come only from Parliament, and Shelburne proposed that this be incorporated in the peace treaty which would then be subject to approval by that body.[44]

To the Americans a share in the fisheries, the cession of the Western lands, and the navigation of the Mississippi were all "indispensable necessities," to borrow the redundant phrase

---

[43] AAE cp Angleterre, vol. 537, no. 163, ff. 385–398; vol. 538, nos. 54 and 65, ff. 122–123, 146–194; Rayneval to Vergennes, Dec. 25, 1782, Wharton, VI, pp. 166–167.
[44] Aug. 29, Sept. 13 and 19, 1782. Fortescue, nos. 3907, 3918, 3928.

they often employed. These ideas were quite different from those entertained at Versailles. Adams, coming to Paris from Holland only at the very end of October, seems to have taken the lead in the argument with the British envoys. At least he was the most vocal on the subject, and he and Jay took credit for what they believed was a weakness in Franklin for France. Franklin, moreover, was a sick man at this time and in no position to keep ahead of his younger colleagues. Adams was eloquent on the subject of future wars if America was kept away from the fisheries and the Mississippi. The fisheries were so involved with the internal economy of the country and with its foreign trade that if they were taken away, the effect would be to enkindle a new war with the conquest of Nova Scotia and Newfoundland as the prime object. As for the Mississippi, the spread of the population would be so rapid, and the need for using the river so great, that the people could not be restrained from taking the law into their own hands. No treaty could last long in the teeth of such inexorable forces.[45]

Adams earned a reputation as "the Washington of the negotiation," a sobriquet which pleased him greatly. With the British his arguments prevailed over the French. Where legal claims were unimpressive—Adams did not use them, and Shelburne spoke of them as "nonsense"—Adams's realistic warnings were more convincing than Rayneval's caution. Shelburne himself had a knowledge of the trans-Allegheny West, extending back many years before the war, and the American argument of population pressure counted more with him than French theories of keeping the United States to the seaboard. But the British statesman appreciated the plight of the American loyalists and the unpaid debts still owing British merchants since prewar days, and he thought of the hinterland as a region where land could be sold and new provinces started for the benefit of these people who had lost so heavily. In other words, transfer of the West to the United States was to be made conditional upon a satisfactory settlement in behalf of the loyalists.[46]

---

[45] Adams's Journ., Nov. 30, 1782, Wharton, VI, pp. 90–93.
[46] Cabinet Minute, Oct. 17, Fortescue, no. 3956; Shelburne to Oswald, private, Oct. 21, 1782, Shelburne Mss.

In Paris the loyalists were the center of frequent controversy, even Vergennes taking their part with the British against the Americans. Among the Americans there was a split, Jay and Adams with their strong conservative instincts being more sympathetic than Franklin. The old doctor was unmoved, being as insensitive as was Robert Livingston, who was frank enough to tell Franklin he wanted to see the loyalists driven out of the country. The patriot party needed to be sure of itself, but could not be if the loyalists remained: the party would be in constant jeopardy from the presence of a large subversive element. Livingston, however, made an interesting confession: "in the mass of our people," he told Jay, there appeared to be "a great number who, though resolved on independence, prefer an alliance with England to one with France . . ." But in the government, he continued, "independence and the alliance with France connect themselves so closely together that we never speak of them separately." [47]

In the end the Americans got what they wanted without offering a *quid pro quo* for the loyalists. They were readmitted to a full share in the fisheries and were granted a simple cession of the trans-Allegheny hinterland south of the Great Lakes with the right to participate on equal terms in the navigation of the Mississippi. Shelburne put reconciliation first, and so did not risk a deadlock for the sake of the loyalists. But a separate and secret article relating to the boundary of West Florida may be the clue to his willingness to retreat without further argument. Oswald's article stipulated that, if West Florida remained British as it had been since 1763, its northern boundary would be drawn from the mouth of the Yazoo along a line extending due east to the Appalachicola River. Oswald explained to Shelburne that should West Florida reach so far up the Mississippi it would provide ample means for compensating the loyalists without burdening the British public.[48] The scheme never materialized, however, since it was subsequently

[47] Livingston to Franklin, Jan. 7, Wharton, V, p. 93; to Jay, Nov. 23, 1782, *ibid.*, VI, p. 71; Franklin to Oswald, Nov. 26, and Adams' Journ., *ibid.*, pp. 80, 84.
[48] Oswald to Shelburne, Dec. 4, 1782, Shelburne Mss.

decided to return West Florida to Spain and, as agreed on with the Americans, the province was shrunk to a boundary extending along the thirty-second parallel north latitude. In other words, with West Florida reverting to Spain, the American position in the West was much better, at least on paper, than it could have been if the province had remained British.

All that the loyalists got from the peace treaty was a weak clause which pledged the Congress to "recommend" to the state legislatures compensation or restitution to those who were found to be "real British subjects." The number of these being negligible the vast majority, who were native-born, were helpless against state governments wholly controlled by their enemies. Moreover, an organized campaign against them reopened in the states, pressure being brought on the legislatures to enact exclusion laws. Alexander Hamilton, observing this new persecution, expressed his disgust. But, as Livingston admitted, the wartime confiscations had resulted in the emergence of a powerful class which had enriched itself at loyalist expense; and by the following September 1783, when the definitive peace was concluded, a mass migration from the United States had begun. Relative to the total population, this was one of the largest movements of its kind in modern history. Hamilton's comments on the popular frenzy against these refugees suggest a situation similar to the flight of the Huguenots from France just a century before; and Livingston was ready to agree that sordid personal motives were involved. Reversing himself completely, he now regretted the loss of those people who, he admitted, were the principal victims of the war. "It is a sad misfortune," he belatedly concluded, "that the more we know of our fellow creatures the less reason we have to esteem them." [49]

Lord Shelburne, with one eye on the approaching fall session of Parliament, agreed to the preliminary articles of peace which Oswald had signed with the three American envoys in Paris on November 30, 1782. With the king he shared the feeling almost

---

[49] Hamilton to George Clinton, June 1, to Livingston, Aug. 13, Livingston to Hamilton, Aug. 30, 1783, Hamilton Papers, III, pp. 372, 431, 434–435; Livingston to Carmichael, May 7, 1783, Wharton, VI, p. 409.

universal in Britain, that he was privy to a serious dismemberment of the Empire. It was impossible to foretell, he confided to his majesty, the good or bad consequences which might follow. Parliament received the news in the speech from the throne, December 5, 1782, and debated the treaty both before and after the Christmas recess. Fox, who had used the term "independence" several times in previous debates but without defining it, agreed that it was "an evil of great magnitude," but saw no alternative.

Lord North supplied the most pungent criticism. The boundaries granted to the United States, were "not only new in nature, but extremely generous in their principle." Twenty-four Indian nations were abandoned, as were the loyalists. Canada was affected by the shrinkage of its boundaries as provided by the Quebec Act of 1774, and, under the agreement to turn over the forts on the south side of the Great Lakes, it was directly exposed to future encroachment. The former prime minister was also observant enough to notice that the British right to navigate the Mississippi was now worthless, the boundary being drawn north of the river's source. As another Member of Parliament sarcastically put it, Shelburne had "certainly proved himself a great Christian, for he had not only parted with his cloak to America, but he had given his coat likewise." [50] There seemed to be but one solace: Shelburne had driven a wedge between France and America, and had at least opened the door to reconciliation.

Both the terms of the peace and the secretiveness of the American envoys in keeping them from the French until after the treaty was signed were a disagreeable shock to Vergennes. To Rayneval, who was in London on his second visit, the minister wrote:

You will notice that the English buy the peace more than they make it. Their concessions, in fact, as much as to the boundaries as to the fisheries and the loyalists, exceed all that I should have thought possible. What can be the motive, that could have brought terms so easy, that they could have been interpreted as a kind of surrender?

Two weeks after this outburst Vergennes had still not re-

---

[50] Fortescue, nos. 3977–3978; *PR*, IX, pp. 246–253.

covered. Franklin, his old friend, had let him down, while Jay and Adams were downright discourteous. It had been understood that, while the negotiations were to be separate, the French were to come in on the final agreement. "If we may judge of the future from what has passed here under our eyes," he remarked bitterly, "we shall be but poorly paid for all we have done for the United States and for securing to them a national existence." [51]

Yet Vergennes, putting aside his irritation, went ahead with a new loan of six million livres which had been authorized while the negotiations were in progress. Morris had hoped for twenty million livres, but the French had cut this down to six million, payable in quarters through the year 1783. The motive for this final burst of generosity is not apparent except in terms of the lurking fear of an American collapse and of the chain of consequences it would bring. Franklin had pressed hard for the whole sum, but was glad to get what he was offered. The war might still go on, he thought, since the other powers had not yet come to terms; and the British government had been so liberal that Parliament might vote it down. "Our people certainly ought to do more for themselves," Franklin reflected. "It is absurd the pretending to be lovers of liberty while they grudge paying for the defence of it." Ironically Franklin's success in getting money out of the French was never equaled by the Congress in its feeble efforts to induce the revolutionary state governments to levy taxes and make grants for the support of the war. [52] And it is amusing to read Luzerne's private report to Vergennes of his attempt to discourage the Congress from reprimanding its emissaries for their discourtesy toward France. The appearances of harmony between the two allies must be preserved; the English must not be allowed to think there had been a breach. [53]

---

[51] Vergennes to Rayneval, Dec. 4, to Franklin, Dec. 15, to Luzerne, Dec. 19, 1782, Wharton, VI, pp. 107, 140, 150–152.
[52] Franklin to Morris, Dec. 23, 1782, Morris to Luzerne, Jan. 13, 1783, Wharton, VI, pp. 159–160, 206–210; Allan Nevins, *The American States during and after the Revolution, 1775–1789*, New York, 1924, pp. 470–478.
[53] Luzerne to Vergennes, Mar. 22, 1783, AAE cp Etats Unis, vol. 23, no. 26, ff. 355–362.

Nevertheless, in advising Robert Morris of the new French loan, Luzerne felt it necessary to take a very firm line. The deteriorating financial situation in America was personally embarrassing, he declared—he had been assuring Versailles that it would improve. Warning again that France could no longer carry the burden, he underscored his previous admonition: *"Without the speedy establishment of a substantial public revenue, and without the exact execution of the engagements entered into by Congress, the hope of obtaining loans in Europe must be given up."* Morris had been telling the Congress the same thing, but without results, and he now underscored his own warnings. Every member should realize the French were not bluffing; there was *"no hope of any further pecuniary aid from Europe. . . . our public credit is gone."* The Congress had to come to a decision. "They cannot borrow, and the States will not pay. *The thing has happened which was expected. . . ."* [54] Morris's own remedy was a national bank and a general excise tax.

If Lord Shelburne really did foresee all the doubts and suspicions springing up between Britain's enemies—and the evidence that he did is wanting—he was truly a master craftsman. The Spanish court was taken by surprise, and was both chagrined and resentful toward the French, whom it blamed for starting the war and then turning into Shelburne's dupes. Spain needed peace, but still harbored illusions about capturing Gibraltar. William Carmichael, whom Jay had left in Madrid, was a great social success but was disappointed at not getting official recognition. Lafayette, who looked at himself almost as a symbol of Franco-American friendship, went to Spain to help Carmichael out. The Spaniards cordially hated the French, he knew, and they had no sentiment for the Americans, but it was good policy to have them as allies. It was unfortunate they were to have the Floridas; they were dead set against sharing the Mississippi and did not want the Americans as neighbors. But Shelburne's stroke in settling with the United States had forced them to consider their own position very seriously. Lafayette and the French ambassador in Madrid mustered all the argu-

---

[54] Luzerne to Morris, Mar. 15, Morris to president of congress, Mar. 17, 1783, Wharton, VI, pp. 301–303, 308–311.

ments they could think of in favor of recognition—the Spaniards, observed Lafayette, "wanted to procrastinate, and yet
they knew it must be done." Finally on March 2, 1783, Floridablanca rewarded them with the announcement that the king
would receive the American envoy.[55]

The French themselves were confronted with a serious dilemma. Luzerne's advice to the Congress was to make a friend and
an ally of Spain, but the Americans, knowing the Spanish attitude, felt that France should side with them. The French were
trying to hold the alliance together and to bring Spain into it,
but this was impossible—American and Spanish interests were
too far apart. Yet if the French took the American part against
Spain, they would find themselves falling in step behind the
British. Misgivings in regard to France, first expressed in Philadelphia in August of 1782, emerged again in December in more
virulent form before the Congress knew of the peace treaty
signed in Paris. A letter from John Jay, filled with distrust and
containing an intercepted document to prove it, found its mark.
Madison, who recorded the effect and was sympathetic to
France, realized how extremely perplexing it all was to the
French mind. French blood and money had been poured out
not only for the sake of independence, but also for the commerce and gratitude of America. A liberal British policy could
spoil it all, however; America would come to feel an obligation
to Britain, rather than to France. Like Livingston, Madison was
ready to believe the worst of the British, but if the British decided to be generous, the French were helpless to prevent it.
Luzerne intervened with a tactful message to the Congress on
the last day of the year; Rochambeau and his army meanwhile
embarked for the West Indies with a vote of thanks and an
expression of regret at their leaving; and it was with a feeling
of relief that Madison recorded that anti-French sentiment had
abated.[56]

---

[55] Carmichael to Livingston, Dec. 30, 1782, Jan. 18 and Feb. 21, 1783;
Lafayette to Carmichael, Jan. 20 and to Livingston, Feb. 5 and Mar. 2, 1783,
Wharton, VI, pp. 184–187, 215–218, 222–223, 238–240, 256–257, 259–260,
268–270.
[56] Madison's reports of the debates in congress, Dec. 24 and 30, 1782, Jan.
1 and 3, 1783, Wharton, VI, pp. 161–162, 182–184, 189–190, 193.

More than three months elapsed from the time the provisional treaty was signed in Paris to the time when the text of the treaty was received in Philadelphia on March 12, 1783. The same vessel brought copies of the first debates in Parliament over the treaty. Livingston, Hamilton, and especially Madison gave expression to the mixed feelings of the Congress. Rumors of peace had already been started by intelligence received from London, and popular joy at the prospect was universal. But at the top there was something like consternation, a feeling that Lord Shelburne had set out a most effective decoy that would sow distrust among the allies and intensify the divisions in America between the party which hankered after a British connection and those whose confidence in France savored of credulity. Prudent men, feared Hamilton, would find it difficult to steer a proper course. The separate and secret article particularly alarmed Livingston; if avowed by the United States, it would "fully justify Spain in making a separate peace without the least regard to our interest." Madison remarked on the divisions among the commissioners in Paris: Jay taking the lead in zeal for the British offer, Adams following cordially, Franklin dragged into it, and Laurens violently suspicious of Britain and full of confidence in France. And Madison concluded:

The dilemma to which Congress are reduced is infinitely perplexing. If they abet the proceedings of their ministers, all confidence with France is at an end, which, in the event of a renewal of the war, must be as dreadful as in that of peace it may be dishonorable. If they disavow the conduct of their ministers by their usual frankness of communication, the most serious inconveniences also present themselves. The torment of this dilemma can not be justly conveyed without a fuller recital of facts than is permitted. . . .[57]

Further dissension ensued: the American envoys in Paris were accused of kicking down the ladder by which they had been elevated, and Adams was singled out in particular for his *volte face* in favor of Britain. Madison thought the contents of the separate article should be divulged to Spain, but the divi-

---

[57] Luzerne to Vergennes, Feb. 25, 1783, AAE cp Etats Unis, vol. 23, no. 63, ff. 180–186; Hamilton to Washington, Mar. 17, Livingston to president of congress, Madison to E. Randolph, Mar. 18, 1783, Wharton, VI, pp. 311–317.

sions in the Congress were so sharp that a vote on the matter was not possible. Luzerne, apprehensive of a break, sent a warning against British attempts to divide the allies and suggested that British overtures to resume trade be turned down. Livingston obviously was torn between his strong wartime prejudices against Britain and his realization that the United States stood to benefit heavily from the provisional treaty. Fortunately this embarrassing situation lasted only a week; intelligence reached Philadelphia on March 23, 1783, that Britain had signed a general peace with France and Spain in the preceding January. So Livingston was now in a position to compliment the envoys in Paris on their success and at the same time reproach them for mistrusting the French. But he was not above hoping that the British West Indies would be thrown open to American trade, and that this act of Britain would compel France to follow suit.[58]

Lord Shelburne resigned and Fox, through an astonishing coalition with his old political enemy, Lord North, formed a new government at Westminster. In a fine position to cash in on Shelburne's diplomacy, Fox somewhat to Franklin's regret replaced Richard Oswald with David Hartley as Britain's principal negotiator in Paris. Like the merchants, Hartley was anxious to resume trade and intercourse with the Americans, and found himself at last in a position to advance the ideas of reconciliation he had so long propounded. It is amusing to observe how his old friend Franklin, clinging to his partiality for France, treated Hartley's proposals with reserve, while Adams, who had formerly regarded Hartley with a jealous eye, warmed to his basic ideas. Franklin, confronted in June with the prospect of another default on overdue bills, went hat in hand to Vergennes for an additional credit of a million livres, repeating what he had said before that this would be "absolutely the last that will be asked." Jay overcame his anti-French feelings sufficiently to put his name to this plea, but was receptive to one

[58] Madison's Reports, Mar. 22 and 24; Luzerne to Livingston, Mar. 22; Livingston to commissioners, Mar. 25, and to Franklin, Mar. 26, Wharton, VI, pp. 330–340, 343–345; Luzerne to Vergennes, Mar. 22, 1783, AAE cp Etats Unis, vol. 23, no. 126, ff. 355–362.

228 EMPIRE AND INDEPENDENCE

of Hartley's favorite proposals—the establishment of a common citizenship between the British and the Americans. Suspecting Spain of a desire for a mutual security agreement with Britain against the United States, Jay believed immediate advantage should be taken of the prevailing British wish for a rapprochement so as to head off any such possibility.[59]

Vergennes turned cold at Franklin's plea for money, and to Luzerne he wrote with some asperity on the turn things had taken. He was especially aroused over the jealousy between Jay and Adams on the one side and Franklin on the other; and apprehensive should Franklin be replaced at the French court by Jay, "un homme avec qui j'aimerais le moins traiter des affaires." Luzerne was cautioned to use his influence with the Congress on Franklin's behalf, but beyond expressing a hope that the Congress could be saved in any change that might occur in America the French foreign minister felt there was nothing he could do.[60]

To Franklin, Adams had come to be a "mischievous madman" bent on forcing apart the Franco-American union on which, Franklin believed, the United States depended for its importance in Europe. In a calmer mood the old doctor conceded that Adams was "an honest man, often a wise one, but sometimes and in some things absolutely out of his senses." But, learning from his friend Samuel Cooper of Boston, whom Luzerne had paid for his Francophile articles, that Adams and Jay had spread the notion in America that they had won the peace in spite of Vergennes and himself, Franklin lost his temper and demanded a retraction. The French court, he wrote the Congress in September 1783, ten days after the definitive treaty of peace with Great Britain, was America's friend. American safety depended on the country's remaining faithful to the alliance. Britain would never cease trying to separate the two.[61]

---

[59] Franklin to Livingston, Apr. 15; Jay to Livingston, Apr. 22; Franklin and Jay to Vergennes, June 28, 1783, Wharton, VI, pp. 378, 388–390, 508.
[60] Vergennes to Luzerne, July 21 and Sept. 7, 1783, AAE cp Etats Unis, vol. 25, ff. 63–71, 261–265.
[61] Franklin to Morris, Mar. 7, to Livingston, July 22, Wharton, VI, pp. 277, 581–582; to Jay and to E. Boudinot, Sept. 10 and 13, 1783, Smyth, IX, nos. 1438, 1440.

Adams, on the other hand, once so strong a believer in France as the "natural ally" and in Britain as the "natural enemy," had traveled full circle. His changed mood becomes apparent by February 1783, when he evinced an eagerness for a commercial treaty and for an exchange of ministers with Britain. Adams grounded his argument on the importance of foreign trade, and it is plain to see that he put at the top the opportunities arising from intercourse with Britain. Moreover, the court of London was "the best station to collect intelligence from every part, and by means of the freedom of the press to communicate information for the benefit of our country to every part of the world." Then, after stating that "it is our part to be the first to send a minister to Great Britain, which is the older and as yet the superior State," he launched into a vigorous exposition of the qualities such a minister must have. Naturally Adams was gazing in the mirror at himself.[62]

When Hartley arrived in Paris with an invitation to all the American ministers to visit London and be received at court like the ministers of any other sovereign state, Adams was all cordiality. Arguments, slightly modified to meet the new situation, which Hartley had vainly used on Franklin during the war, found a ready listener in Adams. Between Britain and America, Hartley declared, there was a natural communion of intercourse. France could not take the place of Great Britain. The alliance with America was temporary, and was now "completed and terminated without leaving behind it any political principle of future permanent connexion between them." Against a special relationship between America and Spain the case was even stronger. Spain's only activity in the war had been to procure a barrier by annexing West Florida and, by means of obtaining the mouth of the Mississippi, to establish "a strong and jealous boundary against any future progress of the American States in those parts."

Warming to his theme, Hartley pointed out that, its independence established, the United States would "cast about for some natural, permanent, and powerful ally, with whom they

---

[62] Adams to Livingston, Feb. 5 and May 24, 1783, Wharton, VI, pp. 242–247, 447.

may interchange all cementing reciprocities, both commercial and political." Britain was just such an ally—"the first of European nations in riches . . . industry, commerce, manufactures . . . together with civil liberty, which is the source of all, and naval power, which is the support of all." The United States, on its part, reaching from the Atlantic to the Mississippi, contained an inexhaustible source of riches and future power. "These will be the foundations of great events in the new page of life. . . . Great Britain and America must be still inseparable, either as friends and foes. This is an awful and important truth . . . not to be prejudged in passion, nor the arrangements of them to be hastily foreclosed."

Determined not to relax his effort at reconciliation, on which he had worked for so many years, Hartley returned to the attack two weeks later. Britain and America, he pointed out, were the two great powers dividing the continent of North America. Since geography threw them so closely together, they should be friends; and, knowing Franklin's attitude, Hartley took pains to say that the connection with France did not preclude good relations with Britain. Forebearance should be observed. "After a war of animosities, time should be allowed for recollection." To presume in favor of conciliation may help it forward; to presume against it may destroy its chances forever.[63]

Adams chimed in with all of this. Adams and Hartley paired off well together in making the definitive treaty of peace. They shared an interest in foreign trade, Adams being especially eager for the advantages the British West Indies could give, and Hartley holding out hope that the Americans would get them. Serious objections emanating from shipping interests arose on the British side over this issue; but Hartley could at least remind the commissioners that, even under the existing system, the Americans had more privileges in the trade of the British islands than in the French. Adams appreciated the difficulties—the British ministry, he said, was "afraid of every knot of merchants"—but he was impatient to go to London.

---

[63] Hartley's Memorial to the commissioners, June 1 and 13, 1783, *ibid.*, pp. 465–469, 483–487.

"An American minister," he was sure, "would be a formidable being to any British minister whatever. He would converse with all parties, and if he is a prudent, cautious man, he would at this moment have more influence there than you can imagine." But France, he was equally positive, saw "with pain every appearance of returning real and cordial friendship" between Britain and America. Adams was so obsessed with the West India trade that he told his former French colleague in Holland, the duc de la Vauguyon, that "the English were a parcel of sots to exclude us [from it], for the consequence would be that in fifteen or twenty years we should have another war with them. *'Tant Mieux! tant mieux! je vous en félicité,* cried the duke with pleasure. . . . And in this wish he expressed the feelings and the vows of every Frenchman upon the face of the earth." [64]

Adams greatly enjoyed contemplating the problems of history, especially the role of chance in shaping the direction they might take. And so it seems appropriate to end this book, as it was begun, with an extract from one of his letters. Deeply gratified with the peace, he indulged himself in the following bit of retrospection. To Robert Morris he wrote in July 1783:

I cannot look back upon this event without the most affecting sentiments, when I consider the number of nations concerned, the complications of interests extending all over the globe, the characters of actors, the difficulties which attended every step of the progress, how everything labored in England, France, Spain, and Holland; . . . and that all these difficulties were dissipated by one decided step of the British and American ministers. I feel too strongly a gratitude to Heaven for having been conducted safely through the storm to be very solicitous whether we have the approbation of mortals or not.

A delay of one day might, and probably would, have changed the ministry in England, in which case all would have been lost. If, after we had agreed with Mr. Oswald, we had gone to Versailles to show the result to the Count de Vergennes, you would have been this moment at war; and God knows how or when you would have got out. . . . We must have waited for France and Spain, which would have changed the ministry in England, and lost the whole peace as certainly as there is a world in being. When a few frail vessels are

---

[64] Adams to Livingston, June 23 (two letters), and July 10, 1783, *ibid.*, VI, pp. 499–502, 532–534.

navigating among innumerable mountains of ice, driven by various winds, and drawn by various currents, and a narrow crevice appears to one by which all may escape, if that one improves the moment, and sets the example, it will not do to stand upon ceremonies and ask which shall go first, or that all may go together.[65]

---

[65] *Ibid.*, pp. 515–516.

# Bibliographical Essay

This essay comments on the many authorities whose books and articles have been utilized in this study but, who for the most part, have not been cited in the footnotes. The authors and their works are discussed generally in the order in which I have used them in the book, rather than in alphabetical order.

G. M. Waller's, *Samuel Vetch, Colonial Enterpriser*, Chapel Hill, 1960, is an invaluable study of the imperial ambitions of Massachusetts in the early eighteenth century. Lawrence H. Leder's, *Robert Livingston 1654–1728 and the Politics of Colonial New York*, Chapel Hill, 1961, is a good companion volume to Waller. Joseph E. Johnson's, "A Quaker Imperialist's View of the British Colonies in America, 1732," *Penn. Mag. of Hist. and Biog.*, LX, Apr. 1936, pp. 97–130, demonstrates the similar influence of James Logan in Pennsylvania. Of the ten volumes thus far published of Lawrence Henry Gipson's monumental *The British Empire before the American Revolution*, New York, 1958–1961, I have relied heavily on vols. vi, vii and viii on the *Great War for the Empire* (vi: *The Years of Defeat, 1754–1757*; vii: *The Victorious Years, 1758–1760*; viii: *The Culmination, 1760–1763*), and on vols. ix and x on *The Triumphant Empire* (ix: *New Responsibilities within the Enlarged Empire, 1763–1766*; x: *Thunder-Clouds gather in the West, 1763–1766*). Very suggestive, furthermore, is Professor Gipson's essay, "The American Revolution as an Aftermath of the Great War for the Empire, 1754–1763," *Polit. Sci. Quart.*, LXV, 1950–1951, pp. 86–104.

On the speculative activity relating to Western lands, Clarence W. Alvord's, *The Mississippi Valley in British Politics*, 2 vols., Cleveland, O., 1917, is the pioneer work. Carrying the subject

233

much farther are: Albert T. Volwiler's, *George Croghan and the Westward Movement, 1741–1782*, Cleveland, O., 1926; Thomas P. Abernethy's, *Western Lands and the American Revolution*, New York, 1937; Kenneth P. Bailey's, *The Ohio Company of Virginia and the Westward Movement, 1748–1792. A Chapter in the History of the Colonial Frontier*, Glendale, Calif., 1939, and by the same author *The Ohio Company Papers, 1753–1817, being primarily Papers of 'the Suffering Traders' of Pennsylvania*, Arcata, Calif., 1947; and especially Jack M. Sosin's, *Whitehall and the Wilderness, the Middle West in British Colonial Policy, 1760–1775*, Lincoln, Neb., 1961, a searching re-examination of the pressures exerted by land-hungry speculators on the British government and their effect on British American policy. Equally candid is Professor Sosin's article, "The Massachusetts Acts of 1774: Coercive or Preventive?" *Hunt. Lib. Quart.*, XXVI, 1963, pp. 235–252.

Suggestive in indicating that revolutionary anti-British feeling, clearly the beginning of nationalism, was deeply rooted among the American masses are the two works by Stanley M. Pargellis, *Lord Loudoun in North America*, New Haven, Conn., 1933, and *Military Affairs in North America, 1748–1765*, New York, 1936. Volume III of Douglas Southall Freeman's, *George Washington, a Biography*, 7 vols., New York, 1948–1953, is important for the interwar years and gives the facts relating to Washington's land speculations. Howard H. Peckham's, *Pontiac and the Indian Uprising*, Princeton, 1947, is the best work on that subject.

A. M. Schlesinger's, *The Colonial Merchants and the American Revolution, 1763–1776*, New York, 1918, and his *Prelude to Independence. The Newspaper War on Britain 1764–1776*, New York, 1958, are both very informative. Also informative is Robert A. East's *Business Enterprise in the American Revolutionary Era*, New York, 1938. Schlesinger's books throw considerable light on Colonial mobs and the men who incited them to violence. Edmund S. and Helen M. Morgan's, *The Stamp Act Crisis. Prologue to Revolution*, Chapel Hill, 1953, is the principal work on that subject, although it has been successfully challenged by Sosin, *supra*.

On Canada and the Quebec Act of 1774 the works of the following Canadian historians are indispensable: A. L. Burt, *The Old Province of Quebec*, Toronto, 1933; D. G. Creighton, *The Commercial Empire of the St. Lawrence, 1760–1850*, New Haven, 1937, and A. R. M. Lower, *Colony to Nation. A History of Canada*, Toronto, 1947. Charles H. Metzger, S. J., *The Quebec Act. A Primary Cause of the American Revolution*, New York, 1936, is convincing in showing how religious bigotry, especially in New England, contributed to national feeling at the time of crisis. In a recent monograph, *Catholics and the American Revolution, A Study in Religious Climate*, Chicago, 1962, Father Metzger has ably extended his research. Finally, for a brief, condensed treatment of the whole subject of the background of the Revolution, see R. W. Van Alstyne's, *The Rising American Empire*, New York, 1960, pp. 1–27.

Indicative of a desire for a better appreciation of the British situation, a number of important works have been published in recent years. Heading this list is Sir Lewis Namier's and John Brooke's, *The House of Commons, 1754–1790*, 3 vols., London, 1964. An admirable new edition of *The Correspondence of Edmund Burke*, Thomas W. Copeland, gen. ed., Cambridge, Eng. and Chicago, Ill., is now in progress. Margaret Marion Spector's *The American Department of the British Government, 1768–1782*, New York, 1940, is an excellent study of the internal workings of the government and of the personalities involved. Two books by Herbert Butterfield rank high: *George III, Lord North and the People*, London, 1949, and *George III and the Historians*, London, 1957. Also stimulating is Richard Pares's, *King George III and the Politicians*, Oxford, 1953. John Brooke's, *The Chatham Administration, 1766–1768*, London, 1956, and Ian R. Christie's, *The End of North's Ministry, 1780–1782*, London, 1958, are important monographs. See also Charles R. Ritcheson's, *British Politics and the American Revolution*, Norman, Okla., 1954, and Eric Robson's, *The American Revolution in its Political and Military Aspects, 1763–1783*, London, 1955. W. E. Minchinton's, *The Trade of Bristol in the Eighteenth Century*, Bristol Record Society's Publications, XX (1957), gives insight into the workings of British foreign trade. Similar studies of other British ports would be desirable. Three articles written by me which appeared in the *Hunt. Lib. Quart.* draw heavily on British manuscript collections: "Europe, the Rockingham Whigs, and the War for American Independence: Some Documents," XXV (Nov., 1961), pp. 1–28; "Parliamentary Supremacy versus Independence: Notes and Documents," XXVI (May, 1963), pp. 201–233; "Great Britain, the War for Independence, and the 'Gathering Storm' in Europe, 1775–1778," XXVII (Aug., 1964), pp. 311–346. *Correspondence of William Pitt, Earl of Chatham,* William S. Taylor and J. H. Pringle, eds., 4 vols., London, 1838–1840, is an important collection.

Focusing on the military aspects of the war, but refreshingly international in its treatment, is Piers Mackesy's, *The War for America, 1775–1783,* Cambridge, Mass., 1964. The works of William B. Willcox are of prime importance, viz.: "British Strategy in America, 1778," *Journ. Mod. Hist.,* XIX (1947), pp. 97–121; "Rhode Island in British Strategy, 1780–1781," *ibid.,* XVII (1945), pp. 304–331; "The British Road to Yorktown: a study in divided command," *Amer. Hist. Rev.,* LII (1946), pp. 1–35; *The American Rebellion. Sir Henry Clinton's Narrative of His Campaigns, 1775–1782,* New Haven, Conn., 1954; and *Portrait of a General. Sir Henry Clinton in the War of Independence,* New York, 1964. From these works the reader should turn to A. Temple Patterson's, *The Other Armada. The Franco-Spanish Attempt to Invade Britain in 1779,* Manchester, Eng., 1960; and for a splendid collection of documents with introduction to *The Private Papers of John Earl of Sandwich, First Lord of the Admiralty, 1771–1782,* G. R. Barnes and J. H. Owen, eds., 4 vols., The Navy Records Society, 1932–1938. A complete set of photostats of the British Admiralty Papers for the war period is available in the Division of Manuscripts of the Library of Congress. *The Despatches of Molyneux Shuldam,* Robert W. Neeser, ed., New York, The Naval History Society, 1913, is also an important collection of documents. Still of value, although dated in scholarship are: A. T. Mahan's, *Major Operations of the Navies in the War of American Independence,* London, 1913, and W. M. James, R.N., *The British Navy in Adversity. A Study of the War of American Independence,* London, 1926. Two books by G. Lacour-Gayet are essential for study of French naval policy: *La Marine Militaire de la France sous le Règne de Louis XV*, Paris, 1902, and *La Marine Militaire de la France sous le Règne de Louis XVI*, Paris, 1905. Commandant André Lasseray, *Les Français sous les Treize Etoiles* (1775–1783), 2 vols., Paris, 1935, furnishes biographical material on all Frenchmen, civilians and armed forces, who participated in the American War. Louis Gottschalk's monographs on Lafayette, Chicago, 1935–1942, are to be mentioned in this connection.

American loyalists are at last attracting scholarly attention, and of the several books recently published about them, Paul H. Smith's *Loyalists and Redcoats. A Study in British Revolutionary Policy*, Chapel Hill, N. C., 1964, is the most meritorious. Anecdotal but lacking in depth is North Callahan's *Royal Raiders. The Tories of the American Revolution*, Indianapolis, 1963. Frances Acomb's, *Anglophobia in France, 1763–1789. An Essay in the History of Constitutionalism and Nationalism*, Durham, N. C., 1950, is a fine study. John J. Meng's, *Despatches and Instruction of Conrad Alexandre Gérard, 1778–1780*, Baltimore, 1939, a large volume of French diplomatic documents preceded by a careful introduction by Mr. Meng, is indispensable. William Emmett O'Donnell's, *The Chevalier de La Luzerne. French Minister to the United States 1779–1784*, Bruges et Louvain, 1938, is likewise important. Isabel de Madariaga's, *Britain, Russia and the Armed Neutrality of 1780*, London, 1962, is a searching study of that subject. *American Independence through Prussian Eyes. A Neutral View of the Peace Negotiations of 1782–1783*, Marvin L. Brown, trans. & ed., Durham, N. C., 1959, is a fascinating selection of documents from the Prussian diplomatic correspondence including King Frederick's own shrewd appraisal of the war and its consequences. *The Revolutionary Journal of Baron Ludwig von Closen, 1780–1783*, Evelyn M. Acomb, trans. & ed., Chapel Hill, N. C., 1958, is interesting for its sidelights on the French and American armed forces. Von Closen was aide-de-camp to Rochambeau. Vera Lee Brown's, *Studies in the History of Spain in the Second Half of the Eighteenth Century*, Smith College Studies in History, XV (1929), pp. 3–92, is very helpful, especially in relation to Portugal.

Older works focusing narrowly on American diplomatic

relations during the War for Independence have been of little value in the writing of this volume. Edward S. Corwin's, *French Policy and the American Alliance of 1778*, Princeton, N. J., 1916, and Samuel Flagg Bemis's, *The Diplomacy of the American Revolution*, New York, 1935, rest heavily on Henri Doniol's, *Histoire de la Participation de la France a l'Establissement des Etats-Unis d'Amérique. Correspondance Diplomatique et Documents*, 5 vols., Paris, 1886–1892. Both of these monographs are outdated in scholarship and limited in scope, but Corwin achieves an urbane temper and cosmopolitan spirit not to be found in either Doniol or Bemis. Bemis displays the same strong brand of national bias for which he indicts the Frenchman, betraying himself through his adjectives and his frequent use of exclamation points. Elizabeth S. Kite's, *Beaumarchais and the War of American Independence*, 2 vols., Boston, 1918, is likewise obsolete, having used no original French sources but leaning almost entirely on Doniol and on a still older French author, who published a book on Beaumarchais in 1850. More thorough in his search of the French archives, and still helpful although needing revision, is C. H. Van Tyne's, "Influences which determined the French Government to make the Treaty with America, 1778," and "French Aid before the Alliance of 1778," *Amer. Hist. Rev.*, XXI (1915–1916), pp. 528–541 and XXXI (1925–1926), pp. 20–40. Thomas P. Abernethy's, "Commercial Activities of Silas Deane in France," *ibid.*, XXXIX (1933–1934), pp. 477–485, is interesting but, having made little use of Deane's own papers, is lacking in many areas. Clarence L. Ver Steeg's, *Robert Morris, Revolutionary Financier*, Philadelphia, 1954, is thorough but leaves out of account Morris's activity on the Marine Committee of the Continental Congress. Edward Everett Hale's, *Franklin in France*, 2 vols., Boston, Mass., 1888, contains original material and throws interesting sidelights on Franklin's personal relationships in Paris.

# Bibliography of Original Sources

## MANUSCRIPTS

AMERICA

I. *The National Archives and the Library of Congress*
Papers of the Continental Congress (*PCC*):
Index to foreign correspondence 1775–1789
President's Letterbooks: John Hancock, 2 vols., 1775 – Oct. 1777;
Henry Laurens, 2 vols., 1777–1778; John Jay, Dec. 11,
1778 – May 19, 1780; Samuel Huntington, May 19, 1780 –
May 25, 1781
Reports of the Committee of Foreign Affairs, 2 vols.
Reports of Committees on Prisoners' Department, Admiralty,
and Agent of Marine.
Marine Committee Letterbook, 1776–1780; Reports of the Marine
Committee and Board of Admiralty.
Letters, Committee of Foreign Affairs and R. R. Livingston,
1776–1782.
Letters of Benjamin Franklin, 4 vols.
Index to Reports and Letters of the Executive Departments, 2
vols., 1776–1782.
Letters of Arthur Lee, 2 vols.
Letters of the Commissioners
Letters of La Luzerne, 2 vols.
Diplomatic and Other Letters of William Lee, Benjamin Franklin,
John Adams, C. F. Dumas et al.
Robert Morris Papers
Samuel Curwen Letters (Force Transcripts)
Joseph Galloway Letters
George Washington Papers
II. *American Philosophical Society and the Historical Society of*
*Pennsylvania*
Franklin Collection of the A. P. S.
Benjamin Vaughan Papers
Henry Laurens Correspondence, 1762–1780

John Langdon Papers
Franklin Papers. Miscellaneous, 1750–1780, 3 vols.
William Henry Drayton. Manuscript of his treatise, "The Confederation of the United States" (1776).
III.   *Alderman Library (University of Virginia)*
Lee Papers
IV.   *William L. Clements Library*
Clinton Papers
Lord George Germain Papers
William Knox Papers
Shelburne Papers
Wedderburn Papers
Sydney Papers (Thomas Townshend)
V.   *Henry E. Huntington Library*
Samuel Cooper Papers
Sir William Pulteney Papers


# BRITAIN

*Note*: B. F. Stevens, *Facsimiles of Manuscripts in European Archives relating to America 1773–1783*, 25 vols., London, 1889–1898, is included here, although it reproduces some material from the Continental archives also. Invaluable as this great set is, it is far from being complete.

I.   *Public Record Office*
Admiralty Papers: In Letters, vols. 486–489; Out Letters, vols. 1333–1341.
Amherst Papers (War Office, series 34, vols. 118, 144, 148)
Chatham Papers, series 30, vols. 8, 95–98
Colonial Office, series 5, vols. 40, 139–141, 167–169
Grenville Papers (2nd Earl Gower), series 29, bundle 1 (1775–1796)
Headquarters Papers, British Army, series 30/55, vols. 7–11
Manchester, Duke of, Papers, series 30/15, no. 909 (Notebook of Intelligence in the form of a diary, Mar. 10, 1778–Dec. 21, 1779)
State Papers, series 78 (France), vols. 296–306; 84 (Holland), vols. 553–566; 89 (Portugal), vols. 81–84; 90 (Prussia), vols. 99–101; 94 (Spain), vols. 200–209.
War Office, series 1, vol. 10; series 4, vols. 273–274
II.   *Bodleian Library*
North Papers
III.   *British Museum*
Almon Papers (1766–1805)
Auckland Papers, vols. III-IV (June 1777–July 1778)
Bridport Papers (Adm. Hood), vols. I-III (1773–1781)

George III, Correspondence with John Robinson, vols. I-III (1772–1784)

Hardwicke Papers, vols. XXIII, XLII, LXXVI, LXXIX, LXXXV-LXXXVI, XCV, CCI-CCIII (includes a very rich collection of letters from Thomas Hutchinson, 1774–1779; Sir Joseph Yorke and James Harris; diplomatic letterbooks of Sir R. M. Keith, head of the British mission at Vienna, 1774–1778).

Liverpool (Charles Jenkinson, 1st Earl of) Papers, 1774–1782.

Wilkes Papers, vols. V-VI (1770–1780), a few scattered letters of interest.

IV. *National Maritime Museum, Greenwich*

Sandwich Papers: San T/6–8, Transcripts of material collected for the projected vol. V of the Navy Records Society's *Sandwich Papers* (see *infra*), which was never published; and transcripts of manuscripts owned by the Viscount Hinchingbrooke.

V. *University of Nottingham*

Newcastle Papers, Bundles 1–2, Correspondence relating to the American War 1776–1782.

Portland Papers

VI. *Sheffield Central Library*

Letters and Papers of the 2nd Marquis of Rockingham

VII. *West Suffolk County Record Office, Bury St. Edmunds*

Grafton Papers

VIII. *Private Holdings*

Richmond and Gordon Papers, Goodwood, Chichester

Shelburne Papers, Bowood, Wilts

Thynne Papers (3rd. Visct. Weymouth), Longleat, Wilts.

Thomas Walpole Papers in possession of Mr. David Holland.


FRANCE

I. *Archives des Affaires Etrangères (AAE). Correspondance Politique [cp]*.

Angleterre, vols. 450–451, 471, 474–475, 479, 507–508, 510–511, 517, 536–539, 540, 544–545

Etats Unis, vols. 1–3, 11, 13–14, 19–23, 25

Mémoires et Documents (MD)

Angleterre, vols. 52–53, 55–56, 73

Etats Unis, vols. 5, 7

France et Divers Etats, vols. 446, 584, 2114–2115

II. *Archives Nationales (AN). Serial Letter K.* vols. 157–159, 164, 1301, 1340.

III. *Bibliothèque Nationale (BN). Nouvelles Acquisitions (NA)*, vols. 1927–1928, 6498, 9409, 9412, 9416, 9430

IV. *Archives Historiques de la Guerre (Vincennes).* vols. 3732–3733.

## PRINTED MATERIALS

### AMERICAN

*The Adams Papers,* L. H. Butterfield, ed., series I, 4 vols.; series II, 2 vols., Cambridge, Mass., 1961, 1963.

American Archives, Peter Force, ed., 4th and 5th series, 9 vols., Washington, D. C., 1837–1853.

*Letters of Members of the Continental Congress,* Edmund C. Burnett, ed., 8 vols., Washington, D. C., 1921–1936.

Continental Congress, *Journals,* 34 vols., Washington, D. C., 1904–1937.

Deane, Silas, *Correspondence,* in Collections of the Connecticut Historical Society, vols. II and XXIII.

*The Deane Papers,* Charles Isham, ed., 4 vols., in Collections of the New York Historical Society for the year 1886.

Franklin, Benjamin, *Calendar of the Franklin Papers in the Library of the American Philosophical Society,* 5 vols., Philadelphia, 1908.

*The Writings of Benjamin Franklin,* Albert H. Smyth, ed., 10 vols., New York, 1905–1907.

Hamilton, Alexander, *Papers of,* Harold C. Syrett and Jacob E. Cooke, eds., 7 vols. published, New York, 1961–1963.

Jefferson, Thomas, *Papers of,* Julian P. Boyd, ed., 16 vols. published, Princeton, N. J., 1950–1961.

*Out-Letters of the Continental Marine Committee and Board of Admiralty, August, 1776-September, 1780,* Charles Oscar Paullin, ed., 2 vols., New York, The Naval History Society, 1914.

*The Diary and Letters of His Excellency Thomas Hutchinson,* Peter Orlando Hutchinson, ed., 2 vols., Boston, Mass., 1884.

Washington, George, *The Writings of,* John C. Fitzpatrick, ed., 39 vols., Washington, D. C., 1931–1934.

*The Revolutionary Diplomatic Correspondence of the United States,* Wharton, Francis, ed., 6 vols., Washington, D. C., 1889.

### BRITISH

British Museum, Burney Collection of Newspapers, notably in connection with this book, *The London Evening Post,* the *Morning Post and Daily Advertiser,* the *Gazeteer and New Daily Advertiser,* and *Lloyd's Evening Post.*

Burke, Edmund, *Correspondence,* Thomas W. Copeland, gen. ed., 5 vols. pub., Cambridge, Eng. and Chicago, Ill., 1961–1964.

*The Correspondence of King George III,* John Fortescue, ed., 6 vols., London, 1928.

*The Correspondence of General Thomas Gage with the Secretaries of State 1763–1775,* Clarence E. Carter, ed., 2 vols., New Haven, Conn., 1933.

Historical Manuscripts Commission, 11th, 14th and 15th Reports on the Dartmouth Papers and the Carlisle Papers.

*Parliamentary History of England (PH),* 36 vols., London, 1806–1820.

*Parliamentary Register (PR),* 60 vols., 1774–1801, London, 1775–1801.

*The Private Papers of John Earl of Sandwich, First Lord of the Admiralty 1771–1782,* G. R. Barnes and J. H. Owen, eds., 4 vols. The Navy Records Society, 1932–1938.

Walpole, Horace, *Journal of the Reign of King George the Third from the Year 1771 to 1783,* 2 vols., London, 1859.

*Memoirs of the Reign of King George the Third,* G. F. R. Barker, ed., 4 vols., London, 1894.

# Index

Abingdon, Bertie Willoughby, Earl of, influence as a writer, 130, 142

Adams, John, and British envoys, 219–220; and desire for French fleet, 171–172, 173, 174, 178, 179–181, 183, 185–186, 201, 202, 207, 209, 212, 213; and French alliance, 88, 106, 107; and Galloway's Plan, 39, 55; and idea of empire, 1, 5, 12, 21, 26; on "natural allies" and "natural enemies," 161, 162–163, 164, 167, 169; new attitude toward France, 214, 215; and peace negotiations, 223, 226–231; wants extreme action, 66, 67, 70, 82

Adams, Samuel, 35, 66

Admiralty, British, and French ports, 121; and interception of enemy shipping, 121–122, 129, 133, 156; and offensive in the West Indies, 197–198; and transport problems, 86

Albany, New York, 3; and Canada, 104; Plan of Union, 12, 16

Allegheny Mountains, as natural boundary, 5, 7, 8, 16, 17, 177, 211

Almon, John, London editor, 12–13, 32n; fear of France, 65; suspects secret French-American alliance, 132, 136–137

America, and the balance of Europe, 75; and British victory in the West Indies, 209, 210, 211; and British Whigs, 76, 79, 80; and Canada, 104, 107, 108, 109; concludes alliance with France, 137–138, 139, 141, 142; and contraband trade, 122, 123, 124; and Dutch powder trade, 84, 87, 98; and French munitions ships, 128, 129–130, 136; and land sales, 99; and Morris, 115, 119; "natural ally" of France, 101–102, 103; and peace negotiations, 212, 213, 214, 215, 216, 217, 218, 219–220, 222, 223–224, 225–231; reveals intention to be independent, 68, 72, 73, 74; as seat of empire, 1, 2, 13, 14; and the Toulon fleet, 143, 144, 147, 154, 156, 158, 162–163, 164, 166, 171, 172, 173, 174, 176, 177, 178, 179, 180, 181, 182, 183, 185, 186, 187, 191, 192, 194, 195–197, 198–200, 201, 202, 203, 204, 205, 206, 207; and Vergennes, 110, 111, 113; as viewed from Britain, 28–30, 43, 45, 55, 63, 64, 65

Amsterdam, and banking, 125, 173, 181, 201, 207; and Dutch powder trade, 83, 84–85

Arnold, Benedict, and the Canadian expedition, 104

Bancroft, Dr. Edward, 41, 56, 90; and David Hartley, 106; and Silas

Deane, 95–96, 101, 102n; and William Eden, 134–135, 138

Beaumarchais, Pierre-Augustin, Caron de, 49, 70; ties with Vergennes and Gerard, 91, 96–97, 111, 128

Bilbao, Spanish port, 85, 125, 133

Bingham, William, American agent in French West Indies, 82, 98, 99, 113; and privateering, 127–128

Biscay, Bay of, 50, 98; and British frigates, 121; and privateering, 127

Blackstone, Sir William, 150

Board of Trade, 2; and the American West, 5, 7, 10, 16, 17, 18

Bordeaux, 85, 90, 98, 105, 121, 127, 146

Boston, Mass., 2, 3; "Boston Massacre," 33; "Boston Tea Party," 35; distrust of, 6, 21, 23, 24; and Franklin, 40, 43, 46, 64, 66, 67, 74, 86, 157, 176, 228; and religious intolerance, 38, 39; as viewed from Britain, 36, 37

Bouquet, Colonel Henry, 6; effort to protect the Indians, 16, 17, 22

Braddock, Major General Edward, 7, 30

Brest, French naval base, 50, 93, 124, 137; armed convoy from, 138, 156, 165, 168; and attempted invasion of Britain, 169, 178, 179

Bristol, West of England port, 70; and contacts with America, 75

Britain, 1, 2, 3, 4, 7, 8, 9, 10, 11, 14; dismayed over effects of Stamp Act, 27–29; fear of dismemberment, 61–63, 67, 68, 73, 74, 75, 76, 77, 79, 81, 86, 87, 89, 90, 91, 92; fiscal problem, 24; and Franco-Spanish armada, 168–170, 171, 176, 178, 179, 183, 185, 186, 191, 192–193, 195, 198–200, 201, 202, 205, 207, 209, 210, 211, 212, 213, 214, 215, 217, 220; and Franklin,

34, 35, 36, 38, 41, 42, 43–44; French attitude toward, 47–53, 55–56, 57; and the navy, 122, 123, 124, 126, 128–129, 130, 131; and news of Saratoga, 132, 135, 136, 137, 138, 139, 141, 142, 145, 147, 156, 158, 161, 162–163, 164, 167; and optimism in 1763, 15, 21, 22; and peace negotiations, 224–231; and policy toward France, 108, 109, 110, 113, 114, 117, 118, 121; position analyzed, 45–46; and the Spanish-Portuguese crisis, 93–94, 98, 101, 103, 106

Broglie, Victor-François, duc de, maréchal de France, 102, 111

Brown, John, Rhode Island merchant, 23

Bunker Hill, 70, 84

Burgoyne, General John, 105; and Saratoga, 123, 130, 131, 132, 133, 134, 141, 142, 174, 195

Burke, Edmund, views approaching crisis, 36–37, 62, 75, 108; and Whig party, 117, 142, 144, 192, 196, 203, 205, 206

Cadiz, 93; and Spanish fleet, 109

Camden, Charles Pratt, Baron, fear of war, 62–63, 77, 109; on sea power, 203–204; and Western lands, 19

Canada, 1, 2, 3; continued American desire for, 115, 123, 131, 144, 154, 158–159, 161, 162, 165, 166, 167, 171, 176, 179, 193, 199, 204, 206, 210, 222; and Governor Shirley, 5, 11, 13; invasion of, 79, 104–107, 110; rebirth of, 20, 37, 38, 50, 66, 71

Caribbean Sea, 2, 3, 6, 165, 202

Carleton, Sir Guy, governor of Quebec, 66; and reconciliation, 206, 209–210, 211

Carlisle, Frederick Howard, Earl of, 151

Tobacco, export of, 110, 116, 127, 133, 197

Toulon, French naval base, 50, 93, 137, 143; and comte d'Estaing, 155–156

Townshend, Charles, Chancellor of the Exchequer, and the Townshend duties, 32, 33

Tucker, Josiah, Dean of Gloucester, views America, 28–29, 57, 74, 198

Turgot, Etienne-François, Marquis de, French finance minister, 48, 53; and war policy, 92

Utrecht, Peace of, 4

Vandalia Company, 19, 33

Vergennes, Charles Gravier, comte de, French foreign minister, 53; and Bonvouloir, 84, 89; and Deane, 90, 92–93, 97, 103; and John Adams, 173, 174, 175, 179, 181; and John Jay, 183, 184, 188, 199, 201–202; and peace negotiations, 213, 214, 216, 217, 218, 220, 222–223, 227, 228, 231; reacts to Declaration of Independence, 110, 116, 119–120, 124, 127, 128, 132–133, 134, 135; and secret treaty negotiation, 136–137, 145, 166, 167, 168, 169, 170, 172

Versailles, seat of the government of Louis XVI, 52, 89, 90, 93, 102, 109, 120, 131; secret negotiations at, 135–138, 144, 161, 164, 172, 184, 187, 210, 217, 218, 219, 224, 231

Vetch, Samuel, 2; and conquest of Acadia, 3, 4, 5

Virginia, 5, 6, 7; and the Ohio Company, 9, 15, 16, 110, 170, 175, 182, 188, 197, 207

Voltaire (François-Marie Arouet), 47

Wabash River, 13

Walpole, Horace, 142

Walpole, Thomas, M.P., London merchant banker, 9, 19, 83; peace efforts, 95–96, 99; reacts to Franklin's arrival in France, 116

Walpole Associates, speculative group, 19, 32, 37, 41, 83

Washington, George, 7; and British peace mission, 154, 155; disappointed by de Grasse, 200–201, 202, 209, 211, 219; fears collapse, 170, 174, 175, 176, 178, 179; and French alliance, 162; and invasion of Canada, 104, 105, 107, 115, 131, 142, 149, 153; landed interests of, 9, 16, 26; named general, 66, 79; wants French naval help, 181–182, 184, 188–189, 199

Wedderburn, Alexander, and the conciliatory bills, 148; and speculative interests, 19

Wentworth, Paul, 143, 144, 145, 146, 147, 150; and the Toulon fleet, 155

Wesley, John, Methodist leader, defines his position towards the Revolution, 71–72

West, American, and conflicting interest groups, 15, 16, 17, 18, 19, 22; and the British army, 25, 32, 33, 37; and Quebec Act, 38, 40, 202, 211, 217, 218, 219, 220

West Indies, 2, 12, 23, 82, 83, 85; and blockade problem, 86, 87, 91, 98, 103, 107, 110, 114; and French naval reinforcement, 172, 178, 179, 180, 181, 188, 189, 193, 198, 200, 201, 204, 206, 207, 208, 209, 216, 225, 227, 230, 231; and warfare at sea, 121, 122, 126, 127, 128, 130, 132, 133, 138, 151, 152, 155, 158, 165, 166, 167

Weymouth, Thomas Thynne, Viscount, Secretary of State for the Southern Department, 96, 99n; 120, 121, 127, 128–129, 133, 134, 135, 137, 138